D1034363

Rhetoric and the Republic

Rhetoric, Culture, and Social Critique

Series Editor
John Louis Lucaites

Editorial Board
Richard Bauman
Barbara Biesecker
Carole Blair
Dilip Gaonkar
Robert Hariman
Steven Mailloux
Raymie E. McKerrow
Toby Miller
Austin Sarat
Janet Staiger
Barbie Zelizer

Rhetoric and the Republic

Politics, Civic Discourse, and Education in Early America

MARK GARRETT LONGAKER

THE UNIVERSITY OF ALABAMA PRESS

Tuscaloosa

Copyright © 2007
The University of Alabama Press
Tuscaloosa, Alabama 35487-0380
All rights reserved
Manufactured in the United States of America

Typeface: Perpetua

∞

The paper on which this book is printed meets the minimum requirements of American
National Standard for Information Sciences-Permanence of Paper for Printed Library
Materials, ANSI Z39.48-1984.

Library of Congress Cataloging-in-Publication Data

Longaker, Mark Garrett, 1974–
Rhetoric and the republic : politics, civic discourse, and education in
early America / Mark Garrett Longaker.
p.   cm. — (Rhetoric, culture, and social critique)
Includes bibliographical references and index.
ISBN-13: 978-0-8173-1547-4 (cloth : alk. paper)
ISBN-10: 0-8173-1547-0 (cloth : alk. paper)
1. English language—Rhetoric—Study and teaching—United States. 2. Rhetoric—Study
and teaching—United States. 3. Rhetoric—Political aspects—United States. 4. English
language—United States—Rhetoric. 5. Rhetoric—Social aspects—United States.
6. Education, Higher—United States—History—18th century. 7. United States—
History—Colonial period, ca. 1600–1775. I. Title.
PE1405.U6L66 2007
808.0071′173—dc22

2006017692

Contents

Tables

Acknowledgments

Acknowledgments customarily begin with mention of the professional support that has contributed to a project, and they typically end with recognition of those most central to an author's personal life. By no means do I intend to downplay the importance of those who have read and offered comments about this argument or the research presented herein. Still, I have to break tradition. The greatest support for my work has come from my mother, Patricia Longaker; my wife, Michelle Meaux; and my daughter, Rosalind Longaker Meaux. My mother has taught me to be proud of my own past; Michelle has taught me to seek joy in the present; and Rosalind has made me hopeful about the future.

This book began as an essay written for a graduate seminar and has continued to grow, to change, and to assume its present, radically altered shape. The archival research presented in chapter 3 was largely funded by a Penn State Research and Graduate Studies Dissertation Support grant and also by an award from the Philip Young Memorial Endowment for study in American literature. Both of these organizations deserve many thanks for helping scholars to pursue valuable, though perhaps not lucrative, writing projects. The book's publication has been made possible by a generous grant from the University Co-operative Society in Austin, Texas. I hope that the final product sheds favorable light on those who contributed monetary support to its completion. Several readers deserve thanks for helping me initially to synthesize a mountain of historical research. I am particularly indebted to Cheryl Glenn, Clement Hawes, Stephen Browne, Jeffrey Walker, and Marie Secor. Marie also deserves recognition for being the best professional adviser and mentor a young scholar could ever hope for. Several of my coworkers at the University of Texas offered valuable feedback on various early drafts of the book's introduction. Joan Mullin, Patricia Roberts-Miller, Judith Rosenberg, and Janice Fernheimer all helped me to negotiate the difficult task of succinctly introducing a long argument. Getting the book ready for a publisher was another difficult task, one that I could not have managed without assistance. Thomas P. Miller offered pointers on writing a persuasive book proposal. Jeffrey Walker deserves thanks again for reading and giving feedback on the entire manuscript just before I sent it off for review at the University of Alabama Press. Finally, in recent months, I have received helpful advice from the staff at UA Press, from the anonymous reviewers, and from Mindy Wilson. I have spoken to and received interesting feedback from countless people in casual conversations, at academic conferences, and in e-mail correspondence. It is a great sin not to list them all, but the time for acknowledgments is brief, and my memory is poor. I can therefore only offer widespread thanks to anyone who has listened or been gracious enough to respond to my ramblings about rhetorical education in early America.

Acknowledgments pages typically end with a disclaimer that everything good in the book to follow comes as a result of outside support, and everything bad comes as a result of the author's personal shortcomings. I like this practice, and I will follow suit. Anything worth reading in these pages comes as a result of the support I've received from many sources. Any oversight, overstatement, any flagrantly insipid remark belongs to me alone.

Introduction
Now that We're Civic

The poet and the historian differ not in writing in verse or in prose [. . .]. The true difference is that one relates what has happened, the other what may happen. Poetry, therefore, is a more philosophical and a higher thing than history: for poetry tends to express the universal, history the particular.

—Aristotle

It may seem strange to begin and end a book about eighteenth-century American rhetoric, politics, and pedagogy with an extended reflection on contemporary education. After all, history is, as Aristotle tells us, about the past. This introduction proposes, however, that history deals with what was and with what can be. It is factual and poetical. This introductory chapter and the conclusion reflect on and explain the poetical function performed by the encapsulated historical narrative: Why is this story important right now?

Right now, at universities generally, there is an effort to connect higher education with contemporary civic concerns. Academics are encouraged to research public issues, to design classes that engage national, state, and local communities, to teach students responsible democratic citizenship. Despite the occasional charge of "partisan advocacy" (Fish), most today would agree with the 528 university presidents who endorsed a 1999 declaration encouraging "higher education to re-examine its public purposes and its commitments to the democratic ideal" ("Presidents' Declaration"). The university, for the better part of the twentieth century, has been metaphorically captured in the cold, distant image of the ivory tower, but in recent years it has tried to fashion a new image: the urban outreach center. University workers claim to produce both knowledge and citizens. They champion active involvement over intellectual distance, political over scholastic relevance.

Among rhetoric teachers, the civic turn manifests itself most prominently in efforts to research, theorize, and promote public discourse, an important component in any democratic order where citizens must come together to decide, discuss, and deal with their shared concerns.[1] This promising scholarly and pedagogical reconsideration of how to theorize and teach public discourse is encouraged by recent Edenic narratives about the history of rhetorical education. The story, essentially, is that teachers of rhetoric, particularly those in the eighteenth-century American academy, had students engage one another in public deliberation. Rhetoric helped to shape national identity by offering the necessary tools of public debate. Typically this golden age precedes a fall, sometimes into belletrism, sometimes into liberal individualism, sometimes into formalism. But contemporary rhetoricians hope to revitalize rhetoric's civic mission. If rhetorical education was once a civic project, it can become so again.[2] Civic rhetoric, imagined as a return to a once dominant pedagogical model, marches today to the Edenic drum, redrawing disciplinary maps and classroom syllabi alike. And looking back to a time when disciplinary divides did not separate writing from oratory, we can see that rhetorical education is the common ground shared by a number of university workers. We all teach rhetoric, and therefore we are all engaged in the civic project of forming citizens for a healthy democracy. As it was in 1750, so it should be today.

Doubtless, this familiar narrative is based on indisputable facts. Students in eighteenth-century American higher education composed orations and disputed politically salient topics such as the divine rights of kings, economic policy conducive to a healthy republic, or the value of sumptuary laws. (These topics and their relevance to American public life will be discussed in later chapters.) And surely, in the nineteenth century, rhetorical education became much less concerned with public issues and much more focused on the students' personal experiences.[3] Confronted with nineteenth-century rhetoric primers and their suggested topics such as "describe the lake near your house on a summer evening" and comparing this to early American rhetorical education, one must notice a shift away from the political toward the personal. For those wanting to promote a more politically relevant pedagogy, this change must look like a decline, and its recognition as such should incite hope for a return to the golden age of civic rhetoric. The Edenic narrative thereby brings pedagogy back to civic relevance, and it brings many teachers-scholars in disparate fields to the common ground of rhetoric.

However, though this narrative has supported the civic turn in American rhetorical pedagogy, though it helps various scholars and teachers to find common ground, it does not encourage the kind of reflection requisite to responsible democratic education. Now that we're civic, we need a narrative to parse the various connections among education, politics, economic interests, and cultural and intellectual trends. In order to more fully consider the politics of rhetorical education, we need something more than a narrative celebrating the possible return to a prelapsarian paradise. Rather than returning to the untroubled days of civic rhetoric in the early American academy, we should consider how rhetoric engages the politics of each particular moment in history.

The majority of this book is an examination of public discourse and rhetorical pedagogy in the late eighteenth and early nineteenth centuries. It offers a critical narrative about rhetoric's place in early American civic education, one told in the present to supplement the Edenic narrative told so often among contemporary historians of rhetoric. This introduction and the first chapter, however, will focus not on education per se but on the many factors that deserve consideration when examining education in historical context. We need a manner of explaining how a number of social factors connect to one another in a given moment and in a given practice. We also need to explain how something so locally performed, like rhetorical education, can affect seemingly larger and more pressing historical developments. For such an understanding, Gramscian Marxism seems particularly helpful.

Rhetorical Education: An Articulated Site of Hegemony

Antonio Gramsci argued that, at any moment in the history of modern society, a given set of political, social, and economic developments come together in a hegemonic order. In democratic societies like twenty-first-

or eighteenth-century America, hegemony is not the violent imposition of interests or ideas, nor is it achieved by duping most of the population into acquiescence and ignorance. Rather, for one reason or another, in one manner or another, every person in a social formation participates in the construction, maintenance, and possible alteration of hegemony. Though hegemony might privilege a given political or economic elite, its constitution requires everyone's labor, as performed in a variety of circumstances. Hegemony might not offer the best odds to an individual player, but it is the only game in town. And to play, citizens must, to some degree, reify the rules of the game; thus citizens' participation in hegemonic social and cultural institutions entails their implicit consent. Furthermore, the persistence of a hegemonic order is never guaranteed. There is no determining factor in a social formation, only local choices that (re)construct the network of power inhabited by all. People might consent to a hegemonic game, but they might not stick with the established betting strategies. They may even find a way to beat the house (Gramsci, *Selections from the Prison Notebooks* 400–14).

Recent efforts to revitalize the Gramscian notion of hegemony have emphasized the field of power emergent in any modern social formation and the contingent relationships among otherwise semiautonomous institutions such as education and parliamentary politics. Hegemony relies not just on the institutions that one engages but also on the connections among these institutions. A hegemonic order is the result of various efforts to articulate inherited social, economic, and political conditions, to change the field of power by reconnecting its elements. In this discussion, the term *articulation* refers to contingent relationships drawn by historical agents among separate and semiautonomous institutions in order to actuate political agency in a unique historical context.[4] Articulation theory has been most fully explored in the works of Stuart Hall, Ernesto Laclau, Chantal Mouffe, and Lawrence Grossberg. These theorists adopted the term to discuss the discursive effort to connect rhetorical elements key to a given power structure. Laclau and Mouffe, for instance, define articulation as "any practice establishing a relation among elements such that their identity is modified as a result of the articulatory practice," and they limit the effects of articulation to the realm of discourse. The only elements open to "articulatory practice" are the rhetorical components of a "discursive formation" (105). Grossberg similarly defines articulation as "the construction of one set of relations out of another" (*We Gotta* 54). Hall follows Laclau and Mouffe by limiting the practice of articulation. According to all four thinkers, articulation can only effect rhetorical relationships among discursive elements. Hall, in a now famous example, argued that Jamaican blacks rearticulated the discursive notion of blackness (once connoting inferiority, incivility, and dispossession) to national pride, liberation, and beauty. According to Hall, rearticulating these discursive elements allowed Jamaican blacks to claim a radical political agency during the 1970s ("Signification" 107–8). Recent appropriation of articulation theory among rhetoricians has followed in this discursive vein, focusing on the rhetorical arena and positing that articulatory practice has application to linguistic artifacts, like definitions.[5]

Articulation theory has been useful among rhetorical theorists who are interested, as I am, in analyzing the role rhetoric plays in constructing contingent fields of power among semiautonomous institutions in a social formation. From this perspective, power appears to entail more than the norms of a rhetorical culture or a widely accepted political discourse. Power arises out of the connections between the two and their connections to other elements, such as a particular variation of capitalism (for instance, Fordism), a particular political party, even a social movement or a spontaneous rebellion. Cultural formations such as a political discourse, a set of rhetorical norms, or a rhetorical pedagogy are sites where these semiautonomous elements get connected to one another in interesting and effective ways. For instance, the Republican Party's recent control over U.S. political and cultural developments has resulted from the party's ability to articulate variations of American fundamentalist Christianity to an aggressive foreign policy and an unevenly applied laissez-faire economics. Articulation theory would attribute all of these connections to the pithy rhetoric of an "ownership society," a contingent discursive formation that ties various institutions together into a totalizing discursive formation that shapes the field of modern hegemony. Each of these institutions exists semiautonomously from the others, but Republican strategists, cultural workers, rhetors, and politicians began to suture them together in 2000.

Though very useful to the rhetorical theorist who is interested in analyzing the role of discourse in a hegemonic order, articulation theory forgets an important part of Gramsci's theory of hegemony: the key role allotted to economic institutions. Articulation theory, as communication studies scholars have inherited it from Hall, Grossberg, Laclau, and Mouffe, focuses on discourse, often losing track of economic variables such as classes, industries, and whole systems of production. Hall's discursive analysis of political hegemony in Thatcherite England openly derides consideration of economic institutions and instead focuses on the realm of culture (see *The Hard Road*). Grossberg likewise focuses his analysis on discursive articulations between cultural institutions, like rock music, and political discourses, like Ronald Reagan's neoliberal talk of ending the 1950s era of big government (*We Gotta*). Kevin DeLuca insists that nondiscursive reality, such as the industrial mode of capitalism, exists, but political work can only occur through the "hegemonic discourse of Industrialism" (342). The emphasis that all three place on the discursive realm tends to downplay economic factors.

Gramsci reminds us, however, that "though hegemony is ethical-political, it must also be economic, must necessarily be based on the decisive function exercised by the leading group in the decisive nucleus of economic activity" (*Selections from the Prison Notebooks* 161). Gramsci's theory of hegemony points to the "superstructures of civil society" as the "trench-systems of modern warfare" (235), but this emphasis on cultural and political institutions should not lead us to imagine economic variables as similar or subordinate to elements like religion, education, or rhetorical practice. Rather, economic institutions—though identifiably removed and though developing somewhat independently of cultural institutions—get articulated in interesting and productive ways to and in discursive formations. I am proposing, therefore, an articulation theory that does not forget the semiautonomous realm of the economic, an articulation theory that recognizes that, though a great deal of political work happens when people discursively relate rhetorical concepts to one another, economic variables such as classes, technologies, and whole modes of production are also involved in articulatory practice. Economic variables are an essential—if not *the* essential—component in any hegemonic articulation of various elements, some discursive, many not. That the articulation among these components often happens through discourse does not mean that hegemony is entirely a rhetorical production.

Of course, this is not to say that various rhetorical norms or political discourses are epiphenomena of economic variables, as some communication studies scholars have implied (Cloud "The Materiality"; Garnham), nor is it to say that discursive effects are comparable to those of an economic recession or a crisis of overproduction (Greene); and it is certainly not to say that all articulation is a discursive phenomenon (Laclau and Mouffe 67–71, 105–22; Hall "The Problem," "Signification," *The Hard Road* 12–13). Rather, a Gramscian theory of hegemony, when coupled to recent articulation theory, can account for rhetoric and economics while allowing that both are woven into contingent efforts by particular actors who encounter and interact with their conflicted historical situations— discursive and nondiscursive. Though in the "last instance" material interest trumps all other motivators, this "last instance" never arrives.[6] Therefore, while it is useful to map the economic foundation of a political struggle, it is also foolish to assume that such a foundation can ever exist or even be viewed without weighty cultural and social striations contributing to its composition. A shared discursive formation, though not a strictly economic variable, is particularly important in any hegemonic order, since a common language can bring together subjects with different interests and affiliations. Many recent theorists of hegemony have noticed that in civil society language holds great sway and operates as a central institution guiding and unifying people by encouraging common identification along a set terrain of argumentative topics, a shared understanding of the world, allowing both collective action and disagreement.[7] Hegemony, built of economic bricks, relies on rhetorical mortar.[8]

Key Sites of Articulation:
Rhetorical Publicity and Rhetorical Pedagogy

One of this book's principal arguments is that two key sites of articulation should be of interest to rhetoricians: rhetorical publicity (defined more fully in chapter 1) and rhetorical pedagogy. Just as a political discourse can be articulated to various inherited institutions, so also can rhetorical education become a site where people articulate cultural variables and economic interests in an effort to alter, enforce, or resist the hegemonic order that they have inherited. A given pedagogy, in one sense, is an effort to teach people how to communicate effectively. But in a broader sense, any program of rhetorical education is a nexus where political discourse, economic interests, and social and partisan agendas get connected in very local acts such as debate topics or evaluative criteria to determine "good" writing.

In sum, Gramsci's understanding of hegemony when brought into conversation with recent articulation theory teaches us that public discourse and rhetorical education are important sites where a host of forces come together. Rhetorical education in any democratic society must therefore be civic. Rhetorical educators should not settle for a narrative that calls them back to their civic roots. We should wonder about the possible ways to become civic. We should question the motives behind, the shapes of, the political affiliations made possible by, and the articulations made between variations on public discourse and civic education. The better part of this book is an exploration of the politics of republicanism in eighteenth-century rhetorical education. The argument, in a nutshell, is that early American republicanism was a contested political terrain that allowed multiple and conflicting positions to arise, leading to numerous rhetorical practices and numerous understandings of how to train citizens to participate in public deliberation. In the republican public space, people articulated various economic and political interests to a common republican political discourse. This struggle depended on and was resolved through local actions by specific republican rhetors. Likewise a number of rhetorical pedagogies in the late eighteenth century were also sites where people struggled over hegemony, articulating republican political discourse, class-based proclivities, and partisan ideologies to one another, all in an effort to shape the future of the American republic by shaping its future citizens.

The first chapter examines republicanism as a political discourse articulated to various economic interests and partisan affiliations. By "political discourse," I mean a rhetorically constructed set of beliefs about what constitutes good government. This refers to more than vocabulary. Though political discourses depend on key definitions, they also depend on people to relate these definitions to one another and to their particular historical conditions. My use of the terms *republicanism* and *liberalism* does not invoke the popular definitions common in the contemporary American lexicon, nor do I refer to any political parties. Capital *R* Republicans belong to a political party that articulates contemporary developments such as a

Christian variety of social conservatism to corporate cronyism and to in-constantly pursued free market globalism. And those self-identifying as contemporary liberals are likely to articulate a modicum of economic (Keynesian) state interventionism to a libertarian insistence on the pro-tection of civil and reproductive rights. Liberalism will be defined more fully in the conclusion, and chapter 1 will offer a full explanation of re-publican political discourse. At present, before delving into either, I have to concede that I find neither comforting. In fact, I have strong reserva-tions about both. Nonetheless, my main purpose here is not to criticize. It is to critique, to understand the variety of pedagogies and economic interests articulated to these political discourses.

If a political discourse and a rhetorical pedagogy have a variety of ar-ticulations to one another and to economic institutions in American so-ciety, then we should not hope for a revival of civic republicanism before considering the economic implications of such an effort. And the best way to illustrate that republican political discourse, public rhetorical norms, and pedagogies are not innocent or necessarily desirable institutions is to examine their initial dominance in early American society against the eco-nomic conditions along the eighteenth-century British Atlantic. Chapter 1 analyzes the various economic interests of early American society and the debates about what a good American republic should look like. These de-bates created a public space to discuss the formation of a government and a national character, but this space was influenced by the economic inter-ests present along the British Atlantic. Republican political discourse pro-vided the common ground over which disagreements about economic and political interests could occur. In the end, a variation of laissez-faire capi-talism became dominant, but this could only happen by articulating free market economic policy to republicanism in a public space where citi-zens were debating the fate of their national experiment. The Democratic-Republican Party eventually achieved hegemony in the nineteenth century by articulating specific economic interests to a commonly understood re-publican discourse in a public space where others were articulating very different interests to the same vocabulary. Also, any hegemony won in this contest was not guaranteed. The Democratic-Republican articulation of economic interest, public rhetorical practice, and political discourse re-mained dominant for twenty-eight years, but in 1829 Jacksonian Democrats articulated a new hegemony, ousting the Democratic-Republicans and ending their presence on the American stage. The shift to Jacksonian democracy, as others have argued (Clark and Halloran; Schlesinger), inaugurated the era of liberal dominance in American political discourse, thus ousting republicanism from its dominant position in the field of articulatory hegemonic practice. Though this shift is important to American history, the present study concludes just before it begins.

Chapter 2 discusses early American rhetorical education, as it was articulated to the discourse of republicanism, but in varying ways, again reflecting the many possibilities of republican political discourse. Republican political discourse was articulated to various pedagogical practices and economic interests in eighteenth-century America. Chapters three, four, and five closely examine particular sites of rhetorical instruction to show the complicated interaction of political discourse, public rhetorical norms, pedagogy, and economic interests in specific colleges (Yale, the College of Philadelphia, King's College New York, and the College of New Jersey) over the latter half of the eighteenth century. Each site examined is unique. Though republicanism was a common element among these schools, at different points in their development, instructors at each site articulated this political discourse to a pedagogical practice for singular economic-political effects. These three chapters reinforce my claim that republicanism comes in many pedagogical shapes and sizes and can be articulated to a variety of interests. Its plasticity makes it neither politically desirable nor repulsive. It is, like all political discourses, interesting and open. The conclusion returns to the present effort to revive republican pedagogy and political discourse to show how this effort is also multiply constructed, how the variations on republicanism have articulations to differing contemporary economic interests. All these chapters amount to an argument that republicanism is not the heavenly moment of rhetoric's apotheosis. We should not look back to it fondly nor try to revive it presently. We should consider it critically in relation to rhetorical pedagogy, economic interests, and, especially, to rhetoric's key points of concern: public discourse and pedagogy. What becomes of rhetoric and the republic has less to do with the political discourse or the rhetorical theory that we adopt and more to do with our individual efforts at pedagogical and political articulation.

Rhetoric and the Republic

I

One Republic, Many Republicanisms

Early American Political Discourse and Publicity

If you would persuade, you must appeal to interest rather than intellect.
—Benjamin Franklin

Given the impact that republican political discourse had on early American public argument, and given the hegemonic articulations among dominant rhetorical norms, a common political discourse, and a variety of rhetorical pedagogies, it is fitting to begin a study of eighteenth-century rhetorical education not with education at all but with two significant and related factors: republicanism and public argument. If early Americans imagined themselves as republican citizens and if they engaged one another through a common republican vocabulary, then they also would have created curricula to prepare future citizens for similar engagement in a similar vocabulary.[1] Exploring the perimeters of republicanism and public argument, therefore, sets the stage for subsequent chapters that explore how this political discourse was articulated not only to rhetorical norms of public exchange but also to efforts at preparing young citizens for their civic lives.

This first chapter, to an extent, accepts the scholarly consensus that republicanism was a principal factor in early American public debate.[2] Immediately following, in fact, is an exploration of this discourse's importance before the American Revolution. However, this chapter also challenges this consensus by considering another factor important to both the creation of early American public discourse and to the formation of early American rhetorical pedagogy. National unity was not just the product of a shared republican discourse. It was also the product of a complicated negotiation among several economic formations. Early American civic identity therefore resulted from a manner of public rhetorical exchange, a political discourse, and a host of economic interests, all interrelated factors that shaped a nation and its efforts to educate citizens.

What follows is an exploration of various early American efforts to negotiate conflicting economic interests through a common republican vocabulary. I argue that republican unity was neither a discursive nor an economic effect, and it would be irresponsible to say that republican political discourse was either a psychagogic elixir inducing rhetorical intoxication or a cosmetic powder masking pockmarked economic interests. Rather, republicanism spurred common identification, provided a sense of common mission, and supplied a vocabulary for understanding national purpose. Republicanism also created a discursive space where citizens could wrestle over their nondiscursive investments in economic institutions such as trade policy, duties, and slavery. If economic factors deserve attention, then rhetorical education of the era did not simply pursue republican ideals nor did it solely endorse republican rhetorical norms. And early American rhetorical education, just like early American public argument, negotiated conflicting economic interests through the common vocabulary that republicanism provided.

This chapter proposes that people's methods of becoming public agents are sites of articulation where actors often connect a commonly held political discourse to norms of rhetorical exchange and to economic and political affiliations. This contested site of articulation will hereafter be referred to as *publicity,* a term that I use very differently from its contemporary appropriation. In the following discussion, publicity has nothing to do with the public relations industry, though it does relate to one's public exposure. Publicity, in my use, is more akin to publicness, a manner of embodying and performing good public citizenship through public argument. But publicity references more than a discursive effect. It references the articulation, through this discursive effort, of economic and partisan affiliations to a commonly held discourse about good government. A republican publicity, therefore, rhetorically engages in the struggle over what it means to be a good republican rhetor. A republican publicity, like a republican pedagogy, is not a consistent practice. Rather, at any moment, one might encounter several conflicting republican publicities, individual efforts to articulate a host of factors (some rhetorical, some economic) to a common political discourse in the hopes of suturing these connections into a hegemonic fabric that others will accept as the only manner of publicly, rhetorically enacting good republican argumentation. In order to explore republican publicity as a contested site of articulation, this book will begin with the common rhetorical ground that all republican publicities share: republican political discourse. It will then explore the economic factors at play in early American society to demonstrate how various arguments about republican citizenship were tied to these conflicting interests while employing the same publicly accepted discourse about what constitutes effective democratic governance. Finally, three warring republican publicities will be analyzed (Timothy Dwight's millennial republicanism, Alexander Hamilton's manufacturing republicanism, and Thomas Jefferson's agrarian republicanism) to show that republican public rhetorical practice varied depending on the speaker's ability to make a public argument about good citizenship through a commonly accepted political discourse while endorsing a specific economic interest.

Republican Publicity and Political Discourse: The Rhetorical Perimeters of Republicanism

Rhetoricians have often wondered about the discursive conditions necessary for people to disagree productively without these arguments degenerating into hopeless schism, faction, and violence. Some consensus clearly is necessary to bring people into conversation, and some speaker(s) must voice that consensus, in effect, asking others to join the debate. Language shapes public spaces and citizens because, for strangers to come together as a public, they must be addressed as a public (Warner, *Publics* 87–92). Articulation of a publicity therefore requires a commonly accepted, though multivalent, discourse outlining the perimeters of good civic participation. A political discourse is a necessary component to any publicity. In fact, a public sphere's viability in part hinges on its participants' ability to recognize and debate shared concerns in a mutually intelligible discourse (Hauser, *Vernacular* 68–9). Also, a public sphere's character can be determined and judged at least in part by its rhetorical culture, the still developing conditions and conventions that its participants share and utilize in their efforts at persuasion (Farrell 7). And the shape of the language that hails citizens into a particular mode of publicity deserves analysis because that language sets the terms for further debate. Of course, a variety of discourses hail people as public citizens in a variety of ways every day, so it would be simplistic to assume that only the most overtly politicized language deserves analysis as "public" or that citizenship can be easily tallied by measuring the number of letters to the editor one submits in a given year (Asen 189–91). Without devaluing other public spaces/discourses in early American society and in the interest of understanding one discourse contributing to early American articulatory practices of publicity, we should analyze the political discourse of republicanism, the language hailing people as republican citizens.

Republican discourse offered early Americans a body of appeals that made possible a cohesive public sphere, and this discourse also encouraged a set of rhetorical norms that shaped the debate over what the republic would become. People along the British Atlantic were encouraged to imagine themselves as consubstantial and to participate in a conversation about how the republic should progress. In the process of identification, those finding common ground also divided themselves from others. Those identifying as American republicans agreed discursively about their collective existence and also agreed that they were not monarchists, certainly not French, Spanish, or British (Burke, *Rhetoric* 21). Kenneth Burke used a number of terms to describe the backdrop against which identification occurs, the most famous and perhaps the most useful of which is the parlor conversation to which actors arrive late. The conversation has its own available vocabulary and discursive forms that new participants must learn to employ, but the available conversation does not completely structure a participant's ability to intervene. For Burke, action is the appropriation of available conversational structure for new ends, thereby perpetuating the conversation while changing it.[3] Republican political discourse, in these terms, looks like a conversation about the shape of good government. It began among the Greeks and persisted in various locations, such as fifteenth-century Florence, seventeenth-century England, and finally eighteenth-century America. Citizens along the British Atlantic arrived at this conversation late but collectively identified with one another by appropriating its terms for their own purposes in their own situations.

Early American republicanism was a body of persuasion citizens inherited from previous actors and adopted collectively to guide their deliberations over shared concerns. This body of persuasion was made up of related discursive forms that provided a sense (however multivalent) of good government. The classical term referencing a discursive form is *topos* or topic. Ancient and recent neo-Aristotelian rhetoricians describe topics as places where arguments can be found, common discursive territory over which people can (dis)agree.[4] Burke described topics as relations among people and with respect to material-social environments. In the rhetorical act, Burke argued, the rhetor appropriates an available topic, reconstituting it for particular ends to effect new relationships with others and with the world. The topic, as a found and altered mediator, both shapes and is shaped by human agency.[5] Topics in American political discourse have been constituted for a variety of arguments and in a variety of economic circumstances. Both FDR's Social Security and George W. Bush's Department of Homeland Security were bolstered by appeals to the security topic. The New Deal expansion of entitlement programs appealed to freedom (from want) while twenty-first-century neoconservative militarism also appeals to freedom (from terrorism). Appealing to argumentative topics common to a conversation will get people nodding but will not always get them nodding at the same thing. Collective political action in any modern democracy that does not depend on outright deception always involves some appeal to topics commonly known yet open to various constitutions. In the beginnings of the American republican experiment, collective political action became possible in part because citizens "rummaged through the attic of antiquity [. . . and] mined the resources of the republican tradition" (T. Gustafson 198).

Rhetorically analyzing republican political discourse allows us to see a number of things about its shape and its effect on early American civic identity—that is, what it meant to be and to speak like a republican. This analysis also reveals that within republican political discourse there were many opportunities for disagreement, many chances to articulate hegemonic constellations of republican publicity. Below is a rhetorical analysis of the conversation about republicanism to show its various topics and their capacity to encourage collective identification along a set of shared concerns. Then, by analyzing two very different arguments, both appropriating republican topics, I demonstrate that in eighteenth-century British Atlantic settlements, republicanism did not lead everyone to the same political position, though it might have brought them together in a common conversation about their collective political fate. Among a variety of publicities, therefore, there is a common arena of shared concerns, a common discourse, and there are also a great many opportunities for disagreement. In later chapters, this dynamic of republican consensus and dissensus will become important in exploring the various iterations of "good" republican pedagogy.

Republican political discourse begins with the assumption that the principal function of government is to provide for the public good. Unlike the liberal state, which acts principally to protect its citizens' private liberties, the republican state tries to provide for the commonweal in whatever fashion it can. Two British republican political theorists who were very influential among colonial and early national citizens, John Trenchard and Thomas Gordon, best expressed this principle in *Cato's Letters* (1720–23): "The administration of government is nothing else, but the attendance of the trustees of the people upon the interest and affairs of the people" (1: 111); or again, "Nothing is so much the interest of private men, as to see the publick flourish" (2: 638). Republicanism also begins with the assumption that citizenship is earned through active participation in government. Ancient republican theorists, in fact, assumed that people were innately political animals, making active participation in civic affairs not only a prerequisite for citizenship but also an inborn human proclivity. Aristotle averred this view at the beginning of his *Politics:* "he who is unable to live in society, or who has no need because he is sufficient for himself, must either be a beast or a god: he is no part of the state" (14; bk. 1, ch. 2, sec. 25). Aristotle's definition of humans as political animals firmly situates him and republican political discourse in the civic humanist tradition that scholars of rhetoric have recently praised and attempted to revitalize in contemporary rhetorical education (T. Miller, *Formation* 288–89; Sloane; Poulakos). These concerns place republican discourse in orbit around a question: How can active citizens pursue the public good? The conversation constituting republican political discourse offered a number of answers to this question, all sharing a common set of topics: power, liberty, civic virtue, the *vita activa,* and corruption, among others.

Power

Power was often imagined as a necessary component in any republic to ensure unity and to preserve public virtue. Machiavelli even argued that citizens who inhabited a weak or morally bankrupt republic should hand over control to a prince who could restore a virtuous order. Machiavelli's republicanism requires the occasional intervention of a powerful prince to reform recurrent excesses. He advocated a constant rotation of monarchy and democracy, the prince and the republic, saying, "It is while revolving in this cycle that all republics are governed and govern themselves" (13). British republicans likewise afforded power a necessary place, though they did not think absolute power necessary in any circumstances. In fact, Trenchard and Gordon continually argued against such "arbitrary power" because they questioned any single ruler's ability to embody virtue: "the mind of any man, which is weak and limited, ought never to be trusted with a power that is boundless" (1: 180). Rather than allowing a constant dithering between monarchy and republic, as Machiavelli advocated, Trenchard and Gordon believed that a free and inquiring citizenry should keep power in check. The republic, in Trenchard's and Gordon's eyes, required laws and a system of checks and balances to prevent the quick slide into tyranny.[6] Trenchard and Gordon inaugurated the republican principle of the separation between executive and legislative powers. Early American republicans obviously continued this tradition when they constructed the three branches of U.S. government and the constitutional principle of checks and balances. The U.S. executive, judicial, and legislative branches check one another, thereby preserving the necessary republican power without risking despotism. Typically, a tripartite separation of powers is imagined as a central component of republican political discourse, but this is not entirely accurate. The tripartite separation of powers commonly defended in American republican discourse is in fact a distal principle attached to the more central republican notion of power.

Liberty

Republican "liberty" refers to citizens' ability to participate freely in civic activities. "Liberty" in the twenty-first-century lexicon tends to follow the liberal definition: instrumental, utilitarian, rational, individualistic, abstract, and egalitarian. But in the republican tradition, "liberty" means something quite different. It refers to a public capacity, the citizens' ability to actively participate in civic affairs. As republican citizenship requires active engagement in government, republican liberty permits this engagement (Appleby, *Capitalism* 15–21). The citizen gets defined by her possession and her use of liberty. And liberty's exercise is a requisite to check power. Trenchard and Gordon argued vehemently for citizen liberty because they believed that free citizens would check the excesses of power, just as they believed that powerful leaders would preserve virtuous institutions among the citizenry. While an excess of power leads to tyranny, an excess of liberty leads to "licentiousness" and "anarchy" (Trenchard and Gordon 1: 185). Early American republicans likewise imagined that power and liberty had to be kept in balance, and they bickered over how to achieve this equilibrium (Bailyn, *Ideological* 55–67).

In 1787, for instance, many argued that a strong federal government was needed to prevent disorder. In Federalist 6, Alexander Hamilton depicted Shays's Rebellion as a consequence of excessive liberty, and he presented a strong federal government as the necessary power to restore "perfect wisdom and perfect virtue" to the American republic (Madison, Hamilton, and Jay 104–08). Others claimed that a powerful federal government would ruin liberty and establish unwarranted and arbitrary power. The early American insistence on representative government also resulted from the liberty topic in republican political discourse. Like the advocacy for a tripartite separation of powers, the American republican belief in representative government is a distal notion branching from two central topics—liberty and power. Supporters of the U.S. Constitution (Federalists) worried that direct democracy would lead to an excess of liberty and therefore anarchy. Good government, to preserve a balance between citizen liberty and governmental power, needs the buffer of representative agents, elected by, though not immediately accountable to, the people. In fact, in the debates over ratification of the Constitution, Federalists referred to themselves as "republicans" in contrast to the "democrats" who wanted more direct representation. It deserves notice, however, that even anti-Federalists appealed to republican topics when making their arguments against the Constitution. They argued that the Federalists wanted an excess of power, which would disastrously curtail citizen liberty. Despite certain claims to sole ownership of the label, both Federalists and anti-Federalists were republicans insofar as they both appealed to topics like liberty and power.

Civic Virtue

In ancient Greek the word is *arête,* in Latin *virtus,* and in Italian *virtú.* The concept travels from the ancient Greeks, whose word is best translated as *excellence,* to the Romans, particularly the Stoic philosophers, whose word has masculinist resonances (the Latin word for *man* is *vir,* and Roman virtue is a "manly" quality), and finally to the Florentine philosophers, particularly Machiavelli, who imagined virtue as the counterforce to *fortuna* in the struggle to maintain a republic's integrity. The "Machiavellian moment," as J. G. A. Pocock identified it, is the point at which a political philosopher, politician, or citizen realizes that the republic's success is not guaranteed but rather depends on the rock of citizen virtue buffeted by *fortuna*'s corrosive waves. Eighteenth-century Americans inherited the concept of civic virtue from European (and some British) philosophers such as Charles le Secondat Baron de Montesquieu, Adam Ferguson, and Jean-Jacques Rousseau.

Early in his neoclassical treatise on politics, *The Spirit of the Laws* (1750), Montesquieu offered a classic statement about the relationship between the healthy republic and the character of its citizens. He said that the republic depends principally on its citizens' virtue, "but political virtue is a renunciation of oneself which is always a very painful thing" (35). Adam Ferguson also believed citizen virtue essential to the healthy republic, drawing on both classical political and Scottish common sense philosophy. In Ferguson's system, moral sense lays the foundation for civic virtue "to diffuse happiness" (41). While eighteenth-century leaders might have been unwilling and unable to maintain a collective ethos by imposing the harsh strictures found in ancient Greek republics like Sparta, most willfully adopted the classical belief that a republic is built on the soft but potentially stable ground of its citizens' virtue. While they all agreed that civic virtue was important, they did not agree about what constituted virtue. Montesquieu defined it simply as love of one's country. Rousseau believed virtue involved austerity, and Adam Smith, following Ferguson, saw both sympathy and the industrious pursuit of private property as virtuous. Just as present-day politicians all agree about the importance of "values" yet consistently disagree about how to define them, eighteenth-century political thinkers and citizens agreed about the importance of virtue yet disagreed about its constitution.

Vita Activa

The vita activa and civic virtue are related concepts. If virtue is the character necessary to functional republican citizens, the vita activa is the life necessary to preserve civic virtue. As Drew McCoy has illustrated, debates about the vita activa often pointed to economic activities conducive to the ideal republic (19–20). Adam Ferguson, for instance, believed that civilizations pass through a natural progression from hunter-gatherers, to shepherds, to farmers, to merchants and manufacturers. Ferguson argued that the successful republic should encourage trade, but he worried that an excess of commerce would erode civic virtue. Ferguson's solution, therefore, was a vita activa including commerce without allowing it to corrupt or to completely outpace agriculture. (See parts 4–5 of Ferguson's *Essay on the History of Civil Society*.) Adam Smith, Ferguson's compatriot, similarly saw agriculture as the most stable economic activity. Healthy societies progress through agriculture into manufacturing and commerce, but the vita activa of a successful republic should privilege agriculture: "According to the natural course of things, therefore, the greater part of the capital of every growing society's capital is, first, directed to agriculture, afterwards to manufacture, and last of all to foreign commerce." Smith argued for free trade, but he also believed that the soil of virtuous husbandry should underlie any commercial republic (*Wealth* 411, 740–45).

In contrast to those adulating agriculture as a necessary component to the vita activa, many argued for more trade. Though far from advocating free reign to luxury, pride, and greed, Montesquieu believed that commerce in the eighteenth century could do for modern republics what strict codes of conduct and ritual did for ancient republics. According to Montesquieu, "[t]he natural effect of commerce is to lead to peace," and "[t]he spirit of commerce produces in men a certain feeling for exact justice" (338–39). Alexander Hamilton likewise hoped that commerce would promote peace and civic virtue: "Commercial republics, like ours, will never be disposed to waste themselves in ruinous contentions with each other. They will be governed by mutual interest, and will cultivate a spirit of mutual amity and concord" (Madison, Hamilton, and Jay 106).

While debates about the vita activa often focused on economics, many also turned to cultural issues. Rousseau, for instance, worried about the fineries common among "men of taste" in commercial France. At several points in his *First Discourse,* he praised the Spartans for curtailing the arts to focus citizen attention on politics. "While living conveniences multiply, arts are perfected and luxury spreads, true courage is enervated, military virtues disappear" (54). This concern for how cultural life affects civic virtue became particularly important among those in education, since many believed that teaching certain kinds of public interaction could cultivate civic virtue.

Corruption

Just as the vita activa is related to civic virtue, so the topic of corruption relates to them both. While the vita activa represents the ideal life (economic and cultural) to inculcate civic virtue, corruption represents the point at which elements necessary to a republic become excessive and lead to its downfall. Classical republicans believed that to maintain virtue, progress must, to a degree, halt. Republican political discourse often incorporates a belief that governments repeat a cycle of democracy, anarchy, monarchy, and tyranny, with each form of government creating its successor's conditions. Intellectual historians have remarked that this cyclical understanding of history also appeared among early Americans (Pocock 6, 521; Wood 29). Doubtless, the cycles of government (pre)occupied many on both sides of the Atlantic. Rousseau worried that through progress, "souls have been corrupted in proportion to the advancement of our sciences and arts towards perfection" (39). Ferguson dedicated one-third (parts 5 and 6) of his *Essay on the History of Civil Society* to the potential for corruption in commercial republics.

Many believed that progress requires trade, which introduces a certain amount of corruption by cultivating and distributing excess and luxury. Instead of plugging holes in the dikes against commerce, citizens should accept and embrace a modicum of corruption to encourage productivity. David Hume, for instance, worried that a commercial population, amid the excess of modern production, would become indolent, and he viewed sloth as far more corrupting than luxury. His solution, therefore, was "to govern men by other passions, and animate them with a spirit of avarice and industry, art and luxury" ("Of Commerce" 10). Hume, however, never argued that luxury should be encouraged without qualification: "When carried a degree too far, [luxury] is a quality pernicious, though perhaps not the most pernicious, to political society" ("Of Refinement" 16). Hume's political vision was more jaundiced than Rousseau's and Ferguson's, but it appealed to the same topic on which they hung their arguments.

The same can be said of early Americans making public arguments: they all appealed to republican political discourse, though they ended up in very different places. Republicanism's capacity to bring people together without creating complete consensus contributed significantly to the formation of an American public sphere. Citizens made common use of republican topics in the debate over British duties and the possibility of revolution, particularly in two of the most famous arguments after the Stamp Act crisis: Jonathan Dickinson's *Letters from a Farmer* (1767–68) and Thomas Paine's *Common Sense* (1776). Both authors employed a republican vocabulary, but they arrived at very different arguments.

Dickinson and Paine: Publicity and Republican Political Discourse

Dickinson, a Quaker writing in the immediate aftermath of the Stamp Act, conceded that the British government deserved much of its power, particularly the ability to levy duties and to regulate trade. Dickinson described the relationship between the colonies and Great Britain before the end of the Seven Years' War as a mutually beneficial balance of power and liberty. The British parliament exercised due and just authority over trade to everyone's benefit. Colonials preserved liberty in local assemblies and in commerce. In Dickinson's words, "parliament unquestionably possesses a legal authority to *regulate* the trade of *Great Britain,* and all its colonies. Such an authority is essential to the relations between a mother country and its colonies; and necessary to the common good of all" (13). Britain exceeded her power and encroached on colonial liberty in her attempts to levy taxes without allowing colonials direct representation in Parliament (48–49). By defining acceptable exercise of power as pre–Seven Years' War British mercantilism and abuse of power as post–Stamp Act British mercantilism, Dickinson was able to make a case for resistance. Once Dickinson's definition of liberty was established, he spoke conceptually of it, fully trusting the reader to draw connections between his abstract discussion and the concrete political situation. At one point, he seemed directly to channel Trenchard and Gordon, saying "perpetual jealousy respecting liberty, is absolutely requisite in all free states" (117).

A number of Dickinson's arguments also appeal to other republican topics, such as the vita activa and the corrupting influence of luxuries. For instance, Dickinson argued that, in order to preserve the stability of republican government, citizens must constantly police those in power because, "unless the most watchful attention be exerted, a new servitude may be slipped upon us under the sanction of usual and respectable terms" (63). He also forgave British taxes on luxury items because such items were not necessary and, if allowed in excess, may corrupt (74–75). Dickinson even opened his last letter with a reminder that the chief duty of republican government is protection of the public good: "A people is traveling fast to destruction, when individuals consider their interests as distinct from those of the public" (133). Important to note, though, is that Dickinson did not advocate full separation from England, and when the Declaration of Independence was drafted, he abstained from signing, ostensibly out of his religiously driven pacifism but probably also out of his conservatism. Dickinson, like many other colonials, was willing to define some but not all British rule as excessive power, and he worried about the excessive liberty that might result from independence. Even his resistance to independence was based on an appeal to republican topics.

Thomas Paine, on the other hand, similarly appealing to republican topics, arrived at very different conclusions about British control over colonial affairs. Paine opened his pamphlet by distinguishing between government and society, the latter of which appears to arise out of natural liberty, the former out of the need to restrain said liberty for public benefit (1). Paine's distinction appeals to both the liberty and the power topics, claiming an important place for governmental power—maintenance of civic virtue. Paine said that some form of government is eventually necessary "to supply the defect of moral virtue" (3). As power encourages civic virtue and contains excessive liberty, free citizens exercising their liberties must police governmental power, "And as this frequent exchange will establish a common interest with every part of the community, they [government power and citizen liberty] will mutually and naturally support each other, and on this [. . .] depends the *strength of government and the happiness of the governed*" (4).

Unlike Dickinson, who allowed certain forms of British government to stand as reasonable power, Paine defined excessive power as any authority not rooted in direct popular representation, a definition allowing him to paint the British monarchy, regardless of its policy, as a threat to liberty (9–10). Paine also defined the democratic republic as the only government in which the abuse of power would not threaten liberty. He compared the sickly, corrupt British monarchy to strong democracy: "Why is the constitution of England sickly, but because monarchy hath poisoned the republic, the crown hath engrossed the commons." In his depiction of Great Britain as no longer worthy of the name "republic," in his claim that the "corrupt influence of the crown" had poisoned the mother country, Paine again appealed to a common republican topic, and he began an argument for rebellion as appropriate to the vita activa (20). By defining monarchy as an excess of power and the democratic republic as a virtuous balance of power and liberty, Paine was able not only to push for independence but also for the establishment of democracy in the colonies. The vita activa not only included rebellion but also the creation of a more direct democracy.

Dickinson and Paine created two variant arguments appealing to the same republican topics. Their articulations of republican discourse to differing partisan interests and specific reactions to British trade policy present us with differing republican publicities that share a common set of rhetorical appeals. Their public arguments demonstrate how a political discourse can constitute the ideological component of publicity without imposing consensus. They also demonstrate the rhetorical operation of definition arguments in various articulations of republican publicity. Dickenson and Paine agreed about how to define power, liberty, and the vita activa, but they disagreed about how to apply these terms to human events such as the duties on lead and glass, the British monarchy, or the potentially independent American government. They disagreed, for instance, about whether to define recent British actions or all British government as an abuse of power. In defining their circumstances and their opportunities, they attempted to advocate a certain collective sense of the situation and to promote particular actions. There occurred in colonial society a "definitional rupture."[7] As things fell together, Thomas Paine's definition of British monarchy became the most widely accepted, but his definition of direct democracy as the only way to vouchsafe a balance of liberty and power did not fare as well. American political debate through the Constitutional Convention (1787) was riddled with arguments over whether or not direct democracy could be defined as anarchy, tyranny (of the majority), or the only government to successfully balance power and liberty. All parties in these subsequent debates made appeals to the same republican topics that Dickinson and Paine appropriated. All of these arguments, therefore, contributed to the construction and maintenance of a republican public sphere, though this public sphere was home to very different articulations among a common political discourse and a variety of political agendas.

The Edges of Republican Publicity and Rhetorical Analysis

Though illustrative in many capacities, the above analysis of republican political discourse and its importance in the articulation of differing early American publicities overlooks certain racial, class, and gendered biases. Republicanism hailed laborers, women, and people of color as citizens, but, when these people responded by taking up this common discourse, they were often either ignored or denigrated. Rogers M. Smith has noticed an ascriptive strand in American civic practice, a restriction of citizen agency to white, Protestant, propertied males (80–85). In articulations of republicanism to certain rhetorical norms, specifically those norms that afford a voice to certain kinds of participants, this ascriptive tendency had regrettable results. Early American republican publicity was often an articulatory practice only made efficacious if attempted by white propertied men like Jonathan Dickinson and Thomas Paine.

Republican publicities favored the economic elite by privileging the cultural markers of the eighteenth-century bourgeoisie. In America, sociability, respectability, and the pretension to bracketing private interests were all peculiar to the capitalist class and all afforded distinction in the accepted norms of republican rhetorical culture (Shields; Warner, *Letters* 72). The rhetorical norms among laborers, slaves, servants, and frontierspeople were often denigrated by bourgeois revolutionaries like Samuel Adams, James Madison, and Thomas Jefferson.[8] American republicanism's exclusiveness, however, did not cut solely along class lines. People of particular races, genders, and cultures were also left out of the conversation. The republic, as discussed and disagreed over, for instance, was always masculine, civic virtue often openly described as "manly" (Rousseau 111). Popular literature along the British Atlantic often only allowed women civic agency through their husbands and their sons. Novels openly promoted the secondary role of feminine virtue and republican motherhood. (See William Henry Brown's novel *The Power of Sympathy* [1789] and Hannah Webster Foster's *The Coquette* [1797].) The few female actors that did attempt to enter the republican public sphere had to inhabit "a vocabulary of masculine patriotism" in order to gain any audience (S. Gustafson 250). African-American rhetors often appealed to republican topics and to Christian rhetoric in order to claim political agency for themselves, but they were rarely afforded much attention.[9] The ascriptive bias common to American articulations of republican publicity has drawn several criticisms. Certainly, American republican publicity, in all its formations, did not embody tolerance, nor did the republican public sphere along the eighteenth-century British Atlantic have permeable boundaries (Hauser, *Vernacular* 77–80; Benhabib).

Republicanism and Laissez-Faire Capitalism: Political Discourse, Publicity, and Economics

As the preceding discussion suggests, a shared discourse was articulated in various ways by different versions of republican publicity. To this, we must now add a discussion of the economic conditions to which republican discourse was articulated. Publicity is more than an articulation of a political discourse, a set of rhetorical norms, and a partisan agenda. It is an articulation of all these components to an economic interest. To understand the economic component of any republican publicity, one must explore the theories of political economy and the material interests common along the eighteenth-century British Atlantic.

While classical republicanism encouraged heavy government involvement in all aspects of public life (management of economic production and distribution included), in the seventeenth and eighteenth centuries, a variety of people began to promote less government intervention, believing that, if left alone, the free market would efficiently allocate resources and encourage continued prosperity among self-interested actors. These theorists were encouraged by the breakdown of Tudor control in the 1690s, a control that had allowed heavy government intervention in British economic affairs. Free-market enthusiasts were also encouraged by the "promise of prosperity," the relatively newfound ability to produce far more than the population needed to survive, allowing for trade, a division of labor, and the production of unnecessary but desirable goods (Appleby, *Capitalism* 27–28). The economic conditions of free trade encouraged people to imagine themselves as autonomous and self-interested actors, which led to an elaborate theory of the "natural" laws of the marketplace, the possibility of serving the public good by leaving economic matters to the invisible hand of laissez-faire capitalism. An economic theory was articulated to the prosperity growing out of free-market policy.

Joyce Appleby has argued that the principal political parties in the early national period found a common ground in republican political discourse. Like Paine and Dickinson, both Federalists and Democratic-Republicans spoke the same language. But Democratic-Republicans redefined key terms in the republican lexicon to suit the advancement of laissez-faire capitalism. "Capitalism thus disclosed itself in a benign and visionary way to Republicans who drew from its dynamic operation the promise of a new age." Democratic-Republicans appropriated republican topics to advance an economic system that benefited them. They redefined the vita activa, turning away from the classical republican notion that the government is "the noblest activity for men of civic virtue" and celebrating "the informal, voluntary political life open to all" (Appleby, *Capitalism* 50, 19, 67). In each effort at redefinition, each new appropriation of republican discourse, the Democratic-Republicans entered the public sphere and made new use of its available means of persuasion. They articulated an inherited political discourse to a new economic paradigm. Most importantly, for Appleby and for this analysis, "[t]hey did it with words" (78).

Even Dickinson and Paine articulated their differing arguments to colonial capitalism. Dickinson's claims never threatened to dismantle the relationship with British government, so they appealed to established colonial merchants who benefited from the protection of British trade restrictions. The Navigation Acts, passed after 1651 and in force throughout all British colonies until 1849, restricted colonials to trade with British provinces and benefited capitalists particularly in the northeast by shielding them from international, especially Dutch, competition. Though they could only trade with Great Britain, their markets were protected by the mother country's substantial navy. Also many of the agricultural goods that northeastern merchants exported (timber, barreled meat, fish, oil, and grain) were exempted, allowing colonists in New Jersey, Pennsylvania, Massachusetts, and Connecticut to export their agricultural surplus wherever they pleased. The protection from competition and free access to international markets enabled the northern and the middle colonies to handle the high prices of British-produced molasses, sugar, and manufactured goods. Also, the Navigation Acts restricted oceanic trade to British vessels, so northeastern colonials had a steady demand for their vibrant shipbuilding industry (Vickers 245). Colonials exploited all of these opportunities, and by 1740 they had developed a thriving commercial economy along the northeastern seaboard. To threaten separation from the mother country was also to threaten colonial capitalism. Dickinson avoided this by openly defending Great Britain's right to restrict colonial trade, arguing that British "parliament unquestionably possesses a legal authority to *regulate* the trade of *Great-Britain,* and all its colonies. Such an authority is essential to the relations between a mother country and its colonies; and necessary to the common good of all" (13). Dickinson's republican publicity articulated British mercantilism to the interests of northeastern American merchants comforted by the quilted blanket of British trade restrictions, markets, and military protection.

Paine, on the other hand, by demanding independence as the only path to a stable balance between power and liberty, threatened colonial capitalism. Chapter 4 of *Common Sense* tried to mollify merchants who might have resisted such a separation. Analysis of Paine's pamphlet, without an awareness of the economic interests at play, is complicated by this concluding section, an extended and rather tedious argument about the colonies' ability to fund the war and to avoid economic depression while separating from the mother country.[10] Early in the argument, Paine reassured colonial merchants that British markets would not shun colonial goods if ties to the mother country were severed because "[t]he articles of commerce by which she has enriched herself, are the necessities of life, and will always have a market while eating is the custom of Europe" (23). He also argued that independence would open other European markets to American exports (26). The pamphlet's last chapter promised colonials that they could afford a war without risking financial ruin. In the appendix Paine further argued that "[t]he mercantile and reasonable part of England, will still be with us; because, peace *with* trade, is preferable to war, *without* it" (67). Thus, Paine's republican publicity articulated the economic interests of northeastern capitalists to his separatist agenda.

Even in the European conversation, republican discourse was articulated to various economic interests and developments. While Appleby finds that Democratic-Republicans adopted topics like the vita activa and liberty to defend laissez-faire capitalism, in many places republicanism was articulated to a reaction against capitalism's profiteering individualism. Appeals to the public good and to a bourgeois sense of sympathy were often invoked as bulwarks against capitalism's more pernicious motives.[11] Some European political thinkers invoked republican topics in direct reaction against free-market capitalism and all its artifices.[12] Nevertheless, it is unfair to label all eighteenth-century republicanism, particularly American republicanism, "anticapitalistic" or "antimodern" as numerous historians have implied (Wood 53–65; Pocock 506–52; McCoy 23–26). Republican discourse was articulated to a variety of often conflicting economic interests and agendas, sometimes to free-market capitalism, sometimes to its opposite.

While it is a mistake to assume that republicanism was a raw reaction against capitalism, it is equally a mistake to assume that republicanism was a rhetorical gloss for laissez-faire economic policy.[13] Both of these interpretations suffer from the effort to find argumentative consistency in the conflicted terrain of any publicity, in the conflicted articulations of a political discourse to various economic interests. Republican discourse was articulated to a variety of political positions and to a variety of economic interests. Joyce Appleby has aptly demonstrated that a developing market economy affected how people defined republican categories. She has also explained how a complicity with laissez-faire capitalism crept into republican terminology. What her thesis does not account for, however, is the plurality of economic interests in early American society and the variety of appeals made to these various interests through republican topics. Appleby consistently assumes that a free-market economy was taking over all of the British Atlantic. Republicanism either appears wedded to emerging laissez-faire capitalism or to residual economic reaction—mercantilism, medieval state interventionism. Her own analysis of the 1790s partisan division depicts Federalists as elitists partially committed to free-market policies but unwilling to give up their social privileges or their governmental influence over the colonial economy.[14] The Democratic-Republicans, on the other hand, look like hopeful laissez-faire ideologues willing to clear away all the breakers of government intervention so that everyone could ride capitalism's wave to the shores of universal progress. Appleby says, "At the most general level, the Republicans' expectation of a sustained prosperity based upon an ever-expanding global exchange of goods undercut the Federalist rationale for energetic government" (*Capitalism* 92).

Recent economists have found along the eighteenth-century British Atlantic a plurality of economic formations, often in conflict with one another. There was more to the British Atlantic than free-market capitalism and its detractors. There were farmers in the hinterland, semiautonomous yet still dependent on an unregulated overland trade. The Whiskey Rebellion (1794) happened because this economic interest was threatened by a Federalist tax on a product that frontier farmers produced for sale. In the 1780s, Federalists courted frontier citizens by promising that a stronger centralized government would raise a federal army and protect western settlements from Amerindian assaults, which were often directly provoked by Anglo encroachment. The frontier economy, though only marginally tied to early American capitalism, therefore had a great effect on federal policy.

There were plantation owners in the South who depended on the quasi-feudal institution of slavery and also on the free international market where they could seek the best prices for their indigo, tobacco, and rice. These economic interests kept the South out of the revolutionary effort for fear that slaves would revolt when they were no longer threatened with reprisal from the British army. Southern plantation owners also feared exclusion from British markets. At the time of the American Revolution, the southern colonies sent 70 percent of their exports to Britain (Galenson 200). Common arguments against the American Revolution predicted that independence would threaten commerce with Great Britain, an appeal made directly to the southern reliance on British markets. *Plain Truth* (1776), the anonymous and famous loyalist refutation of Thomas Paine's *Common Sense,* made such veiled appeals to southern economic interests, claiming that revolution would sever trade with Great Britain, thereby cutting their commercial lifeline and ending the beneficent flow of British culture and capital (26). Even after the Revolution, the South would continue to depend heavily on British markets, which is why Jefferson's Democratic-Republican Party, strong in the southern states, would resist Federalist efforts to promote local manufacture by imposing tariffs on British goods. South Carolina was the colony least willing to rebel, and its plantation owners only agreed to do so because they were convinced that the new world economy could sustain a market for their agricultural surplus (Menard 294). The South was also pulled into the revolutionary effort by promises to lift British restrictions on traffic in southern staple crops. Later, the Federalist Party would pander to the southern fear of slave revolts by promising to build a strong federal army to suppress any uprising.

There were laborers throughout the colonies who wanted to improve their lives by moving west and settling on "virgin" territory. They resented the British treaty ending the Seven Years' War. By the Proclamation of 1763, the British government forbade any settlements west of the Appalachian divide. This treaty contributed a great deal to proletarian support for the Revolution. In his first move as newly appointed commander and chief of the federal army, George Washington waged war on the Miami and Shawnee (1790), driving them from their lands to secure more territory for Anglo westward expansion. His was the first in a series of American wars, all in an effort to ensure an open frontier. In 1803 Jefferson justified the Louisiana Purchase by appealing to proletarian desire for a better life in frontier agriculture. This land would allow, he claimed, end-less westward expansion for American citizens. The first two states west of the Appalachians added to the union were Kentucky (1792) and Tennes-see (1796), both of which grew out of the Virginian and North Carolinian hinterlands.

Even early American capitalism was not a unified institution. Some merchants in the northeast resisted the Revolution because they feared losing protection of British trade policies. Colonial capitalism experi-enced an extended boom from 1716–51 and recovered quickly to grow again between 1755 and 1764. Even the 1751–55 recession was mild. The colonial economy as a whole experienced tremendous growth between 1740 and 1764 (McCusker and Menard 60, 65). In this time, many estab-lished merchants grew wealthier and more politically aligned with British mercantilism. Some commercial farmers in the middle colonies and the northeast did not fear exclusion from British markets because a manufac-turing industry thrived in this area and because colonial markets could absorb the wheat and grain produced in the mid-Atlantic breadbasket.[15] While established merchants often feared revolution, commercial farmers in the middle colonies supported it. Some northeastern manufacturers and shopkeepers supported the Revolution because they suffered intensely from an extended depression caused by strict British enforcement of trade policy after the Seven Years' War. All of these people—established Con-necticut merchants, Pennsylvanian commercial farmers, Boston shop-keepers—were capitalists, but they occupied different positions in a com-plex economy, so they supported different political efforts.

Surely, there is something to Appleby's argument that capitalism and its laissez-faire ideology steadily infiltrated the American economy and the republican public sphere. All colonials benefited from developing free-market commerce, as is illustrated by widespread prosperity during the Seven Years' War (1756–63). In these years, lax enforcement of mercan-tile restrictions allowed a lively smuggling trade to develop with the Caribbean colonies, and British military presence in New York brought a steady stream of money into the city. Even though the hinterlands did not immediately witness or benefit from commerce like the urban centers, they relied on this trade for their own prosperity. Frontier families needed strong markets to sell their agricultural surplus and to purchase things they could not produce. And smuggling allowed the southern plantations finally to sell their exports outside the British trade circuit. Economists focusing on this era have repeatedly noticed that the myth of the autonomous early American producer (farmer, mill owner, or craftsperson) obscures the irrefutable fact that everyone was tied to domestic and overseas trade (McCusker and Menard 10).

So capitalism, from one important perspective, appears to have been emerging, with unified economic and ideological components. From another perspective, however, the colonial economy appears to have been fragmented and conflicted. Economists writing about this era stress the variety of economic interests present along the British Atlantic. Several historians have noticed that differing economic interests often resulted in differing visions of the ideal republic, differing partisan affiliations, even differing ideologies.[16] In hindsight, free-market capitalism appears to have won the day, but things do not look so neatly determined when considered in the particularity of early American struggles over economic policy. From this latter perspective, republican discourse looks less like a reflection or effect of free-market commerce and more like a common component in the struggle over republican publicity, an articulation that brings together both discursive formations (like rhetorical topics) and extra-discursive pressures (like modes of production or competing positions in a complicated political economy). By presenting differing articulations of republican publicity, citizens engaged one another in a common vocabulary to negotiate differing economic interests, differing political allegiances, and differing definitions of key terms, all in the hopes of affecting what would become of the republic economically, politically, culturally, and rhetorically.

Hegemony and Republican Rhetorical Strategy

This section offers three analyses of different arguments, all made in the late eighteenth century, all appropriating republican topics but with crucial differences. Each of the arguments offers a unique republican publicity, articulating the topics discussed above to a particular economic interest, a particular partisan agenda, and to a variety of other discourses (some religious, some economic). Timothy Dwight's republican publicity articulated topics like virtue and corruption to Puritan Calvinism and to a quasi-medieval economic structure peculiar to Protestant communities in New England, claiming that the virtuous republic should encourage agriculture in small communities where local government sets trade policy to discourage excessive commercial activity. Alexander Hamilton's republican publicity articulated topics like the vita activa to northeastern, principally urban, manufacturing interests and to active federal promotion of local industry. Hamilton's argument positions manufacturing as an important part of a healthy republic and favors government intervention to protect American manufacturers from foreign competition. Thomas Jefferson's republican publicity articulated topics like corruption and liberty to southern economic interests, particularly privileging commercial agriculture as the basis of American prosperity and arguing for free trade to allow maximum profit on the international market. Jefferson's articulation of republican publicity eventually became dominant, but that victory would have never been conceivable without his rhetorical articulation of republican political discourse to a specific economic program. If early American publicity was so contested and if republican rhetors articulated their arguments to differing economic interests, then capitalism was never a guaranteed winner. Its success depended both on economic and rhetorical factors that had to be articulated by particular actors.

Timothy Dwight's Millennial Republican Publicity at Greenfield Hill

The settlers who initially came to and prospered in New England and the middle colonies did not seek wealth nor the means to attain it. Their theological and political leanings led them rather toward a desire for simple family comfort and communal living organized by various authoritarian social structures rooted in seventeeth-century Calvinism, be it Congregational, Baptist, Dutch Reform, or Presbyterian. (The Society of Friends is a notable exception to the common Calvinism among early New England communities.) They were drawn by William Penn's promises of "English husbandry" along the Delaware, Francis Higginson's descriptions of "greene Pease growing in [. . . the Massachusetts governor's] Garden," and the hope of a simple life among like-minded believers (Vickers 210–11). Their desires neatly fit New England's topography, which was too rocky for plantation agriculture or for production of an exportable staple crop (McCusker and Menard 92). The northeastern landscape coupled with these early settlers' political inclinations initially led colonials to advocate community over self-interest. In Massachusetts, for instance, the legislature issued permission to create towns, which included legislative representation and land to distribute among citizens. Local assemblies allowed land grants according to several criteria, including status, family size, and extent of social investment. Such policies tried to prevent lucrative agricultural plantations, which discouraged social unity (Galenson 149–50).

Connecticut provides a good example of one seventeenth-century New England rural Protestant community. Populated largely by Congregationalists migrating from Massachusetts, Connecticut's towns were governed by elders and church leaders who established civic order by imposing a strict social hierarchy and moral code. The Connecticut Puritan character was deferential or authoritative depending on its possessor's rank. Town leaders determined mores and economic practices as well. They afforded land grants to new citizens. To promote industriousness, they encouraged certain forms of market-based commerce, like trade in lumber, corn, and cattle. Connecticut political economy, however, involved efforts to curb "excessive" commercialism. Heavy taxes, for instance, were levied against improved lands, making lumbering a very prosperous effort initially but foolish in the long run unless one was willing to farm the land after clearing it (Bushman, *From Puritan* 26–35). Resulting were tightly knit, interdependent settlements built on the foundation of agriculture but pursuing various efforts such as simple manufacture and commerce. Though a few wealthy resident families lived in every settlement, great economic distances did not separate people into widely disparate classes. As a result, well into the eighteenth century, Connecticut society can be characterized as economically "equalitarian."[17]

Puritan communities like those in Connecticut adhered to a federal theology, which developed in part out of Calvinist covenant theology. They believed in a special covenant of grace between God and the regenerate or—in the case of the new nation—a covenant between God and the American republic. In the mid- to late eighteenth century, this federal theology was folded into a unique variation of republicanism, one that catered to the economic policies of Protestant New England towns while also incorporating the common rhetorical topics such as the vita activa, virtue, and corruption. Nathan Hatch has called this "amalgam of traditional Puritan apocalyptic rhetoric and eighteenth-century political discourse" a "civil millennialism" (*Sacred* 23–24). Connecticut Puritans thus articulated a system of religious belief to a political discourse and to certain efforts like the Revolution or to partisan institutions like the Federalist Party. (See Hatch's *The Sacred Cause of Liberty* chs. 1–3.) The public arguments that brought together these elements articulated a millennial republican publicity, a unique iteration of republican discourse sutured to religious beliefs and to a specific political economy.

New England's early settlements shared an authoritarian and anticommercial bent that continued well into the nineteenth century, forming one of the principal reactionary forces against eighteenth-century capitalism and direct democracy. Throughout the eighteenth century, the Connecticut elite dominated an increasingly inclusive and noisy public space of print culture. Nevertheless, figures like Jonathan Edwards, Thomas Clap, and Jared Eliot continually tried to assert a moralistic influence over social developments (Grasso 88–228). Their hope for benign authoritarian rule, though curiously anachronistic in capitalist eighteenth-century America, appeared in many places and shaped Connecticut politics through the early nineteenth century. In the early national period the Federalist Party, allied with Congregationalist leaders, formed what was popularly known as the Federalist-Congregationalist Party. Through 1817, Federalist-Congregationalists fought a written constitution that might take power away from the dominant upper house—the Council—or that might institute laws contradicting their moral order. Their efforts to impose ecclesiastical control resulted in a vigorous opposition to one point in the 1819 constitution: a new provision outlawing state financial support of any particular church (Purcell 232–61). The constitution passed with support from Democratic-Republicans, then allied with the Anglican Church.

In the late eighteenth century, Timothy Dwight, himself a Calvinist and a descendant of the ministerial elite that ruled Connecticut, still embodied this millennial republican publicity, including its authoritative leanings and its reservations about capitalism. His public arguments depicted his own town of Greenfield Hill as a model for the new republic. Dwight's definition of civic virtue appeared in his *Sermon on the Means of Public Happiness* (1795): "The primary means of originating and establishing happiness, in free communities is [. . .] the formation of good personal character" (12). Dwight, however, was not pushing for Spartan *arête* or Stoic *virtus.* He certainly did not advocate the virtue of acquisition. (Early in the sermon, he listed the evils of wealth and greed [8].) Like many millennial republicans of his era, Dwight defined civic virtue with a Protestant inflection (Rahe 748–72). He connected civic virtue to "piety" (21), which citizens can attain through "revelation," religious education, and personal and public worship (24–35). Dwight, through republican argumentative topics, defined the virtuous citizen as a pious Calvinist. He even went so far as to advocate governmental control of religious education in schools to disseminate civic virtue among the citizenry (38).

While Dwight defined civic virtue as Christian piety, he depicted New England's communal political economy as the proper vita activa. His long poem *Greenfield Hill* (1794) describes a humble, equalitarian economy led by divine order to productive, abstemiously commercial obedience. Dwight's vision is both economically egalitarian in its hope for simple community life and socially authoritative in its insistence that everyone follow the same moral order. In Greenfield Hill, he said, "one extended class embraces all" (36). He also held up the pious farmer and the minister as his guides to the good life. Through the farmer character, for instance, Dwight promoted individual and household discipline (133–34). At one point the farmer offers typically communitarian advice about avoiding the excesses of commerce: "*In merchants' books from year to year, / Be careful how your names appear*" (131). The minister, like the farmer, leads a life of daily chores performed for love of God and community. In both *Greenfield Hill* and the *Sermon on the Means of Public Happiness,* Dwight expressed his notion of corruption, which involves any distraction from religion. Excessive capitalism is a prime culprit.

The last part (part 7) of *Greenfield Hill* is particularly important because it offers a look at how Dwight rewrote the republican tradition. In this section, Dwight broke away from the circular notion of time often attributed to both classical republicanism and to his own work.[18] Instead, he waxed millennialistic, arguing that America, the promised nation, the new Eden, would achieve the divinely promised, unending heaven on earth. History is no longer beset by cycles of democracy, anarchy, monarchy, and tyranny. Rather, the republic can enjoy a steady march toward an unending city on a hill. This revision of republican time was common among clergy, who likewise appropriated republican rhetoric to promote their own political economy (Wood 114–24). Recently, other rhetorical analyses find Dwight promoting a similar vision of "the New England ideal [. . .] the sort of social interaction and community life he believed would follow if his political principles were enacted" (Clark, *Rhetorical* 23). Nathan Hatch has found in Dwight's writings a rhetorical appropriation of republican discourse to promote a particularly Protestant vision of the new nation (*Sacred* 112–13). However, without an understanding of the political economy in Protestant New England settlements, Dwight's persuasive efforts look like just another version of republican rhetorical topics. In fact, Dwight's millennial republican publicity appealed to a commonly understood vocabulary and to a set of extra-discursive economic interests. His unique republican publicity articulated a commonly understood discourse about good democratic government to a commercially abstemious political economy and to a Puritan social hierarchy.

Alexander Hamilton's Manufacturing Republican Publicity

In the *Federalist Papers* Hamilton articulated republicanism to capitalist principles such as free trade, promoting a commercial republic of citizen-merchants. He argued, for instance, that the sense of mutual dependence and interest necessary for a healthy republic could arise from commercial exchange (Madison, Hamilton, and Jay 106). Hamilton learned from the Revolution, however, that a very important and relatively new kind of capitalist was emerging, the manufacturer. The economic trouble that followed the Seven Years' War (1756–63) affected manufacturers more than established merchants. Initially, defiance came from those yoked to commerce but carrying the least fat to weather lean years: manufacturers, shopkeepers, and local craftspeople. This disgruntled lot made up the majority of Samuel Adams's Sons of Liberty in Boston. They won the repeal of the Stamp Act, but in 1767 Charles Townshend, chancellor of the exchequer, proposed and passed the Townshend duties on paper, paint, lead, glass, and tea. Manufacturers fought again, this time with a proposed and successful boycott on British manufactured goods, eventually reducing colonial trade with Britain by half. As colonials consumed fewer British manufactured goods, they consumed more locally produced products, directly benefiting colonial manufacturers. In many regards, especially in the urban centers, manufacturing capitalists spearheaded the Revolution (Bridenbaugh, *Cities in Revolt* 334–45, 425). As a result, the center of post-revolutionary eighteenth-century American political economy would never be the nation-state. It would thereafter be the independent producer (McCusker 341).

The influence of a colonial manufacturing class has led many historians to label the Revolution a "middle-class" endeavor (Wood 85–86; Bridenbaugh, *Cities in Revolt;* Bridenbaugh and Bridenbaugh, *Rebels and Gentlemen*). However, despite its political heft, the manufacturing economic interest did not dominate American policy formation until well into the nineteenth century. Hamilton's proposals to encourage manufacturing failed in Congress in the early 1790s, and Jefferson only reluctantly agreed to federally promote manufacturing when his hostility to Great Britain caused a slump in trade, demonstrating how much the United States needed independence from foreign (particularly British) manufactured goods. Manufacturing capitalists would eventually develop into the "manufacturing aristocracy" that Alexis de Tocqueville found and feared in the 1830s. (de Tocqueville presciently worried that this aristocracy would separate from the rest of U.S. society and threaten democracy.) But even in de Tocqueville's account, well into the nineteenth century, the manufacturing capitalist class was still "rising before our eyes," not yet holding the dominant position it would occupy by the 1860s (555–58).

Though it was an emergent economic interest, manufacturing capitalism did have its advocates who articulated republican discourse to a political economy quite different from what Dwight encouraged in his own millennial republican publicity. In 1791, for instance, Alexander Hamilton, anxious to turn America into a commercially prosperous nation, argued before Congress in his now famous "Report on Manufactures" that the federal government should encourage local production by imposing restrictions on American commerce. Hamilton's report articulated a publicity whose elements included a manufacturing economic interest and the same republican topics that Dwight had articulated to a commercially stunted political economy. Early in his report, Hamilton presented Congress with a definition of the vita activa that focused on maximum production in an industry. While he was careful to concede that agriculture was very important, he also argued that manufacturing, in a complementary fashion, could be a productive American industry. Furthermore, he argued that a robust manufacturing economy would bolster constant local demand for agricultural surplus, thereby ensuring a sustainable farming industry (95–96). Hamilton's virtuous citizen soon appears as a productively employed citizen. He owed much to Scottish thinkers like David Hume (whom he admired) and Adam Smith (whose *Wealth of Nations* he had studied carefully). Like these men, he made rhetorical use of republican topics while promoting economic policy. At one point in the "Report," he criticized the farmer for being "careless in the mode of cultivation," a trait not permissible in manufacturing and reprehensible overall, as it leads to waste and indolence (78). Manufacturing encourages virtue in agriculture insofar as it makes the farmer more productive (85).

Hamilton defined the vita activa as productive and diverse industry, civic virtue as industriousness, and corruption as laziness. One of manufacturing's most important effects is its ability to give work to those idle souls unable to toil at the plow. Hamilton pointed particularly to women, the elderly, the infirm, and children, too weak to perform much agricultural labor, whiling away their hours in useless pursuits, "and in many cases a burthen on the community, either from the bias of temper, habit, infirmity of body, or some other cause, indisposing or disqualifying them for the toils of the country" (91). Economic arguments in the seventeenth and eighteenth centuries commonly promoted population growth and full employment by appealing to a belief that more workers would produce more surplus.[19] These arguments appealed to people's desire for greater material comfort, but Hamilton's argument appealed to something very different, something very republican: citizen virtue and corruption. The lazy "burthen" escapes corruption and becomes a virtuous producer when manufacturing presents a form of labor that s/he can perform.

Hamilton's efforts at federally promoting manufactures failed in part because the opposition (principally southern commercial farmers) painted his "Report" as an effort to return to corrupt British mercantilist practices of trade restriction. Commercial farmers in the South defined Hamilton's policies as an encroachment of power upon liberty, therefore a corruption of virtue, a cascading into degenerate English conditions. Many even called him an American Walpole, alluding to the British prime minister who regularized and consolidated the British financial system and was allegedly responsible for the mid-eighteenth-century English social decline. When Hamilton's proposals failed, the Federalist government shifted its economic attention from developing manufactures (a program that benefited New England manufacturing capitalists). Thereafter, Federalists decided to develop and reap the benefits of free international trade in agricultural products (a program that benefited New England established merchants and southern commercial farmers). Both economic programs, however, were articulated to republican discourse (McCoy 152–65).

Thomas Jefferson's Commercial Agrarian Republican Publicity

In the mythos of Americana, Alexander Hamilton typically appears as a progressive capitalist and Thomas Jefferson as a regressive agrarian. Hamilton is the champion of industry, the precursor to Henry Ford; Jefferson is the bucolic reactionary, the forerunner to William Jennings Bryan. This interpretation is based principally on the nineteenth query in Jefferson's *Notes on the State of Virginia* (1787), where he articulated republican topics to an agrarian political economy. Contrary to Hamilton, Jefferson defined the vita activa as agricultural production, claiming, in a now famous passage, that "[t]hose who labor in the earth are the chosen people of God, if ever he had a chosen people, whose breasts he has made his peculiar deposit for substantial and genuine virtue." To value agriculture over manufacturing, Jefferson raised typical republican concerns about the corrupting nature of luxury and commercialism, allowing that the United States would lose some industry by not developing manufactures, but insisting that this "loss by transportation of commodities across the Atlantic will be made up in happiness and permanence of government" (217). While Hamilton, like David Hume, accepted that a certain amount of luxury was necessary to offset more corrupting sloth, Jefferson argued that no corrupting luxury should tempt virtuous agrarian austerity.

It is a mistake, however, to label Jefferson a reactionary. Though Democratic-Republicans might have often alluded to Virgilian myths of bucolic splendor, in policy they were more capitalists than ancient farmers (Richard 161–4). In fact, Jefferson's publicity articulated republican political discourse to economic policies that mimicked Hamilton's platform exactly, excepting the provisions to promote manufacturing. Jefferson and his kind were free marketeers of the Adam Smith variety. Hamilton focused on the manufacturing chapters in *The Wealth of Nations,* developing an industrial economic policy closer to David Ricardo's capitalism. Jefferson focused on Smith's critiques of mercantilism and on the argument that a broad agricultural base would stabilize a healthy republic. In fact, Jefferson's commercial agrarian publicity was so convincing in the late eighteenth century because it articulated republicanism to economic developments that made American agricultural export a much more secure and profitable enterprise. Europe's burgeoning population opened a number of stable markets for U.S. agricultural surplus, while upper and frontier southern farmers switched to grain production, a more stable and certainly more widely exportable crop. Jefferson's republican publicity directly endorsed the production of grain for export. He worried that excessive investment in other crops, like sugar and tobacco, would corrupt the colonies. He said these economic efforts produced a "culture productive of infinite economic wretchedness." He also praised the production of wheat as a virtuous endeavor (*Notes* 218–21). When Jefferson said that "it is the manners and spirit of a people which preserve a republic in vigour" (*Notes* 217), he was carefully fashioning a publicity that articulated republican discourse to a capitalist interest, one favoring free-trade policy and thereby benefiting plantation owners in the southern states.

By articulating his republicanism to commercial production of grain, Jefferson also appealed to economic interests in the middle colonies. Grain production offset the fluctuating, although profitable, markets for tobacco, rice, and indigo in the south. Commercial grain production was also the principal economic effort in Delaware, Pennsylvania, Maryland, and New Jersey. Finally, free-market policies appealed to established merchants in the northeast who did not want any restrictions on their ability to trade for profit. The Democratic-Republican Party eventually achieved hegemony in part because Jeffersonian publicity articulated its policies to republican discourse and to a number of material interests. Seen in this manner, the competition between Hamilton and Jefferson, as well as the competition between the Federalists and the Democratic-Republicans, looks like a competition between two competing modes of capitalism, a commercial agrarian capitalism privileging southern and middle-state farmers (while also appealing to northeastern merchants) and an industrial capitalism privileging New England manufactures (Appleby, *Liberalism* 257–69). Most importantly to the analysis at hand, the competition between Hamilton and Jefferson, Federalism and Democratic-Republicanism, industrialism and free-market agrarian capitalism occurred through common appeals to republican topics. This was a contest over the contested terrain of republican publicity, the hegemonic articulatory practice of public argument. When Jefferson's commercial agrarian policy became dominant, it began to look like there was only one way to be a public republican citizen: Jefferson's way. Once hegemonic, Jefferson's articulatory quilt became totalizing. Others entering the republican public sphere would have trouble finding gaps in the tightly woven sutures that Jefferson's publicity fashioned among the Democratic-Republican Party, its free-trade policy, the various U.S. economic interests, and Jefferson's agrarian version of republican topics.

Scholars focusing strictly on political discourse tend to deride economic analyses as vulgar arguments about material interests determining cultural artifacts and rhetorical claims. Rhetorical theorists, when they acknowledge the importance of extra-discursive factors, tend to proceed without keeping economic developments and interests in view.[20] Both approaches are faulted, the former for ignoring the economic base as an important component of any publicity and the latter for acknowledging its presence but for then proceeding as if this acknowledgement fulfils the analyst's obligation. Though certainly a factor contributing to articulations of early American publicity, economic interest did not determine early American thought or the arguments over what the republic would become. In fact, republican discourse shaped the perimeters of what was publicly appealing. Republicanism enabled actors to promote their economic interests. It is therefore important to consider both economic and rhetorical factors as interactive components of a public debate over the early republic and its ideal methods of enacting public citizenship. The outcome of any historical moment is not determined by an economic, a political-philosophical, or a rhetorical variable. It depends on the articulation of these variables, and this articulation depends on individual acts in a tense moment of struggle over publicity.

This chapter has focused on republican discourse and its appropriations in public arguments about early American politics and economics—its participation in a hegemonic order that eventually privileged commercial farmers over communal New England Protestant settlements and over manufacturers who advocated some trade restriction. The above analyses, informed by consideration of economic interests, demonstrate that republican topics appealed not just by invocation of a common vocabulary but also by rhetorical articulation to a variety of economic interests, social mores, and cultural practices. Hegemony involves an economic base variously connected to and affected by civil society. Along the eighteenth-century British Atlantic, the economic base included a variety of interests, many in conflict with one another. Though one variation of capitalism won the field, it was contested, and the eventual Jeffersonian hegemonic articulation of republicanism to commercial agrarianism was not guaranteed. It was a contingent victory won rhetorically. Republican publicity, therefore, is one important part of early American civil society where hegemony was won and lost.

Just as various groups struggled over how publicly to enact good republican citizenship, so did they struggle over how to teach virtuous republican citizens. In the eighteenth century there was great concern over how to teach republican rhetors because early Americans saw a vital connection between one's civic capacities and one's rhetorical training.[21] They understood that, though citizens are not powerless over language, they are only powerful through it. Early American citizens fought over various publicities and rhetorical pedagogies, whose instantiations and enactments tried to articulate some connection between an economic interest, a common republican discourse, and a pedagogical program to shape good citizens.

And, perhaps most importantly, the struggle over how to enact republican citizenship and the struggle over how to teach rhetoric to American republican citizens were related both in the causal dynamics of eighteenth-century history and in the minds of eighteenth-century citizens. Jefferson and Dwight actively shaped rhetorical pedagogy and rhetorical theory in the early republic with differences that reflected their differing material and political allegiances. Economic interest, public discourse, and rhetorical pedagogy were all vital and interrelated components of what became a cohesive republic. America became a nation and an identity *rhetorically,* in all three senses of the word: through a body of common discourse, through a body of theory about how discourse works, and through efforts to teach the art of discourse to virtuous citizens.

2

One Republic, Many Paideiai

Political Discourse, Publicity, and Education in Early America

Under governments purely republican, where every citizen has a deep interest in the affairs of the nation, and, in some form of public assembly or other, has the means and opportunity of delivering his opinions, and of communicating his sentiments by speech; where government itself has no army but those of persuasion; where prejudice has not acquired an uncontrolled ascendancy, and faction is yet confined within the barriers of peace; the voice of eloquence will not be heard in vain.

—John Quincy Adams

Since the ancient Greeks, education has often been tied to the dissemination of civic virtue in a prosperous republic. In his "Areopagiticus" (355 BCE), Isocrates argued that the fate of Athenian society lay in its ability to teach citizens the virtue of private sacrifice for the public good. He said the properly educated citizen would "not regard a charge over public affairs as a chance for private gain but as a service to the state" (sec. 25, p. 119). Werner Jaeger has illustrated that from Hesiod through Plato the ancient Greeks believed education should shape the human components of a functional state. They "were the first to recognize that education means deliberately moulding human character in accordance with an ideal" (1: xxii). Beginning with the sophists—the first rhetoric teachers—education in civic virtue principally meant education in rhetoric: "In classical Greek the politician is simply called the *rhétor,* an orator [. . .] Eloquence, then, was the point from which any attempt to educate [. . . one] for political leadership was bound to start" (Jaeger 1: 291). The Greek word for education in the ideals of civic virtue is *paideia.* In ancient Greek societies this education took numerous forms as various thinkers and city-states had differing political inclinations. Athens, an open commercial republic, promoted values different from what one would find among students attending the *agôgê* in Sparta, a principally agricultural and military republic. Similarly, Isocrates and Plato had very different ideas of what constituted *arête,* so they developed differing conceptions of education (Jaeger 2: 87–106, 2: 234–50, 3: 46–70). Even in ancient Greece, republicanism had many forms, each articulated to a different conception of education for good citizenship.

The Romans adopted Greek philosophy and culture for their own purposes, developing another *paideia,* this time in accordance with the construction of a vast empire. Cicero believed that the commonwealth stood or fell depending on the rhetor's virtue: "[B]y the judgment and wisdom of the perfect orator, not only his own honor, but that of many other individuals, and the welfare of the whole state, are principally upheld" (*De Oratore* 14; bk. 1, sec. 8). Cicero speculated on the perfect orator's education but did not offer the most detailed description of the Roman *paideia.* Quintilian owns that honor. His twelve-book *Institutio Oratoria* details the education of the virtuous orator from childhood on. He even dedicated one full book to the development of good moral character. In his definition of the orator, Quintilian foregrounded virtue: *vir bonus dicendi peritus;* the good man [sic] skilled in speaking (bk. 12, ch. 1, sec. 1, 4:355). Of course, the Roman *paideia* differed from the Greek, since these societies differed in their conceptions of how the good republic should appear. Likewise, though they had different political inclinations, when early American thinkers adopted republicanism, they also stressed education in rhetoric. Benjamin Rush consciously echoed classical thinkers when he said that eloquence "is the first accomplishment in a republic and often sets the whole machine of government into motion. Let our youth, therefore, be instructed in this art" ("Of the Mode" 10).

The influence of republicanism on early American education is evident in several post-Revolution efforts to exert state control over colleges and curricula. The state of New York seized King's College in 1784 and established a board of regents able to found other educational institutions. They renamed King's College "Columbia University." The newly established

State University of New York system would receive public money, have no religious affiliation, and would educate citizens for proper participation in republican government (Humphrey 271–80). In 1779 the state of Pennsylvania similarly took over the College of Philadelphia, establishing a state-run and -financed university system and renaming the school the University of Pennsylvania. They revised the curriculum and created periodic external review to ensure that the university functioned in the state's interest (Cheyney 122–45).

Perhaps the most widely known effort to spread republican virtue through state-controlled higher education is Thomas Jefferson's persistent attempt at establishing state-funded and -regulated education in Virginia. Jefferson introduced the Bill for the More General Diffusion of Knowledge to the Virginia legislature in 1778, 1780, and 1786, failing each time to push it through both houses. He also tried to achieve state control over William and Mary College. When these efforts failed, he promoted and was eventually successful in founding the University of Virginia (1818) on nonsectarian, republican principles (Cremin, *The National Experience* 107–14). Benjamin Rush also promoted republican education, publishing his now famous "Plan for Establishing Public Schools in Pennsylvania" in 1786. He wanted publicly funded free schools in every town, four colleges, and a university in the state capitol. Rush argued that republican virtue had to be taught early in citizens' lives, saying, "I consider it possible to convert men into republican machines. This must be done if we expect them to perform their parts properly, in the great machine of the government of the state" ("Of the Mode" 9). Rush was active at the University of Pennsylvania, where he served as faculty at the medical school, and he was instrumental in the founding of Dickinson College in Carlisle, Pennsylvania (1783). In these instances and in countless others, republicanism was clearly articulated to American education.

However, this connection between republican discourse and eighteenth-century higher education, already drawn by historians (Cremin, *The National Experience* 5), should not lead to the facile conclusion that eighteenth-century American rhetorical instruction was the same as or shared common effects with pre-Enlightenment curricula. Both were founded on civic humanism, surely. Both shared a political discourse. But early American republican education was its own creation, able to prosper for various reasons, many not at all connected to republicanism. Just as early American publicity was a site where actors articulated a common political discourse to various economic, political, religious, and cultural concerns, so early American education was also a site where individuals sutured republicanism to various and often opposing interests. While the articulatory practice of publicity happened in public arguments about what constitutes a healthy democracy, the articulatory practice of education happened in pedagogical exercises: lectures, debates, student societies, and compositions.

Faculty at William and Mary and the College of New Jersey shared an understanding of how education related to broader society. They thought education was a component of civil society not dramatically separate from, and definitely vital to, the construction of a functional state. All would have nodded at Montesquieu's statement, "In the republican government [. . .] the full power of education is needed" (35). These colleges shared a commitment to training citizens in civic virtue to promote the public good. And they shared a republican belief in the vita activa as performed through deliberation. Frederick Rudolph's claim that a "commitment to the republic became a guiding obligation of the American college" is certainly accurate (61). But this shared obligation did not preclude disagreement over what virtue or the vita activa involved, so, while the colleges were all republican, they were not republican in the same way. Economic and political differences resulted in various articulations between education, particularly rhetorical education, and republican political discourse. Just as Timothy Dwight's, Alexander Hamilton's, and Thomas Jefferson's differing publicities articulated republicanism to conflicting early American economic interests and political allegiances, so did articulations of curricula suture republican discourse to the conflicted base of economic interests and the partisan affiliations among educators and institutions.

While the previous chapter looked at the disputed enactment of republican publicity, this chapter examines similar political and economic conflicts as they affected republican pedagogy. First, institutional factors made early American rhetorical education particularly well suited to republicanism. Specifically, a number of common practices, such as disputation exercises and literary societies, paved the way for a republican rhetorical *paideia* in the colonies. But this republican *paideia* was not uniform in its political affiliations. To illustrate how rhetorical pedagogies variously articulated economic interests, partisan affiliations, and republican discourse, this chapter covers a variety of efforts to weave republicanism into early American education: the 1750s King's College controversy in which Anglican conservatism and Whiggism were both articulated to republican politics and to education; Noah Webster's efforts to articulate the Federalist political platform to republican politics and to an Americanized English during the early national period; the conflicted republican rhetorical curricula at one academy in Philadelphia between 1760 and 1780; and John Quincy Adams's articulation of republicanism, rhetorical pedagogy, and New England bourgeois rhetorical norms at Harvard in the early nineteenth century. These collected examples illustrate that, just as republican publicity was a contested site where political and economic conflicts were negotiated, so also was republican rhetorical pedagogy a conflicted arena where everyone adopted a common vocabulary while promoting very different agendas.

Politics and *Paideia* before Republicanism

The colonial colleges were particularly well-suited to eighteenth-century republicanism. Even before a vocabulary of the "public good" and "citizen virtue" was commonplace, colonial educators were already participating in efforts to train young leaders for public service. From the very beginning, colonials adhered to the British notion that collegiate training principally prepared people for service in the church or in government. English colleges and universities had close ties to, received funds from, influenced, and were influenced by both the British scepter and crown. The first American colleges (Harvard, William and Mary, Yale) were established for ecclesiastical and state service, and they relied heavily on state support. Early in its history, Harvard received a portion of every family's corn harvest, the "college corn," a system soon replaced with more formal grants (Morison 15). With such public subsidy came an obligation to toe the state line. For instance, in the 1750s government and church conspired to push Harvard and Yale away from orthodox Congregationalism. When Yale's president Thomas Clap refused to do so, he aroused the ire of many Connecticut citizens, among them Benjamin Gale, who pressured the

General Assembly into refusing its annual grant in 1755 (Kelley 61–63). Throughout the seventeenth century, state governments practiced what one historian of early American education has called a "benevolent paternalism" (Robson 20–22), a tradition that laid the groundwork for, and that often constructed institutions permitting, later republican efforts to disseminate civic virtue through an alliance between higher education and government. In fact, private higher education was inconceivable to Americans until 1819 when Dartmouth successfully argued before the Supreme Court that the state could not amend its charter. From that point forward, a charter protected the university from public intervention just as it protected the public from undue obligation to the university.

A number of common pedagogical efforts also suited colonial curricula for a republican political project. College life promoted a sense of community among the students and faculty that developed through common routines that everyone followed. All ate at the same hours, attended Mass together. All attended class together, lived in the same building, even attended the same extracurricular activities (Rudolph 145–47). Republican rhetorical pedagogies built on this sense of community. Republicanism's commitment to commonly held civic virtue and to the commonweal requires a modicum of consensus among citizens. Republican rhetorical norms also encourage like-mindedness among citizens. Publicly developing virtue through rhetorical practice encourages citizens to internalize common beliefs and behaviors. A commitment to the public good encourages citizens to hash out their differences and to arrive at a consensus. A republican curriculum, likewise, stresses common ground and trains students in the art of disagreeing while also pursuing mutual understanding. Three common curricular institutions—lecture, recitation, and disputation—prepared student-citizens by encouraging both a sense of community and the ability to disagree while searching for eventual consensus.

While the present-day university does not encourage a sense of community among its matriculates or its faculty, the colonial college was quite different. The principal change wrought by university education after the Industrial Revolution is the elective system, which allows students to choose their own courses of study. One of the most daunting challenges facing university rhetoric instructors today is the plurality of disciplines, each with its own notion of "good" communication. The university today lacks community, though it is awash in communities. By contrast, prior to the mid-nineteenth century, most colleges had uniform curricula that every student endured (Russell 20–26, 35–69). In the seventeenth and early eighteenth centuries, the dominant method of imparting new knowledge was recitation. Students read texts and attended sessions where tutors asked questions about the material. Though pedagogically troubled, perhaps not effective or efficient, recitation did encourage a sense of community among students who simultaneously encountered the same material and the same, often abusive, tutor. Students typically studied rhetoric in their second and third years, reading classical sources and the occasional vernacular text. In 1783 at Rhode Island College, for instance, students read Longinus's *On the Sublime,* Cicero's *De Oratore,* John Ward's *A System of Oratory* (1759), Robert Lowth's *Short Introduction to English Grammar* (1762), and Thomas Sheridan's *A Course of Lectures on Elocution* (1764) (Bronson 103). Recitation was also used to teach advanced Latin and Greek in the first two years. (Students arrived with some training in classical languages.) In these sessions, students translated portions of classical texts into the vernacular or vice versa and exhibited their translations on demand in the classroom.

In the mid-eighteenth century, American colleges began to shed the regents system in which a tutor was assigned to each individual class of students. Influenced by Scottish universities where each subject was assigned to a specialized professor, American colleges began to establish chairs in particular subjects (Sloan 23–24). Typically, any given college would have chairs in mathematics, the natural sciences, moral philosophy, divinity, and rhetoric. Funds often precluded maintaining so many chaired professors, so the university president often doubled as professor of moral philosophy and rhetoric, delivering lectures to juniors and seniors. Students sharing a class were not assigned to one tutor but rather shifted among specialized instructors throughout the year. Professors lectured by offering commentary on a common text that the students read or by amalgamating a number of ideas on a given topic. If students read Longinus's *On the Sublime,* the professor might agree with Longinus's treatise, point out key passages, raise questions about the argument, openly disagree, or place it in the context of contemporary conversations.

These lectures, though highly derivative and rarely insightful, were a key point in the distribution of knowledge.[1] Books were not as common in the eighteenth century as they are today, and they were expensive. Only the very wealthy could afford copies of what they read. Most families owned only a few books, typically a Bible, some sermons, and perhaps a copy of *Pilgrim's Progress.* Though students often read texts available in college libraries, though some even collected enough to have private libraries later in life, most did not own their books. They did, however, keep their lecture notes. These were more than a nostalgic souvenir. They were an intellectual resource. In class, students meticulously transcribed, often verbatim, what the professor said. After hours, they collected their notes and prepared a master copy. Many such notebooks still exist in university archives and are discussed in later chapters. From these master copies, students made their own, carefully written notes, which they kept and referenced throughout their lives. One professor of rhetoric in the late eighteenth century had a better chance of broadly spreading his theories than Hugh Blair, author of the era's most popular rhetoric textbook.

While recitation and lecture surely created the sense of community requisite for a republican *paideia,* students also learned agonistic debate in disputation exercises. Once or twice a week, the college would gather as a whole to listen to upperclassmen dispute an assigned question. One student would argue the point in the affirmative, the other in the negative. Afterward, a judge, often the college president, would offer criticism of the arguments and declare a winner or promulgate a third position. In the seventeenth and early eighteenth centuries, disputation exercises were conducted in syllogistic form and in Latin. The topics were often theologically inflected, though later in the eighteenth century students began debating more politically charged issues. Disputation alone imparted the skill of productive disagreement, a vital republican rhetorical norm. As disputation topics increasingly engaged colonial politics, students were also encouraged to engage republican discourse. In effect, these politically relevant topics hailed students into the republican public sphere. For instance, in 1776, students at the College of New Jersey debated this point: *mentiri, ut vel Natio conservatur, haud fas est* (lying, even to save one's country, is wrong). There is obvious political relevance to this topic, and the students' arguments demonstrate their willingness to debate public issues.

One respondent focused on theological issues rather than the year's pressing events, arguing that lying is wrong because the Bible teaches as much. Another student engaged the language of citizen virtue, claiming that the public performance of good action creates good citizens. He argued that virtue could be preserved by telling the truth in all circumstances.

In the mid-eighteenth century, a number of forces conspired against the pedagogy of syllogistic disputation: a lack of popularity among students, a turn away from a theological to a more secular curriculum at most colleges, a widespread and increasing attention paid to transcontinental and international politics (issues that syllogistic disputation exercises did not address), and a developing belief that formal logic had little practical use. Syllogistic disputation that persisted after 1750 did often address important political issues of the day, though it might have done so in antiquated form. At Dartmouth in 1792, for instance, Joseph Field, Calvin Ingals, and William Ward debated this point: *An theatrum reipublicae utiliti sit* (Is the theater useful to a republic?). Field made appeals to virtue and corruption in a claim that the theater threatens the republic by taking attention away from virtuous pursuits like agriculture and commerce. He ended his paragraph-long exposition with a truncated syllogistic expression: *Deniquae, qodcunquae virtutem subvertit non reipublicae utilitati est, at theatrum virtutem subvertit. Ergo.* (In short, whatever destroys virtue is not of benefit to the republic; yet the theater does destroy virtue. Therefore.) Ingals and Ward also enlisted the virtue topic to attack Field's minor premise—the theater destroys virtue. Ingals argued that attendance at theatrical performances improves judgment and evokes sympathy for virtuous characters.[2] Though their manner of dispute would certainly prove useless in Congress or in a coffeehouse conversation, the shared rhetorical topics hailed these students as republican citizens, striving toward virtuous existence through agonistic deliberation.

As graduates engaged in public speaking on secular and religious topics, they realized that Latin syllogisms did not sway promiscuous assemblies. Cotton Mather, a product of this curriculum, said that the syllogism might help one to find truth but would offer no assistance in conveying it. By 1750, most colleges had begun to replace syllogistic disputation with forensic exercises—formally loose debates in English. Yale began phasing out syllogistic disputation in 1747, Harvard in the 1750s. King's College,

Table 2.1: Selected questions debated at Harvard commencement exercises, 1740–70 (Morison 90–91)

Year(s)	Question Debated
1743, 47, 51, 61, 62	Does civil government originate from compact?
1759	Is an absolute monarchy contrary to right reason?
1765	Can the new prohibitary duties, which make it useless for the people to engage in commerce, be evaded by them as faithful subjects?
1769	Are the people the sole judges of their rights and liberties?
1770	Is a government tyrannical in which the rulers consult their own interest more than that of their subjects?

Rhode Island College, and the College of New Jersey included forensic disputation from their beginnings. Dartmouth, on the other hand, held onto syllogistic debate until the early nineteenth century (Potter 31–37). Forensic disputes tended toward more secular and (inter)national political topics. College faculty and students often drew their questions from collections like Thomas Johnson's *Quaestiones Philosophicae* (1735). They preferred questions with some immediate relevance, rephrased questions to make them relevant, or simply made up their own. Samuel Adams, for instance, ignored more than four hundred questions in Johnson's book when he decided to dispute on whether resistance was justified (Myers). At Harvard, topics debated in commencement exercises from 1743 to 1770 reflect colonial concerns about the era, encouraging students to imagine their declamations as active participation in republican fora. Students addressed issues like the validity of the English monarchy, the possibility of violating trade restrictions, and the sovereignty of government. (See table 2.1.)

On September 7, 1769, at the first commencement of Rhode Island College, there was a dramatic instance of the pedagogical effort to create, through forensic disputation before a multiform audience, a (re)public(an) space where students could agonistically deliberate shared political concerns.[3] James Mitchel Varnum and William Williams, before the college, the town, parents, families, and government officials, debated this question: "Whether British America can under her present circumstances consistent with good policy, affect to become an independent state?" Varnum argued against separation, repeating many claims Loyalists commonly made: separation would destroy colonial trade; the colonies depended on Great Britain for protection; tariffs were not unbearable. Varnum even quoted Jonathan Dickinson's *Letters from a Farmer* to support his claim that those complaining about British tariffs were lazy and unwilling to manufacture in the colonies. Williams refuted Varnum's claims about the economically debilitating effects of Revolution. He argued that British rule drained the local economy by forcing colonials to pay for an imperial military. Williams also appealed to republican topics, defining British government as an abuse of power and encouraging colonials to exercise their liberty in separation. Varnum, responding to Williams's argument, pursued a peaceful resolution. Varnum said he wanted to appease colonials' valid complaints about British mercantilism without risking the loss of British military protection or access to British markets. This response tried to wrest consensus from the debate by conceding that Williams was genuine in his desire to shed no blood and by appealing to the voice of "mature deliberation" (Guild 295). Nevertheless, Varnum's amended argument stood against separation. The give-and-take evident in the Varnum-Williams debate demonstrates a central early American republican rhetorical norm, which students learned in their debate exercises. Students were encouraged to disagree in the interest of improving arguments, of honing their debating skills, but also in the interest of developing positions that could appeal to everyone. Though Williams never found an ideal common ground, though he lapsed into some very divisive claims in his response, he also gestured toward the possibility of consensus.

In addition to their official weekly debates and annual commencement exercises, students also formed communities of common interest and of agonistic debate in literary societies—student-organized clubs that began to appear in the 1750s and '60s. Members came together regularly to read selections from popular authors, to enact plays, and to debate topics forensically. At Harvard, as early as 1758, students performed plays popular among British gentry, such as Joseph Addison's *Cato* and *The Roman Father* (Morison 91). In 1770, the Speaking Club and the Mercurian Club were formed, and in 1774 the Clistonian Club appeared. In these meetings, students often read to one another passages from urbane British literature. They also read their own poems and essays modeled after popular authors like Alexander Pope, Joseph Addison, and William Shakespeare. In these exercises, students formed communities held together by common knowledge of literary texts and by a common practice of sociability. In their disputes on political issues, students created their own public spaces to agonistically debate issues of common concern. At Harvard, they often disputed or delivered stand-alone orations on topics very similar to those debated in official college exercises (Morison 138–39). At William and Mary, the Phi Beta Kappa society was formed in 1776. Other chapters of this society appeared at other colleges in the late eighteenth and early nineteenth centuries. Every meeting of Phi Beta Kappa between 1776 and 1781 hosted a forensic debate, often on a politically relevant topic and often also framed in republican terms. (See table 2.2.)

All of the curricular institutions discussed so far—lectures, recitation, disputation—existed before republican discourse became the American lingua franca. Only the literary societies were contemporary with the rise of republican politics in the colonies, and these societies repeated a pedagogical method already developed in college debate exercises. Therefore, the republican discourse that was developing currency and shaping early American debate about the nation's future was well-suited to give direction to several curricular endeavors already present in early American rhetorical education. In a sense, even before they had a republican vocabulary to discuss the political implications of their rhetorical pedagogies, American educators and students were already republicans. It should therefore come as no surprise to learn that early American education, particularly rhetorical education, was quickly articulated to republicanism. But this articulation was not uniform. Partisan interests among colonials affected how citizens imagined education for civic virtue. The articulation of particularly partisan agendas to a common republican discourse in early American education can be demonstrated by looking at the King's College debates, where participants advocated very different political and

Table 2.2: Selected questions debated at William and Mary's Phi Beta Kappa Society, 1779–80 ("Early Days" 249–59)

Date	Question Debated
March 27, 1779	Whether agriculture or merchandise was most advantageous to a state?
May 8, 1779	Whether a wise state hath any interest nearer at heart than the education of the youth?
June 12, 1779	Whether an agrarian law is consistent with the principles of a wise republic?
November 27, 1779	Whether a general assessment for the support of religious establishments is or is not repugnant to the principles of a republican government?
June 3, 1780	Whether any form of government is more favorable to public virtue than a commonwealth?
September 23, 1780	Whether avarice or luxury is more beneficial to a republic?

religious beliefs while claiming to pursue education for the common good. Even later in the eighteenth century, people like Noah Webster and Benjamin Rush appealed to republican topics in their arguments for a vernacular *paideia* articulated to the Federalist Party.

The King's College Controversy: Republican Education Contested

The King's College controversy (1753–56) pitted Presbyterian Whigs like William Livingston against Anglican Tories like William Smith, all of whom equally employed republican topics.[4] The Whigs argued for nonsectarian control of the college, while the Anglicans promoted their own leadership. Both sides, though radically different in political and religious affiliation, appropriated republican discourse, thus demonstrating that, as early as the 1750s, republican education was a contested site.

William Livingston and William Smith Jr. (no relation to William Smith), both heavily influenced by Whiggish republicans John Trenchard and Thomas Gordon (Bailyn, *Ideological* 35–37), fought for nonsectarian control of the college. They wanted training in civic virtue without religious inculcation. Modeled on Trenchard's and Gordon's *The Independent Whig,* Livingston published *The Independent Reflector,* where he and others argued that education in the interest of the public good could not have religious affiliation. One author, referencing classical sources such as Quintilian and Horace, said the "true Use of Education, is to qualify Men for the different Employments of Life [. . .] to infuse a public Spirit and Love of their Country; to inspire them with the Principles of Honour and Probity; with a fervent Zeal for Liberty, and a diffusive Benevolence for Mankind; and in a Word, to make them the more extensively serviceable to the Common-Wealth" (Klein 172). Another writer called education "the proper Business of the Public," obligating people "to promote the Felicity of [. . .] Fellow-Creatures." This author wanted a college founded not by royal charter but by an act of the assembly, since such legislation would make the institution more accountable to the popular will, more dedicated to the public interest (Klein 191–95). Education is obliged to serve the public good by disseminating virtue. But to Livingston and his cronies, virtue meant religious toleration and often political dissent. Republican citizens become virtuous by exercising their liberty against official institutions of power, such as the Anglican Church.

Smith, who would later become provost of the College of Philadelphia, published responses in the *New York Mercury,* arguing that an Anglican influence on the college would prevent "Bigotry, Enthusiasm, and Pride," elements that destroyed common civic purpose by dividing citizens into squabbling factions ("Extract"). While Livingston imagined civic virtue as the ability to dissent against tyrannical or unjust power, Smith imagined it as a consistent moral character necessary to avoid anarchy. He referred to Livingston's Whiggism as a "*leveling* Notion" that threatened the republic's stability ("To the Public" 9 July 1753). State imposition of moral character through criminal laws and through sectarian religious education was necessary. Smith, in effect, tied Anglicanism to "the common well-being" ("To the Public" 17 Sept. 1753). Livingston appealed to the republican fear of tyranny, while Smith appealed to the republican fear of anarchy. Both claimed to be preserving a precious and balanced moment in history, one that could easily become corrupted. The King's College controversy demonstrates that citizens began imagining education as a republican effort as early as the 1750s, but varying partisan affiliations led to disagreement about what constituted good republican education.

A Federal English: Rhetorical *Paideia* for Federalist Interests

Looking at another, later application of republican discourse, Noah Webster's call for a "Federal English" demonstrates that republicanism directed citizens to debates over rhetorical education. Colonials inherited from British rhetorical theory a belief that the virtuous republic could be achieved and sustained in part through rhetorical practice and instruction. For instance, while serving as professor of rhetoric at Daventry Academy (a British school for religious dissenters), Joseph Priestley offered a course of lectures on language in which he posited that, like republics, languages have a "kind of *regular growth, improvement,* and *declension*" (164). Monarchical governments hinder linguistic expansion, as they hinder prosperity. Only in the free commercial republic does language prosper and grow, but republics must fear corruption through excessive luxury, just as languages are always in danger of a corrupting emphasis on style. Priestley argued that the Roman republic was corrupted by its citizens' indulgences, just as Roman eloquence had been corrupted by "persons addicted to letters, having no occasion for the ancient manly and free eloquence." These corrupted rhetors "fell, through an affection of novelty, into a number of trifling and puerile refinements in style: analogies, instead of being fetched from nature, were borrowed from language itself; and verbal conceits and turns were admired for true wit and just sentiment" (175). Priestley believed that literary critics and teachers could have significant political effect by teaching virtuous rhetoric (182–83).

These lectures were widely read along the British Atlantic. Noah Webster especially admired Priestley's theory of language development and reiterated his connection between republican virtue and rhetorical education. Webster claimed that Great Britain was corrupt, as evidenced by "the taste of her writers" and by her language, which he described as "on the decline" (*Dissertations* 20). Webster's dictionary and his grammar textbooks codified American English first to demonstrate that Americans already practiced a virtuous language and second to encourage that practice more widely. Webster, like many language reformers of the era, viewed American English as a perfect expression of her citizens' character and also as something needing improvement. Some reformers even proposed that Americans call their language "American language" to differentiate it from corrupted British English (Baron 11–14; Howe 77). During the Federalist era of American politics, Webster articulated his language reform to the Federalist effort at unifying the individual states under one powerful government. Shaken by Shays's Rebellion (1786–87) in Massachusetts, Webster believed that people were not linguistically well-equipped for democratic deliberation. Citizens needed stronger guidance by an educated elite. While the Federalists promised to curb anarchy by putting power in the hands of a politically savvy few, Webster promised to promote virtue by establishing a rhetorical leadership who could sustain public order at least in part by modeling virtuous language (Howe 34–37). Webster openly articulated his republican program for language reform to the Federalist Party, calling his version of American English a "Federal English." Unlike the Democratic-Republican Thomas Jefferson, who thought grammar should be a descriptive exercise to catalog the popular idiom (Howe 37), Webster approached grammar prescriptively, promising to consult the "*rules of the language itself,*" appealing, like Priestley, to a universal grammar (*Dissertations* 27). Unlike William Livingston, whose program of republican education articulated the practice of citizen dissent to a Whiggish notion of liberty, Webster's equally republican rhetorical *paideia* articulated citizen obedience to the Federalist Party and to a republican fear of anarchy.

Politics, Pedagogy, and Economics

This chapter, so far, leads to a conclusion that a number of historians have already reached: early American education was a deeply politicized affair, often affected by or at least articulated to republicanism. (See Hoeveler, Roche, Robson, Cremin.) Like early American publicities, early American pedagogies often articulated a common vocabulary to a variety of partisan efforts and interests. One can take the analysis further, however, by considering economics. For instance, one might argue that Americans became more interested in higher education when they discovered republicanism in the 1750s and when republican beliefs became particularly widespread after the Revolution. In 1718, there were three colleges along the British Atlantic. For nearly thirty years, no new colleges appeared, but between 1747 and 1776, six were founded. After the Revolution ended, American colleges were born in even greater numbers. While republicanism helps to explain the proliferation of American higher education in the second half of the eighteenth century, it does not explain where these colleges were located or why they mostly survived in the northern and middle states. To understand that, one must turn away from republicanism and toward capitalism.

The northeastern and middle colonies developed a rich and variegated economy where educated entrepreneurs could pursue a variety of opportunities. In the South, commercial agriculture was the principal route to material comfort. A plantation-owning aristocracy dominated this industry, and its members had little use for education, except as a burnish to their already achieved status. As a result, the southern colonies before the Revolution showed little concern for higher education. Of the nine colleges founded before 1776, only one, William and Mary, was in a southern colony, and it was often underenrolled, could not afford its meager faculty, and closed periodically for lack of resources.

In the northeast, on the other hand, rocky geography and a short growing season prevented commercial agriculture from becoming the dominant industry. The northeastern economy was much more varied, incorporating an overseas and a carrying trade, manufacturing, fishing, farming, and professional industries such as medicine and law. Though the middle colonies certainly had substantial agricultural resources and though they did export a great deal of a surplus grain, the lure of commercial farming did not attract everyone. The middle colonies had the best of both worlds: a hearty commercial agriculture and a variety of other industries.[5] An enterprising and educated citizen living north of Maryland with little capital could become a professional lawyer, a doctor, a bookkeeper. S/he could ply a trade, earning enough money to open a print shop, a smithy, or a kiln. Parsimonious living, diligent saving, and a little careful planning could lead to ownership of, for instance, a printing press. Benjamin Franklin's bootstraps-capitalist saga never would have happened in the southern colonies where the economy was dominated by a single industry and a wealthy few—where entrepreneurialism had no cachet.

Since the northeastern economy presented more opportunity to the enterprising capitalist, people in this area adopted the bourgeois view of education as a means to acquiring social mobility (Cremin, *The Colonial Experience* 109–10). New England colleges accommodated the bourgeois belief that anyone can scale the economic tiers. Among other things, colleges stopped ranking students by their families' social status. Prior to the mid-eighteenth century, most colleges ranked students in each class by their social standing. A student's rank affected where he sat and how he was treated by faculty. Harvard persisted in this practice until 1772 (Morison 104), Yale until the late 1760s (Kelley 74–75), but Rhode Island College, founded by a commercial class of Baptists in a cosmopolitan city, Providence, never ranked its students by social position (Hoeveler 194–95). Colleges also catered to the bourgeois view of education as professional training. Institutions with overt religious leanings (King's College, Queen's College, the College of Rhode Island, the College of New Jersey) tried to draw students by offering instruction in more "practical" subjects such as bookkeeping, cartography, mathematics, geometry, and rhetoric. The number of graduates entering the ministry steadily declined throughout the eighteenth century. From 1700 through 1750, 50 percent of college graduates took orders, but in 1761 that number reduced to 37 percent, and in 1801, it was down to 22 percent (Brubacher 10).

Virginia, South Carolina, and Georgia, on the other hand did not have enough viable ports (excepting Charleston) for trade to override agriculture. Also, commercial agriculture drew talent toward the plantation. All available economic indicators pointed toward rampant economic growth in the South, even though developed capitalism was largely restricted to production and trade in three crops: tobacco, rice, and indigo.[6] Women married earlier. Populations grew more rapidly. Plantation-owning whites ate better, grew taller, lived in more lavish homes, and wore better clothes than those in other mainland colonies (Menard 250–54). In South Carolina and Georgia, by the mid-eighteenth century, small farm owners had all but disappeared, pushed out by or having grown into plantation owners. This area was closest to the British Caribbean in its makeup and its political allegiances.[7] In the Chesapeake area of Virginia, the small yeoman farmer dominated the agrarian landscape into the 1720s, but between 1720 and 1770, several factors conspired to eradicate small farmers and to create plantation agriculture: improved use of local waterways to allow easier export of staple crops; a warehousing system to control quality and to facilitate transport of tobacco; and the introduction of slaves, which allowed Chesapeake farmers to overcome the high cost of labor, a by-product of easy western settlement (Menard 270–77). These gentrified southern plantation families had no real need for education and stood to gain nothing financially from the endeavor.

Higher education prospered north of the Mason-Dixon Line because a developed professional middle class demanded a practical *paideia*. Southern elites wanted an education to polish their patrician sons (Thomson 400–07). These same citizens railed against William and Mary for teaching a bookish scholasticism rather than the genteel smattering of Latin and Greek needed for a southern plantation owner to circulate in polite company.[8] William and Mary, its faculty almost entirely imported from Oxford and Queens, trained scholars. Students wrote Latin and Greek poems daily on classical topics assigned to them (Canby 245).[9] Plantation owners wanted gentlemen able to converse in polite company. William and Mary offered them bookish scholars able to quote Horace in the original Latin. The college therefore suffered from a lack of enrollment and a paucity of funds. In fact, the American South fought any kind of practical education through the nineteenth century. The first Morrill Act provided public land grants for state universities that offered education in agriculture and engineering. It did not pass through Congress until 1862, after the southern states seceded from the union, allowing northern legislators to vote for it without opposition. The northern professional bourgeoisie, by this time spearheading the Industrial Revolution, continued to favor education as a means to achieve mobility. The northern states wanted education to train their citizens for industry. The southern states, still commercially agrarian, still resisted.

Varying economic interests along the British Atlantic not only explain the locations and the professionalized curricula of many colleges, but they also account for several particular efforts at rhetorical education. For instance, Webster's efforts to develop and teach a Federal English found support not just among Federalists but also among the emergent northern professional bourgeoisie. This *paideia* had political and economic appeal. Many prominent early American citizens, like Webster, argued that rhetorical education in classical languages corrupted citizens by teaching useless skills. They advocated education in the proper and virtuous use of English, invoking republican bromides about a profligate British rhetorical education wallowing in its own obsession with dead languages. American educators also invoked claims about the professional utility of vernacular mastery. Running through these attacks was a specifically bourgeois utilitarianism, which built on John Locke's argument for education in "things not words" (Reinhold 221–22). Thomas Paine voiced this appeal in *The Age of Reason* (1794–96) when he claimed that "[l]earning does not consist, as the schools now make it consist, in the knowledge of languages, but in the knowledge of things to which language gives names" (77).

When Benjamin Rush argued for the necessity of teaching eloquence in a republic, he quickly followed with a plan not for education in Latin and Greek but in English. He appealed both to bourgeois practicality and to republican virtue. Learning vernacular eloquence would enable young men to participate in business that benefited the person and the nation. Eloquent citizens versed in economics and capable of participating in a vernacular public discourse could fight the formation of a landed aristocracy ("Of the Mode" 12). Rush proposed that education should "prepare youth for usefulness here, and for happiness hereafter" ("Observations" 13). The classics accomplish neither, so Rush proposed a program for instruction in English rhetoric. His vernacular republican *paideia* drew on both the northeastern bourgeois desire for social advancement through commercial or industrial achievement and on the belief that indolent citizens (like a landed aristocracy) threaten the state's virtue.

Noah Webster likewise believed that a healthy republic needs proper education. Appropriately cultivating citizens' minds could stave off corruption ("On the Education" 2–3). Webster also claimed that the first error in American education was excessive focus on dead languages. Like Rush, Webster praised the capitalist's vernacular facility: "[D]ead languages are not necessary for men of business, merchants, mechanics, planters, &c." Webster feared that a classical "*liberal Education* disqualifies a man for business" ("On the Education" 5, 14). This argument, like Rush's, strongly resembles Alexander Hamilton's claim that idle hands should be employed by commerce and industry. The variation of rhetorical education most suited to preparing students for these activities was also the most virtuous.

Benjamin Franklin's Bourgeois Republican *Paideia*

Though Webster, Paine, and Rush all clearly favored a vernacular *paideia,* suturing republicanism to a northern bourgeois belief in education as a means of social advancement, the most extended and illustrative effort in this vein happened at the Academy of Philadelphia, where Benjamin Franklin doggedly promoted a rhetorical education in English to suit the interests of men in his economic situation: Philadelphian capitalists, including small merchants, shopkeepers, craftspeople, and professionals. This story begins in the 1740s when a group of Philadelphians decided to build a hall where the famous and influential Methodist George Whitefield could ignite his incendiary sermons. This hall, at Fourth and Arch streets, would also be used as a free school, called the Academy of Philadelphia, for the underprivileged in the local community. Funds for the academy fell short, and the project lay incomplete until Benjamin Franklin rode in with a cavalry of twenty-four new trustees. Franklin's kith of petty merchants and craftsmen wanted a school that would offer practical vocational training. The Philadelphian bourgeoisie invested in education as a manner of achieving status, so they pioneered numerous efforts at self education, such as night schools, subscription libraries, and literary societies (Bridenbaugh, *Cities in the Wilderness* 442–50). Franklin was most interested in an academy where young aspirant capitalists could learn the basics in English and mathematics, much as he had done before his apprenticeship at a printer's shop in Boston (*Autobiography* 53).

But Franklin allied himself with trustees who had different designs. They were established Anglican merchants and landowners, mostly the descendents of the proprietary gentry created when William Penn received and distributed Pennsylvania's lands. They formed a close-knit group of merchants whose social circles, family bonds, and commercial interests led them to form the Proprietary Party, to dominate the Council, and to become cultural poseurs. One historian calls them "as affluent, prestigious, cohesive, and exclusive a social group as ever existed in America" (Brobeck 410). During the Revolution, this gentry would find its greatest challenge, and eventually its defeat, in a political battle with less wealthy and less established merchants, shopkeepers, and manufacturers who formed the Anti-Proprietary Party led by Franklin.[10] While Franklin was committed to education in English and to a pragmatic rhetorical *paideia,* the trustees wanted instruction in classical languages.

Eighteenth-century established merchants imitated England's proprietary aristocracy, using their financial capital to purchase markers of social status. For instance, it became common for New England capitalists to buy land in an effort to establish themselves as proprietary gentry. Many hoped to ply the merchant's trade just long enough to acquire estates in England so that their families could move back and live in aristocratic fashion (Bailyn, *New England Merchants* 102–03). Just as land ownership marked one as genteel, so did cultural capital. Knowledge of classical literature, the ability easily to quote Homer and Cicero, marked social distinction. Of course, deep knowledge of classical literature and developed facility in Latin and Greek were not part of the refinement desired by the colonial established bourgeoisie. No one, not even the southern plantation owners, wanted a truly scholastic *paideia*. Rather, they wanted the veneer of a classical education, the kind of training that would allow one to dimple her conversation with appropriate epithets. Thomas Dale, a South Carolinian poseur who passed among the elite in eighteenth-century Charleston society in part by spouting appropriate Latin quotes in polite company, is an example of the valuable cultural capital Latin and Greek could provide in early American genteel society. Dale's success relied upon the genteel colonial's appreciation for, yet shallow knowledge of, ancient literature and culture (Shields 277–301). The Philadelphia gentry favored the Latin and Greek school over the English because they valued education in classic literature and languages as a manner of marking, not achieving, social status. This same belief persisted through the mid-nineteenth century, helping to keep classical languages and literature a strong if not dominant component of American higher education (Reinhold 226, 233–34).

Because of the differing economic classes and educational visions involved in its formation, the institutional structure at the academy was split. Young men could learn to read and write English and also arithmetic to prepare them for "mechanic arts and other professions." Or they could enter the Latin and Greek school, which prepared them for entrance into the College of Philadelphia, founded shortly thereafter (1754). At the Latin and Greek school, students received the refined knowledge of Horace and Longinus, which marked them as members of the Philadelphia gentry. Alexander Graydon attended the academy (without graduating) in the early 1760s. His experiences illustrate the class tension evident in the curricular structure.

Graydon was born to a middle-class family, and he enrolled in the academy when he was eight years old because, as he said, it was "my father's intention to give me the best education the country could afford." By his memory, most matriculates were social climbers, leaning toward careers as colonial merchants. Their practicality led them away from the classical model of education, represented metonymically by instruction in Greek and Latin: "we were all, therefore, to be merchants, as to be mechanics was too humiliating; and accordingly, when the question was proposed, which of us would enter upon the study of Greek, the grammar of which tongue was about to be put into our hands, there were but two or three who declared for it" (40). True to their bourgeois ethos, these boys fixated on the practical matters of education (as did Franklin). They all recognized that merchants were the wealthy and the most privileged in their society, so they all opted to work in that profession. Graydon's statement that to be a mechanic was "too humiliating" betrays a bourgeois disdain for laborers.

Just as the Philadelphia bourgeoisie and gentry fought over position, so did the Latin and Greek and the English schools compete over resources. This competition, and the continuous trustee privilege given to the Latin and Greek school, strained relations between Franklin and the academy from the beginning (Buxbaum). Toward the end of his life, while writing his autobiography, Franklin did not even mention the college or the Latin and Greek school, and his discussion of the academy amounts to a few phrases (182–83). In 1789, Franklin published a pamphlet denouncing the college and the academy, claiming that they had strayed from the original purpose to provide practical education in English and arithmetic for bourgeois children ("Observations"). He even compared Latin and Greek literacy to other genteel cultural habits like wearing a *chapeau bras,* a hat no longer necessary in an era of wigs and nicely dressed hair. Just as the gentry insisted on carrying their hats tucked beneath their arms, so did they insist on learning dead languages. Neither practice served a purpose. Such cultural leftovers were not only frivolous, they were also corrupting. Franklin noticed that in ancient, virtuous republics, austere citizens were never depicted wearing hats, unless they were soldiers wearing helmets ("Observations" 30–31). In fact, in his original call for an academy in Philadelphia (1749), Franklin expressed a desire for simple education that Webster repeated forty years later: "*Agricultural* and *mechanic arts,* were of the most immediate importance; the *culture* of *minds* by *finer arts* and *sciences,* was necessarily postpon'd to times of more wealth and leisure" ("On the Need").

In other documents, Franklin echoed republican sentiments about education, particularly the hope that citizen virtue could be shaped through an appropriate *paideia*. He wanted students to study history, morality, and religion to develop virtuous characters, and he wanted them to engage in agonistic debates about moral, political, and ethical issues to learn the principles of republican citizenship ("Proposals" 411–13). Though he couched these arguments in republican vocabulary, Franklin in fact advocated a particularly bourgeois version of republicanism.

His earliest proposals about the college and the academy reflect a bourgeois ethos and a hope to train young entrepreneurs. In addition to the emphasis on English over Latin, Franklin also mentioned oratory as a mode of practical address. He was influenced by John Locke's own program for rhetorical education, one articulated to bourgeois interests in England. Locke argued against teaching Latin and poetry on the grounds that such pursuits would never assist the aspirant merchant. Like Locke, Franklin also favored teaching students to speak *ex tempore* over training them to deliver polished orations, because the former would better prepare them for commercial affairs (Locke, *Some Thoughts* 282–85). In America as in England, political, social, and especially economic advantages were not always achieved through written discourse. Printing was laborious and slow. Newspapers and pamphlets took so long to assemble and circulate that they could not provide the most up-to-date information about political, legal, or market matters. Political discourse typically came first orally through speeches or sermons, to be printed only long after the fact. Newspapers delivered information from overseas, from distant colonies, reprinted public documents or speeches, offered entertainment, and at times advertised, but they were not immediately useful in pre-revolutionary Philadelphia's economic and political environment.[11] The man of business had to be a man of conversation.

Influenced by Locke's bourgeois *paideia*, Franklin recommended that students improve their letter-writing skills and their handwriting, both useful to the aspirant capitalist. Franklin wanted students to learn to "write a *fair Hand*," to write in a "*clear*" and "*concise*" style, and to learn to pronounce clearly and properly. Following Locke's *Some Thoughts Concern-*

ing Education (1705), Franklin recommended that students learn to write and speak proper English by studying grammar and imitating Tillotson, Addison, and Pope. He also recommended that students write letters and stories about personal experiences to be reviewed by the tutor and then revised ("Proposals"). Franklin included study of rhetoric and oratory (mostly review and imitation of tropes) on the advice of Samuel Johnson, then president of King's College, New York (Columbia University).[12]

Shortly after the academy was founded, at the request of its trustees, Franklin wrote an additional pamphlet, entitled "The Idea of an English School" (1751), in which he described his ideal curriculum. During the first two years of secondary school, he proposed that students study grammar, spelling, and pronunciation, by parsing passages from Addison's *Spectator* and by reading out loud under a tutor's close supervision. The third year of secondary school included study of tropes and figures, more instruction in public performance, now by recitation of parliament speeches, and finally some required historical reading. Franklin saw the first three years as a time to perfect one's grammar, to improve bad habits of pronunciation, and to learn the art of proper speaking. In the fourth year, when students left the academy and entered the college, they would master pronunciation and then turn to composition. As Franklin said, "Writing one's own Language well, is the next necessary Accomplishment after good Speaking." To educate them for professional careers, Franklin had his students write documents that would prove useful to a merchant or tradesman: letters recounting daily events and letters of congratulation, compliment, request, thanks, recommendation, and excuse. He also insisted that his students learn to write in a clear and concise style "without affected Words, or high-flown Phrases." In the fifth year, they would write essays and poems, and in the sixth year, they would write and publicly perform orations before local citizens, faculty, and other students. Franklin's refusal to entertain ornamental styles demonstrates a republican disdain for the corrupting influences of excessively ornamented language as well as a bourgeois interest in clear, functional prose.

Franklin's beliefs about what constituted good republican citizens extended beyond performance in a competitive commercial economy, however. His proposed pedagogy yoked economic interests to cultural habits.

When Franklin designed a curriculum to teach early American boys how to become successful professionals, he was sure to teach them how to speak like respectable young men. He therefore had them study examples of tasteful rhetoric, such as Addison's *Spectator* essays and various poems. Even the rhetorical style favored in Franklin's curriculum reveals his allegiance to bourgeois culture. As historians of public address have noticed, a hallmark of early American bourgeois rhetoric was directness, a trait that signaled sincerity to the listener. If sincerity is the virtue embodied by good rhetorical delivery, then one's prose style must be clear in order to convey this virtue to the audience. Notions of perspicuity, perspicacity, or clarity arise from eighteenth-century capitalistic constructions of the private self as a participant in the public sphere of intellectual exchange. In order to be rhetorically effective, one only had to be sincere, only had to show that s/he spoke from the private self, and others in the room would emotionally sympathize and privately relate (Fliegelman 24). Franklin, like other bourgeois republicans of the day, emphasized sincerity and sympathy in his conception of virtue, and he tried to encourage both through his rhetorical pedagogy. He wanted students to write clearly, and he devised a long list of historical, moral, and ethical texts to shape their characters. Here he demonstrated a republican concern for citizen virtue, a hope that a well-formed *paideia* could shape this virtue, and a faith that clear rhetorical performance could convey and disseminate it. It is also interesting that Franklin included Joseph Addison's *Spectator* essays among the texts that his students would study and imitate. The essay genre is particular to eighteenth-century bourgeois culture, for it employs the two constructions already mentioned: the private self and the clear style (T. Miller, *Formation* 48). In these essays, Addison positioned himself as one separate from, yet engaged in, society, and he wrote in an "unadorned" and "sincere" style.

While Franklin only briefly mentioned the study of tropes and figures in his "Idea for an English School," he carefully explained the need for teaching proper grammar. He also insisted on proper spelling and handwriting, which were especially important to those entering commercial society. Penmanship displayed strength of character and forthrightness. Handwriting books were constantly present and valuable pedagogical tools in eighteenth-century America, and bourgeois citizens slaved to develop a perfectly presentable, unlabored, and sincere handwriting (Bushman, *Refinement* 92–96).

Finally, and perhaps most importantly, Franklin stressed proper speaking at his English school. Under the close supervision of a tutor correcting them as they stumbled along, students would learn to enunciate their words without bombast or flourish. The eighteenth-century bourgeoisie commonly distrusted the written word as artificial and removed. One cannot sympathize with a rhetor when s/he is not present, so conversation was an important medium of capitalist communication (Shields 69–76). In all, Franklin hoped to prepare his students for success in a bourgeois republic by encouraging them to behave as free individuals who could sincerely display virtue through clearly handwritten letters or sympathetic coffeehouse conversation. Initially, his English school was a great success, appealing to both a common discourse of republican education, to an economic interest among Philadelphian capitalists, and to the cultural/ rhetorical norms commonly adopted by the colonial bourgeoisie.

The academy's first professor of English and oratory was James Dove, who had previously run a successful secondary school. Within a year, he attracted more students than his resources could handle. In 1753, the trustees replaced Dove with Franklin's friend and correspondent, Ebenezer Kinnersley, who would maintain the professorship of English and oratory until 1773. Kinnersley followed Franklin's "Idea of an English School" with some small amendments. Students in their first year of college (the fourth year in Franklin's program) did not begin composition but instead continued to study Cicero, Juvenal, and Homer. (This continued study of Latin and Greek writers shows the trustees' influence on the curriculum.) First-year students did, however, begin declaiming publicly. Composition began in the second year of college, and in the third year, students dedicated their entire afternoons to composition and public speaking. Alexander Graydon fondly recalled parsing sentences under Kinnersley's instruction and also recounted the in-class reading exercises that Franklin insisted would improve student pronunciation. He believed that many of the historical and literary texts the boys read, such as Aesop's fables, educated them morally by instilling the bourgeois virtue of sympathy. He said of reading about one particular literary character, "While the mild wisdom of my Mentor [Kinnersley] called forth my veneration, the noble ardour of the youthful hero excited my *sympathy* and emulation. I took part, like a second friend, in the vicissitudes of his fortune, I participated in his toils, I warmed with his exploits, I wept where he wept, and exulted where he triumphed" (27, italics added). Graydon's account indicates that Franklin's rhetorical pedagogy succeeded at instilling bourgeois virtues.

At a glance, one could easily conclude that everything went as Franklin had planned. Rhetorical education was offered in English. Students learned to speak publicly so they could become successful members of a respectable commercial republic. As Franklin said, "Thus instructed, Youth will come out of this School fitted for learning in any Business, Calling or Profession, except wherein Languages are required; and tho' unacquainted with any antient or foreign Tongue, they will be Masters of their own, which is of more immediate and general Use" ("Idea" 108). A closer look, however, reveals that Franklin's aspirations were not realized. To begin with, Ebenezer Kinnersley had no formal experience as a rhetoric professor prior to his appointment at the academy. He was a Baptist clergyman who, after falling out with the church over theological issues, turned his attention toward electricity and made a living doing experiments for Franklin and giving public lectures on the subject. During his time at the academy, he set up his scientific equipment in an apparatus room where he continued to give public lectures on electricity. He also found time, despite his duties as a professor of English and oratory, to continue his pursuits in the natural sciences, publishing articles in the *American Magazine,* inventing an electric air thermometer, and often receiving credit for discoveries also attributed to Franklin.[13] Kinnersley's inexperience caused many to lose faith in the academy, so enrollment fell at the English school.

In addition to Kinnersley's inexperience, Franklin's program also suffered from a lack of support from the trustees and the provost, who favored the Latin over the English school. In the early 1750s, the trustees paid the English master £150 (per annum) to teach forty students and paid the Latin master £200 to teach twenty. The trustees visited the Latin school more often than they did the English, though they were supposed to visit both equally. In his pamphlet "Observations Relative to the Intentions of the Original Founders of the Academy in Philadelphia" (1789),

Franklin excoriated the trustees for their favoritism. He mentioned the inequitable pay, and he particularly dwelled on parents' complaints that students did not learn to speak publicly, noting a decline in enrollment due to popular dissatisfaction. He even complained that the academy had hired his friend Kinnersley, a man "not possessing the Talents of an English School-master in the same Perfection with Mr. Dove" ("Observations" 15). Franklin mostly worried that oratory was not sufficiently taught: He noted that the public performances, originally a success under James Dove's tenure, had drawn progressively smaller crowds and were eventually discontinued. He complained that, by teaching grammar without application, the college and academy were falling into a model of education not suited for the new nation. Despite its eventual failure, Franklin's curriculum is a remarkable moment in early American rhetorical education, for the story of its appearance and eventual demise illustrates that differing rhetorical pedagogies articulated conflicted economic interests to a common republican discourse.

John Quincy Adams's Bourgeois Republican *Paideia* and the Era of Good Feelings

Other programs of rhetorical education likewise linked republican discourse to specific economic and political interests. For instance, John Quincy Adams's republican *paideia* provides a useful contrast to Franklin's curriculum. While Franklin designed a rhetorical curriculum suitable for aspirant capitalists, social climbers mostly living in Philadelphia, Adams designed a rhetorical curriculum suitable for the children of established capitalists, people who imagined education as both a badge of their social standing and as a manner of achieving professional success. Though both Adams and Franklin appropriated republican topics to discuss their rhetorical pedagogies, and though both articulated their programs of rhetorical education to early American capitalism, they catered to the economic interests of different groups. As a result, their rhetorical pedagogies, though sharing a common republicanism and even a common desire to teach English rhetoric, differed. While serving as Boylston Professor of Rhetoric at Harvard (1806–09), John Quincy Adams taught the principles of republican rhetorical practice to Boston's bourgeois sons. His lectures are typically read as classically republican statements, resuscitating ancient rhetorical theory in the early nineteenth century to combat the divisive political efforts of states'-rights southerners (Rathbun; Roberts-Miller "John Quincy Adams's"). This interpretation is not unwarranted. Adams invoked republican discourse and rhetorical theory in his first lecture to Harvard students, claiming to champion the construction of a national, deliberating polis. Like Cicero, Adams tied the republic's health to its rhetoric, telling Harvard students that "[p]ersuasion [. . .] is the great if not the only instrument, whose operations can affect the acts of all our corporate bodies" (1: 71). In subsequent lectures, Adams also invoked Quintilian's definition of the orator (1: 35–39). He focused on the importance of teaching rhetoric and virtue in a stable republic (1: 160, 344–63). He even compared American democracy and oratory to ancient Greek politics (1: 71).

Adams's lectures followed standard classical patterns, inserting Enlightenment ideas along the way. He covered the five canons of rhetoric: invention, disposition, elocution, memory, and pronunciation (1: 162–63). He discussed the three types of rhetoric that Aristotle first recognized: forensic (focused on the past and appropriate for court trials), epideictic (focused on the present and appropriate for popular assemblies), and deliberative (focused on the future and appropriate for legislative bodies) (1: 178–81). He taught students how to locate the point of controversy in a debate using Cicero's stasis theory (1: 187–99). He taught students how to invent arguments using common topics (1: 209–17), and he discussed the five parts of Ciceronian arrangement: exordium, narration, partition, confirmation/refutation, and conclusion (lectures 17–24, vol. 1). Finally, Adams's treatment of style repeated directly the advice Quintilian offered. He focused on stylistic virtues like perspicuity and purity (2: 144–83), discussed loose and periodic syntactical patterns (2: 230–35), and offered extensive treatment of figures and tropes (lectures 30–34, vol. 2).

Certainly, Adams imagined himself teaching Harvard students the tools of deliberation necessary for their participation in a healthy democracy. He even told students that free agonistic debate is a necessary component to democratic government, saying that collegiate disputation exercises train students in public deliberation as practiced by ancient rhetors (1:

142). It would be a mistake, however, to say, as have some historians (Rathbun 176–77), that Adams shared with Cicero a political vision. At Harvard, Adams lectured largely to the privileged sons of established northeastern capitalists who, like the Philadelphian gentry, viewed education as both a validation of their social status and as a manner of achieving professional success. Dorothy Broaddus has referred to the social class attending early nineteenth-century Harvard as a "Boston gentry," a "social elite" attending college for class conditioning (6–7). Though there are important differences between the Philadelphian gentry in the 1750s and the dominant Boston capitalists of the early nineteenth century, one important similarity persists: a view of education as a social marker. Harvard's students attended college to acquire the cultural capital of bourgeois subjectivity, and Adams offered it to them in his rhetorical pedagogy.

In Adams's deviations from classical rhetorical theory, one finds hints of the economic allegiances entangling his republican *paideia*. For instance, Adams said that a rhetor's virtue must be acquired and maintained in public practice (1: 347–55). In the classical republican tradition, virtue appears, is sustained, and is strictly recognized in public performance. Personally held convictions, privately developed inclinations, and private morality have no connection to a person's ability to act as a good citizen. Adams, however, while repeating a common republican platitude about the public quality of citizen virtue, then claimed that this same virtue depends on private capacities, such as Christian revelation and an individuated conscience. He directly referenced Francis Hutcheson's notion of the moral sense and the Christian notion of a privatized conscience informed by personal knowledge of divine truth. According to Adams, these private qualities form the necessary foundations for good republican citizenship (1: 356; Rathbun 190). One is left wondering whether virtue is a quality constructed in public performance or inherent in the pious soul.

Adams turned away from the republican notion of the citizen as a public actor, and he instead taught students a distinctly bourgeois notion of the individuated self. As public-sphere theorists have noticed, capitalism encourages people to imagine themselves as private actors, encountering others in an open space such as the market. Gerard Hauser demonstrates that in capitalist societies the republican civic-virtue tradition is often replaced by a civil-society tradition, in which bourgeois citizens imagine themselves as autonomous actors encountering others in a free space of discursive or monetary exchange. When Scottish moralists like Francis Hutcheson located virtue in the private self, they laid a philosophical justification for a newly bourgeois publicity whose viability depended on its articulation of a capitalist economic interest to a set of rhetorical norms, including sincere display of a private virtue (*Vernacular* 23–24). When John Quincy Adams likewise located virtue in privately developed capacities, he also contributed to a distinctly bourgeois notion of citizenship, one readily received by the children of Boston capitalists. In effect, by training students rhetorically to enact a privately developed virtue in the public sphere, Adams offered them the habits of bourgeois subjectivity. Adams's rhetorical pedagogy, by emphasizing the private development of virtue, made an important step toward the liberal rhetorical norms and pedagogies that would become dominant during and after the Jacksonian era. In Adams's capitalist rhetorical pedagogy, one sees the beginning of the end for republican rhetorical education in America and the early rumblings of an "emerging individual spirit" that would replace republicanism in American public argument and rhetorical instruction (Clark and Halloran 3). Adams thus paved the way for a new political discourse to shape and eventually dominate American articulations of publicity and pedagogy: liberalism. (The tenets of liberal political discourse and its place in American rhetorical education are discussed in the conclusion.) Though some would locate Adams firmly in the republican tradition, he might more accurately be labeled a transitional figure, one who closed the doors on republican rhetorical norms while he lowered the gates for invading liberal rhetorical practices.

Though it is important to notice that Adams's distinctive take on republican virtue laid the groundwork for a liberal publicity that articulated nascent bourgeois rhetorical norms to capitalist interests, one should also notice that he articulated republican discourse to bourgeois rhetorical norms in part by drawing on Christian notions of revelation and private conscience. Typically, any bourgeois rhetorical practice requires that rhetors bracket private qualities such as religious convictions while discussing public concerns and institutions. This norm of bourgeois rhetorical culture has contributed to modern secularism in political affairs. Adams, however, insisted that Christian conscience made virtuous rhetorical performance possible. Adams, of course, inherited all of the elements mentioned so far. In early-nineteenth-century Boston, Protestantism was dominant, republicanism was discussed, capitalism was ascending, and bourgeois rhetorical norms were practiced in coffeehouses and political assemblies. Adams's achievement is the way in which he arranged these elements into a unique constellation of Christian conscience, republican virtue, bourgeois rhetorical norms, and northeastern capitalist culture. Other elements in his rhetorical pedagogy similarly drew on present rhetorical norms among Boston's bourgeois citizenry.

For instance, Adams's discussion of emotional appeals relates to both classical and bourgeois notions of decorum. Drawing on Roman sources such as Cicero and Quintilian, he distinguished between passions and habits. Habits are sociable "mild and orderly emotions," appropriate for rhetorical invocation (1: 377). Passions are either benevolent or malevolent and always dangerous (1: 373). Even the benevolent, Christian passions— like fear of damnation—can override reason, so the good preacher should appeal to a "nobler [. . .] more generous stimulus to piety and virtue" (1: 388). Like Roman rhetoricians, Adams distinguished the rhetorical appropriateness of certain emotional appeals, but what counted as decorous for Adams depended on his bourgeois sense of what was appropriate in Boston's coffeehouses, taverns, and salons. Though Adams ostensibly articulated his advice about emotional appeal to classical republican rhetorical theory, he was also appealing to a very modern norm of bourgeois rhetorical culture. The Ciceronian notion of decorum stresses rhetorical appropriateness to the situation, encouraging the rhetor to tailor her appeals to the audience, the circumstances, the political and aesthetic dispositions common in a moment of delivery.[14] Adams's notion of decorum was much less flexible, encouraging the rhetor to follow the norms of eighteenth-century bourgeois public culture, as if these norms were universally desirable and rhetorically effective in all circumstances.

David Shields refers to Adams's variety of decorum as "sociability," a quality with origins in bourgeois civil society. Shields says that the bourgeois public sphere depended on a sense of personal autonomy and on "[f]riendship, mutual interest, and shared appetite" (32). The Enlightenment emphasis on civility grows out of an ethical problem peculiar to bourgeois society. If public actors develop their virtue independent of one another and if they encounter other different actors in a public space, they risk explosive exchanges that quickly tumble into violence. With the bourgeois sense of a separate self comes the risk of public hostility. Eighteenth-century theorists developed a number of social and ethical constructions to combat this potential rhetorical violence. Sympathy is one such rhetorical norm, decorum another. Hauser says that bourgeois civil society depends on citizens' willingness "*to regulate themselves in ways consistent with a valuation of difference*" (*Vernacular* 21). By teaching his students to practice "mild and orderly emotions," Adams taught them the rhetorical contrivances that they would need to participate successfully in Boston's bourgeois public spaces such as the local coffeehouse or the commodities exchange. Once again, he paved the way for liberalism by articulating bourgeois rhetorical norms to an economic class in his otherwise republican rhetorical pedagogy.

Adams's eventual successor, Edward Tyrell Channing (Boylston Professor of Rhetoric 1819–51), gave similar advice to young bourgeois boys. Channing, in fact, disparaged ancient oratory for pandering to the audience's "imagination and passion," their "pride" and "frailties" (4–5). Channing also spoke glowingly of rhetorical performance embodying bourgeois restraint and decorum, saying, "the imagination and passions do not predominate in modern eloquence; they are not our turbulent masters" (21). Ralph Waldo Emerson, while attending Harvard and studying rhetoric under Channing, wrote an essay on the character of Socrates. Young Emerson also characterized ancient society as warlike and overly passionate. He imagined Socrates as a forerunner to modern bourgeois rhetorical restraint. Though Channing and Emerson would have very different ideas about rhetorical excellence, they shared with Adams a belief in the rhetorical norm of decorum. Bourgeois sensibilities persisted because capitalism continued to favor Boston's commercial class.

Adams also articulated his theory of rhetorical decorum to a republican fear of faction and to political parties specific to the historical moment that he inhabited. John Quincy Adams, himself born to a New England bourgeois family, was a darling of the Federalist Party at the beginning of his political career, but after the 1800 election, as the Democratic-Republicans forged a working alliance between southern commercial farmers and northeastern merchants, Adams drifted toward Jefferson's party, finally breaking with the Federalists in his support of the Louisiana Purchase and the Embargo Act. He personified the political-economic alliance that made the Democratic-Republican reign possible, an alliance consigning the Federalist Party, once the party of Hamiltonian industrialism, to obsolescence. Adams eventually served as secretary of state under James Monroe, the Democratic-Republican president during the era of good feeling. This period's lack of party strife was partly the achievement of Jefferson's hegemonic republican vision, but the era of good feeling also depended on a belief that America had finally thrown off partisan strife to become a republic of like-minded citizens debating issues of common concern. In his first inaugural address, Jefferson declared the era of partisan strife over, promising to renew the spirit of republican unity (Browne 32). When Adams emphasized decorum, he appealed to a bourgeois sensibility among Boston capitalists, but when he emphasized other rhetorical tenets, like the need to build arguments on consensus, he appealed to the Jeffersonian republican promise. Several points in his lectures on rhetoric emphasize republican consensus as achieved by the Democratic-Republicans: his insistence on the orator's virtue; his belief that rhetoric tends toward "truth" recognizable by all (1: 167); his concerns about appeals to the passions, which might override reason; his hope that every Harvard graduate would actively and vocally participate in the common democratic conversation; his attempt to teach students how to locate the common points of disagreement in a debate; even his insistence that responsible rhetors should only invoke proofs that would be agreeably unquestionable to all (2: 65). Set in the era of good feeling, Adams's emphasis on consensus appealed to the Jeffersonian belief that republican unity had finally won the day.

John Quincy Adams was the last Democratic-Republican president in American history. Despite being elected by a congressional decision (no candidate had a real majority of the popular or electoral vote, and Adams came in second to Andrew Jackson), Adams embarked on an ambitious national program in his first annual message. Invoking republican ideas of government in service of the public good, he proposed a national university, federally funded scientific expeditions, an observatory, and a nationally funded and maintained system of roads and canals. Only the improvements most beneficial to early American capitalists, the roads and canals, were ever seriously pursued and then only partly achieved. In 1828, Adams broke ground for the 185-mile Chesapeake and Ohio Canal. In that same year, he was defeated by Andrew Jackson, who appealed to the varying economic interests of southern plantation owners, frontier settlers, and New England factory laborers (Schlesinger 30–56). Once the New England bourgeoisie was excluded from the Democratic base, Adams found himself outside of the dominant political alliance. Thereafter, he blamed Jacksonian Democrats for the destruction of his ideal republican consensus. Adams, the transitional figure between (Democratic) republican and (Jacksonian) liberal hegemonic orders, soon found that he was on the wrong side of history.

In a long career as a U.S. congressman (1830–48), Adams found himself fighting for New England commercial interests, such as the maintenance of a federal bank. The political division between southern plantation owners and New England capitalists incited Adams tirelessly to assault slavery, and anything deriving therefrom, including the gag rule (which tabled, without discussion, any congressional petition regarding slavery, 1836–40) and the annexation of new slave states like Texas. Adams the bourgeois republican quickly settled on one side of a rift between northeastern and southern capitalisms, a conflict not settled until 1861—and then only with great trauma. In these divided circumstances, Adams's republican rhetoric of consensus, suitable for the one-party era of good feeling, failed him miserably. He repeatedly violated his own advice about preserving decorum and appealing to common ground. When defending a group of African slaves in the case of the Amistad vessel, he elicited strong emotions because, as Patricia Roberts-Miller points out, "reason and argument would not prevail" ("John Quincy Adams's" 16). His defense of the Federal Bank was vitriolic, sulphuric, and unyielding. Based on this performance, Ralph Waldo Emerson called Adams a rhetorical "bruiser," no gentleman of the decorous disposition (Schlesinger 84–85). Daniel Webster and Henry Clay (the latter an Adams supporter), also devotees of decorous republican deliberation, were largely ineffectual orators in the Jacksonian era (Schlesinger 51–52). Decorum, though in many regards a consummately bourgeois rhetorical trait, did not win favor in the Jacksonian Congress.

During Jackson's administration, parliamentary deliberation happened in closed-door meetings where a courtly, intimate, and conversational rhetoric created alliances based on mutual interest and political maneuvering. This rhetorical culture circulated among liberal subjects who did not value the republican practice of seeking consensus in argumentation. The autonomous subject did not need to work toward common understanding. S/he merely needed to express allegiances, desires, and interests. The rest was a labor of bargaining for maximum personal gain. This was the era of the kitchen cabinet, a coterie of unofficial advisers who cascaded whispered counsel into the president's ears (Schlesinger 52, 67–68). Like Adams's emphasis on consensus, his rhetorical pedagogy of decorum advocated the rhetorical norms of the Jeffersonian era. When that era ended, the articulations that Adams forged among a rhetorical pedagogy, a political discourse, certain rhetorical norms, and an economic interest failed to operate effectively. He and others enacting the rhetorical norms of consensus and decorum were praised for their oratorical talent but were wildly ineffective in congressional proceedings. Bourgeois northeastern capitalists found their rhetoric appealing, but the devotees of Jacksonian democracy—frontier farmers, northeastern laborers, and southern plantation owners—were not as impressed. Adams's failure as a rhetor is a fascinating moment in the transition from a republican to a liberal hegemony, a transition that was complicated and uneven. Closer scholarly analysis, though not presented here, is merited. Any further study should also examine the role of rhetorical pedagogy as an articulatory site crucial to the formation of any hegemonic order, liberal, republican, or transitional.

The Edges of Republican Rhetorical *Paideiai*

This chapter so far has argued that efforts to teach people the practices of public discourse were contested sites where teachers sutured rhetorical theories, norms of public address, cultural developments, religious beliefs, economic interests, and political allegiances. The thread of republican discourse stitched these elements together in articulatory practices of rhetorical education. While the previous chapter demonstrated that material and partisan affiliations circulating in early American society were articulated in the sundry rhetorical enactments of republican publicity, this present chapter demonstrates something very similar about republican rhetorical pedagogy. Republican rhetoric teachers, just like republican rhetors, articulated their ideals of good republican discourse to their own politically and materially grounded assumptions. It should be noted, however, that early American republican rhetorical pedagogy, like republican publicity, shared certain norms that limited civic agency for many. Just as the American (re)public(an) sphere lacked the permeable boundaries and the tolerance requisite for sustainable civil deliberation, so did republican rhetorical pedagogies perpetuate a variety of regrettable rhetorical norms. Though economic and political interests might have led to disagreement about what constitutes ideal republican rhetoric and though these disagreements might have contributed to differing rhetorical pedagogies, most agreed about who did not deserve full citizen agency in the republican public sphere: laborers, women, and non-Anglo, non-Caucasian ethnicities or races.

The bias against laborers appears most strongly in eighteenth-century anxieties about manageable rhetorical beauty and unstable sublimity. These categories, the beautiful and the sublime, common in rhetorical theory of the era, betray deep appreciations for bourgeois decorum and fears of proletarian power. Love of the sublime set alongside fear of its volatility also reflects the contradictory position of early American bourgeois revolutionaries: they needed combustible mobs of sailors, laborers, and slaves, yet they worried about how to control this conflagration after it had burned through British imperialism. Thomas Jefferson's negative reaction to Patrick Henry's explosive oratory embodies bourgeois apprehension. Jefferson imagined Henry as a sublime orator whose power erupted from a preliterate connection to raw emotion, qualities that he admired in "uncivilized" Amerindian orators but that he thought inappropriate and potentially dangerous in the new republic.[15] Jefferson's ambivalent response displays the tension between his typically eighteenth-century appreciation for naturalness and his bourgeois sense of decorum (Fliegelman 94–102). He developed his sense of oratorical propriety in the Virginia House of Burgesses, a group of elite plantation owners who made no attempt to address popular audiences. Henry's popular appeal threatened this exclusivity, while his efficacy fired the Revolution's engines (S. Gustafson 160–70). When John Quincy Adams lectured about the properly restrained emotion of decorous oratory, he also explained that zealous oratory, though perhaps sublime, threatened republican stability in the same way that passionate proletarian mobs threatened sound republican leadership.

In addition to their anxieties about early American laborers, republican rhetorical educators also worried about preserving Anglo culture against the variety of peoples surrounding them: Amerindian, German, French, African, Dutch, Scottish, Irish. These anxieties often resulted in an Anglo-American cultural imperialism, an effort to establish Anglo rhetorical norms among neighboring populations. Though eighteenth-century Americans fought British imperialism, they also had in mind an imperial project all their own. In contrast to the schoolbook story of valiant revolutionaries fighting British tyranny, the dominant early American political project might be described more accurately as an effort by a privileged group of Anglo property-holders to claim exclusive position on the crest of an imperial wave that they could ride for a century across an entire continent. (See Jennings's *The Creation of America*.)

Imperial ethnocentrism and racism drove numerous efforts culminating long before the early national period. In the mid-eighteenth century, imperialism drove the Society for the Propagation of the Gospel (SPG) to found schools in non-Anglo areas of the British Atlantic where missionaries taught Anglicanism and most importantly Anglo culture and literacy. William Smith, future provost and professor of rhetoric and natural philosophy at the College of Philadelphia, saw great merit in this endeavor. One of his first publications argued for the need to establish English schools to "civilize" and "Christianize" the "barbarous" Amerindian population (*Indian Songs*). Both Smith and Benjamin Franklin belonged to the Society for Propagating Christian Knowledge among the Germans in Pennsylvania, a small group of privileged white Anglo men who funded and established schools in and around Philadelphia to teach the English language and a non-Quaker, non-Catholic Christianity. In a letter to the SPG (13 Dec. 1753) Smith insisted that education and particularly education in the English language could prevent the evils of foreign faction, promote liberty and freedom among citizens in Pennsylvania, and preserve government. Just as laborers threatened the republic with violent faction and sublime oratory, so did non-Anglos threaten with their polyglot rhetorics. Needless to say, Anglo whites would lead Smith's proposed government, and they would do so in English. He painted his imperialist efforts as universally beneficial, "not the work of any particular party. It is a British work" (Wemyss Smith 30–37). Smith explained that the society decided to teach both Dutch and English, but his subsequent discussion indicates that their primary purpose was to teach English to assimilate the Germans into English culture, "to qualify the Germans for all the advantages of *native English Subjects*" (*Short History* 14).

Republican rhetorical pedagogies, therefore, often aimed to control the sublime power of proletarian rhetoric, to "civilize" the barbarous tongues of non-Anglo peoples, and finally to teach republican rhetoric to women so that they could teach it to their sons. The republican public sphere allowed no space for the female presence, though republican pedagogues often did worry about women's limited political role. Benjamin Rush feared that female ignorance could lead to the republic's corruption, because ignorant women are "governed with the greatest difficulty" and because ignorant women would not be able "to concur in instructing their sons in the principles of liberty and government" (*Thoughts* 24, 5). Noah Webster, likewise, believed that women should be educated in republican principles so that they could teach virtuous rhetorical norms to their sons. He also argued that women should study the belles lettres but not novels, which could corrupt their sensibilities ("On the Education" 29). In short, Webster and Rush both allowed women a limited and decidedly subservient role in the dissemination of republican rhetoric.

One of the few early American secondary institutions for female education, the Young Ladies Academy of Philadelphia, was founded to educate women for their proper, rhetorically stultified positions. The Young Ladies Academy held public speaking exercises, just like its contemporary male schools, but the tenor of these exercises differed dramatically. At commencements, for instance, graduates delivered orations (never debates), which typically began with feminized apologies for appearing in public and presuming to say anything important. The valedictorian in 1789, Ann Luxley, began her speech by admitting her young age and her "foibles." Her brief oration essentially advised the students to be attendant, obedient, and modest. Eliza Schrapp, valedictorian in 1791, also opened her oration with apologies, as did 1792 valedictorian Molly Wallace, who said, "[M]y sex, my youth, my inexperience all conspire to make me tremble at the talk which I have undertaken." Wallace's oration is particularly interesting because, unlike the others, who typically offered only gratitude and sentimental good-byes, she promoted women's participation in public debate, hoping for "a female Pitt, Cicero, or Demosthenes." Repeating the masculinist assumptions of her era, she said women should not presume to speak in promiscuous assemblies. Instead, in private conversations, women should rhetorically exhibit charity and modesty. Clearly, none of these women felt empowered to participate in the public spaces where republican agon led to policy. They were imagining and participating in a republican *paideia* that only allowed women limited civic-rhetorical agency. Exposure to rhetorical training, however, did give some women an expanded sense of civic agency. Miss Mason, giving the 1794 salutary oration, argued that women should equally share rights of public address, saying, "Man; despotic man, first made us incapable of the duty, and then forbid us to exercise." Mason wanted women to become lawyers, senators, and ministers. Though her training may have given her a sense of civic agency, the norms of republican public argument did not allow her the kind of rhetorical power that she hoped to garner for all women. Her valiant protofeminist speech was immediately followed by a simpering valedictorian address by Miss Laskey, who advocated female modesty, obedience, and "proper decorum and decency" (*Rise and Progress* 39–41, 49, 73–74, 76–79, 93, 97). Republican masculinism would not be overthrown in one oration.

The gender bias of early American rhetorical theory and pedagogy should come as no great surprise, given that historians have noticed a similar bias dating back to ancient rhetorical theory and the construction of the Roman republic. (See, for instance, Brody's *Manly Writing.*) Certainly there is something admirable in efforts to locate female republican agency in rhetorical avenues not traditionally recognized—private conversations, novels—however much these new roles "played out in a liminal way in the public realm" (Eldred and Mortenson 14). Nevertheless, whatever silver lining one sees, the cloud still remains. Articulations of republican publicity and pedagogy shared the era's classist, racist, and gendered biases.

This chapter demonstrates the systemic biases and the interest-driven differences among republican rhetorical pedagogies in early American higher education, but the presentation so far hinges on analysis of isolated intellectual trends, such as the drive for rhetorical education in vernacular English, and particular individuals, such as Benjamin Franklin or John Quincy Adams.[16] The economic and political circumstances tend to look like a scenic backdrop in the drama of an individual's life. Economic developments seem to complement rather than interact with trends in rhetorical theory. The remainder of this study, however, will focus not on intellectual trends nor on influential rhetorical educators but instead on sites, foregrounding the circumstances of articulation.

My decision to focus the principal analyses of this study on institutional sites is consistent with the Gramscian Marxism that informs this entire study. Looking at a pedagogy in the context of its environment forces us to see connections among rhetorical education and a variety of other factors. This analytic focus is also consistent with a rhetorical principle: *kairos*. The concept of *kairos* teaches that the effectiveness of a rhetorical action, be it a speech, a pamphlet, or a pedagogy, depends on its timeliness, its appropriateness to the situation. Jefferson was not an influential rhetor because of his own genius at *ex nihilo* discursive genesis. He was influential because his rhetorical performances spoke to and with the common vocabulary, the political and economic interests, available at the moment. He was influential because his rhetoric was timely. Likewise, John Quincy Adams was a popular rhetorical educator because his pedagogy suited the economic and partisan interests circulating in early nineteenth-century Boston. When these factors changed, Adams's rhetoric was no longer timely, and it failed, dramatically. By focusing on institutional sites, subsequent chapters illustrate the kairotic articulation that differing rhetorical pedagogies managed among economic, political, institutional, and local geographic situations, as well as intellectual factors and individuals' lives. Though intellectual trends (like rhetorical theories) persist, though economic developments (like capitalism) are lasting, each effort at public rhetorical performance or pedagogy engages these diachronically enduring factors differently, changing the social fabric. Republicanism gets rescripted every time someone claims that a manner of disputation ameliorates citizen virtue or the vita activa. The manner of incorporation matters, the manner of rescripting matters, at times more than the economic or intellectual trends, because our material and intellectual lives get remade every time they are rewoven into social circumstances.

The perspective taken in the following chapters demonstrates that rhetorical educators, though often responding to the conditions that they inherit, though often constrained by their local institutional and demographic circumstances, occupy important and influential positions in any social network. Rhetorical educators sit at the nexus of a variety of forces, some enormous and persistent, some particular and fleeting. They tie all of these things together with a pedagogical articulation of "good" speaking. For this reason, pedagogy—*paideia*—is perhaps the most important work that professors engage, both in the eighteenth century and in the present.

3

Yale 1701–1817

Lux et Veritas
—Yale University motto

In 1700, Connecticut was largely filled with farming communities led by church elders. Though there were strict social distinctions, people's lives were marked by economic austerity and common piety. By 1800, commerce had crept into even the most remote corners of Connecticut life. Markets not only affected every endeavor, but some people made their principal living trading, manufacturing, or selling some non-ministerial professional service. Christian piety was challenged by urban cosmopolitanism. Puritan plainness was being replaced by bourgeois elegance. At the perimeter of these dramatic cultural and economic changes, a national government was taking shape. Connecticut's citizens worried about what they would become and how they would fit into the United States. Connecticut's economy was changing, its culture, likewise. Its governing citizens scrambled to manage these events without losing their privilege. To say the least, eighteenth-century Connecticut was bursting with possibility.

In the midst of all this was the third university founded in British America (est. 1701), a tense site where the aforementioned changes were negotiated and where Connecticut's privileged sons struggled over hegemony. In Connecticut more broadly tension existed between the residual political economy of seventeenth-century Puritan settlements and the emergent political economy of bourgeois capitalism.[1] Commercially temperate, principally agricultural communities would find themselves steadily confronted with new markets, new opportunities to accumulate wealth, new cultural sophistication. The governing Connecticut order flinched at capitalism's profiteering, its self-serving market participants, its externalities: luxury and secular urbanity. They were even more aghast at the potential for liberal democratic reform. In various cultural institutions, Connecticut's elite struggled over the colony's economic, cultural, and political fate. Some were conservatives, unwilling to entertain the most innocent bourgeois bauble. Some welcomed refinement and elegance but refused liberal political reforms. They fought over how to accommodate their changing economic circumstances, their new cultural interests, their authoritarian social hierarchy, and their deeply rooted religious beliefs. These struggles played out at Yale as several efforts at rhetorical education articulated the different economic circumstances in eighteenth-century Connecticut to the bourgeois mores creeping into her taverns and salons, to the Puritan tenor of Connecticut's leadership, and to the developing national republican vocabulary.

Tracing the century-long history of rhetorical education at Yale demonstrates that changes regularly happen in hegemonic orders. Over the course of 120 years, Connecticut witnessed three distinct hegemonic blocs: an austere Puritan government as articulated to subsistence agriculture; a bourgeois Puritan genteel leadership as articulated to a tempered New England capitalism and to the Federalist Party in national U.S. politics; a bourgeois, religiously plural alliance among dissenters as articulated to free-market capitalism and to the Democratic-Republican Party. Each was a contingent intersection of economic and political interests that depended on local work performed in cultural institutions like the university. Each effort at rhetorical education connected these various semiautonomous social factors in an effort to advance a hegemonic constellation at Yale.

Setting Yale's rhetorical education in its historic and hegemonic circumstances demonstrates that rhetorical pedagogies contributed to various hegemonic blocs. This analysis also shows how specific rhetoricians participated in large developments through local actions in the classroom. Rhetoric professors did not simply accommodate the shift from subsistence agriculture to commercial capitalism. They often resisted, often accepted parts of the new political economy while refusing others. They did not necessarily welcome coffeehouse sociability. Some countered with a distinctly Puritan vision of public exchange, one marked by devotion, prayer, and collective worship. Some educators tried to advance bourgeois civility by teaching its rhetorical norms. This chapter offers the long history of Yale's rhetorical *paideia* in the interest of demonstrating two points already mentioned. First, hegemony is contingent on its articulations among cultural institutions. Pedagogy and publicity are two important sites where these articulations get formed. Second, hegemony is dependent on the local actions performed by citizens engaged in what Gramsci called the "trench warfare" of modern political struggle. This struggle might better be termed "the agon of everyday life," a locution that emphasizes the push and pull that happens whenever disparate political and economic interests clash over local sites such as rhetorical education. By recounting and situating Yale's curricular struggles in these contested circumstances, this chapter demonstrates that any effort at rhetorical education engages, constitutes, and sometimes challenges the hegemonic shape of a historical moment. The work of rhetorical education is a principal site where actors forge articulations, where they find agency.

Connecticut Political Economy, 1700–40

It is true, as Alexis de Tocqueville stated in 1848, that America did not have Europe's feudal legions firing reactionary charges against an onslaught of liberal democracy and laissez-faire capitalism (de Tocqueville 10–18). But the onslaught of liberal democracy and laissez-faire capitalism was not met, as some twentieth-century political theorists claim, by cheering crowds and rose petal parades. Though reaction in eighteenth-century New England might not have resembled the ancien regime's resistance in revolutionary France, one cannot conclude that America "lacks a tradition of reaction" (Hartz 5). In New England, especially in the area's most conservative university, many communities founded on religious principles resisted the emergent commercial economy and democratic political reforms of the eighteenth century. Bernard Bailyn has illustrated that Puritan merchants in the seventeenth century, even those in commercial hubs, tempered their business practices with moral directives. Those who did not were maligned, even pursued as criminals. One New England merchant, Robert Keayne, profited from a wave of inflation between 1635 and 1639, but in the last year the Massachusetts General Court prosecuted him for excessive profiteering. He was punished by both the civil government and by the church—he was both lawbreaker and sinner. This victory for the prosecution set off a wave of similar trials (Bailyn, *New England Merchants* 44).

By the eighteenth century, people in thriving urban hubs, such as Boston, welcomed the cultural artifacts, the tolerant mores, the profiteering motives, the fashions, and the refinements drifting in Great Britain's trade circuits. Royal control, exerted in 1691, allowed for an increasing Anglicanization. More English merchants established themselves in colonial harbors. Bernard Bailyn says of these new cosmopolitan capitalists:

> In the larger port towns of provincial New England, particularly those in continuous touch with Europe, the business community represented the spirit of a new age. Its guiding principles were not social stability, order, and the discipline of the senses, but mobility, growth, and the enjoyment of life. Citizens of an international trading world as well as of New England colonies, the merchants took the pattern for their conduct not from the Bible or from parental teachings but from their picture of life in Restoration England. To the watchmen of the holy citadel nothing could have been more insidious. (*New England Merchants* 139)

Many in Connecticut would not embrace capitalism or its cosmopolitan cronies so readily. Connecticut lagged behind Boston throughout the eighteenth century, her citizens often openly resisting what they witnessed in the great Massachusetts harbor. They fought to preserve their city on a hill.

Connecticut did not have the fishing industry vital to northern New England, and it did not have a major urban center like Boston, where skilled craftsmen could congregate and form markets. New Haven did develop some trade along the Atlantic coast, but its poor harbor (often too shallow for ships to dock) and its subservience to nearby Boston harbor made it a minor trading post up until the Seven Years' War. In the 1760s, Boston lost some of its continental traffic to New Haven (Bridenbaugh, *Cities in Revolt* 56; Taylor 96–97). Nevertheless, Connecticut did not develop a lasting trade anywhere beyond the northern Atlantic coast until the early nineteenth century (Purcell 76–77). Since capitalism developed more slowly in Connecticut than in Massachusetts, her communities tended to safeguard traditional cultural and economic institutions. Orthodox religion thrived in Connecticut and at Yale while Harvard was becoming "godless" in the eyes of many. Towns continued to restrict trade or industry in order to preserve their moral vision. Church elders ran local governments, and a small ministerial elite continued to occupy many political offices.

Without a thriving port to encourage growth in manufacture and community formation on a nonagricultural basis, or to import cultural cosmopolitanism (as happened in both Boston and Philadelphia), Connecticut society remained staunchly a seventeenth-century Puritan construction. Spillover from the Massachusetts colony populated the area, and though Connecticut received a charter in 1662, its socioeconomic shape was very similar to and dependent on Massachusetts Puritanism. This was a hierarchized society with a privileged few on top and numerous layers underneath, all deferring to some greater authority, either immediate or transcendent. In the early nineteenth century, Congregationalists manifested themselves politically in the Connecticut Federalist Party, opposed by the much weaker Democratic-Republican Party, which allied with dissenting religions (all non-Congregationalists, including, ironically, Anglicans). In the early eighteenth century, not even this weak opposition existed. Politically, there was the speaking Congregational aristocracy and the obedient silent majority, as evidenced by extreme limitations placed on civic participation. There were two types of voters in colonial Connecticut society: freemen and admitted inhabitants. The latter had to be male householders over twenty-one with estates worth at least £30; they could not vote for magistrates or governor. Freemen were an even more exclusive group, whose civic status depended on official acceptance by the General Court and derived from position in the church hierarchy.

The Congregational Church was the primary organizing force, instantiated civically in the General Assembly, which handled large colony-wide issues. Town assemblies handled local issues like allocation of land and determination of sumptuary laws. Each town possessed all lands in common, which it distributed to individuals depending on need and ability to contribute to community well-being. Though this semifeudalistic economic structure was constantly challenged and steadily shifted to a more proprietary structure necessary to capitalism, it remained dominant well into the mid-eighteenth century. Connecticut citizens accepted their social stratification in part because they believed this hierarchy had divine origins. God's law foreordained all: from the hierarchization of civic and social status to the hierarchization of church membership (into regenerate, unregenerate, full members, halfway members, deacons, ministers, assemblymen, and so on). The Puritan system of technologia, the divinely ordained structure of available knowledge, intellectually justified prevailing authority. Puritan intellectuals believed that

> [w]hen God created the world, He formed a plan or scheme of it in His mind, of which the universe is the embodiment; in His mind the plan was single, but in the universe it is reflected through the concrete objects and so seems diverse to the eye of human reason; these apparently diverse and temporal segments of the single and timeless divine order are the various arts; the principles are arranged into series of axiomatical propositions according to sequences determined by the laws of method. (P. Miller, *New England Mind* 161)

In textbooks like Alexander Richardson's *The Logicians School-Master*, students at Yale learned the technologia, a *paideia* shaping them as Puritan leaders. In early eighteenth-century Connecticut, a residual social formation stood at least in part because of a Puritan *paideia* that taught the intellectual and political elite that their privilege was part of divine order. This *paideia,* of course, included instruction in rhetoric.

The Old Order: Rhetoric at Yale before 1740

Historians of early American education and culture, particularly in New England, know that Ramistic rhetoric dominated Harvard and Yale through the seventeenth and into the eighteenth centuries. Early American Calvinists followed British thinkers like William Ames, who was influenced by Peter Ramus's sixteenth-century rhetorical theory. Perry Miller's argument to that effect, published in 1939, rightly remains the definitive statement on American Ramism and rhetoric prior to 1700 (*New England Mind* 111–206, 300–64). Ramus's rhetorical theory did away with the common topics and separated logic from rhetoric, claiming that invention should seek out truth through a dialectical process of definition and division. While certain Renaissance humanist rhetoricians (such as Desiderius Erasmus and Thomas Wilson) believed that arguments are invented, refined, altered, and debated in a collective process of discursively constructing the world, Ramus believed that truth exists independent of language. Language, for Ramus, was a vehicle for divine truth. Reason sniffs out certainty dialectically: "The whole of dialectic concerns the mind and reason, whereas rhetoric and grammar concern language and speech" (104). Rhetoric, for Ramus, involved the ornamentation of indisputable and divine verity with tropes, figures, and adequate delivery. Subsequent Ramistic rhetorical theories likewise positioned dialectic first, as the instrument for locating truth, and rhetoric second, as the method of making it palatable. Ramistic rhetorical theory, of course, leaves no room for dialogue with others, because dialectic, performed in solitary reflection, reveals all the world's mysteries.

Because the basis of democracy is consent, and because democratic government requires some input from a body of citizens, this consent should be developed deliberatively (Bohman 26–30). Historians of rhetoric notice, however, that Ramistic rhetorical theory short-circuits dialogue, thereby inhibiting one of the crucial rhetorical norms in any democratic society (Ong 289–91). Why try to negotiate with others when one can dialectically arrive at divinely stamped certitude? Such a faith in one truth found outside of human influence, therefore, often serves authoritarian politics (Arendt, "What is Authority?"). For the young Puritan, truth lay in the good book, and virtue in God's directives. Rhetoric just conveyed these ideals to a (hopefully obedient) people. Ramistic logic and rhetorical theory are parts of an authoritative *paideia,* an antidemocratic pedagogy that persisted in a number of curricular initiatives, such as the Lancasterian system of surveillance and control, a favored pedagogy among early nineteenth-century Calvinists like Lyman Beecher. (See Vasquéz's *Authority and Reform,* particularly chs. 1 and 2.)

The Ramistic curriculum in New England marked the beginning of a long string of antidemocratic pedagogies. In the seventeenth and early eighteenth centuries, students at Harvard and Yale did not study Ramus but instead learned his work through the British Ramists, a group of Cambridge-educated Calvinists that took Peter Ramus's revision of scholastic logic and fit it to their own philosophical and political purposes. Chief among these figures are William Ames and Alexander Richardson. The British Ramists shackled the mind to divine art and expressed great faith in language's ability to represent divine archetypes, provided that they travel among regenerate souls.

For the British Ramists, the end of human action, investigation, and communication is art. Art is not separate from philosophy (as was typical in Aristotelian scholasticism) but is rather an amalgam of knowing and therefore following the divine will, a Calvinist variation on the Platonic notion that to know the good is to do the good. Art appears as archetype in God's mind, entype in the world, and ectype in the human intellect.[2] In the *Logicians School-Master* (1629), an English commentary on Ramus's logic that was taught at seventeenth- and eighteenth-century Harvard, Richardson defined art as "[t]he wisdome of God, but yet as it is *energetick* in the thing, so it is called *Ars,* so that marke this, that Art is the Law of God, whereunto he created things, whereby he gouerneth them, and whereunto they yeeld obedience" (15). William Ames borrowed Aristotle's term for good action (*eupraxia*), attaching it not to social norms pragmatically applied but to divine truth. Ames defined art as "the idea of *eupraxia* or good action, methodically delineated by universal rules." Art exists as one idea (an archetype) in God but has many manifestations (entypes) in the perceptible world (*Technometry* 93, 95). Richardson and Ames both conceptualized the whole of human knowledge (the ectypes) and practice as an effort to bring the human will into obedience with the divine. They divided the disciplines into functional parts of this overall effort. Logic (dialectic) becomes the master art through which one invents and orders divine principles. Grammar and rhetoric follow, as the arts of ordering words to allow transmission of these divine archetypes among people.

Only the saved, when filtering the world through Ramistic language games, could see the divine mysteries. Richardson argued that Ramistic logical investigation "teels us first of the simples, and then of disposing them [. . .] So wee know that Logicke caries from the thing to man, and speech from man to man" (7–8). Grammar and rhetoric, the second two general *eupraxia* after logic in Ames's system, convey God's will and must have the capacity to do so accurately. Ames in fact equated eupraxia with the same function classical thinkers attributed to rhetoric, saying it is "Cicero's 'discoursing well'" (*Technometry* 96). He elaborated on the necessity of language as an accurate mediating instrument between God's unified and perfect knowledge and people's fragmented consciousness: "[B]y these mediating appellations or words, things are conveyed from man to man. Hence the principles of speaking and communicating" (*Technometry* 102).

At one point in his most famous religious tract, *The Marrow of Sacred Divinity* (1642), Ames argued that the devil communicates to people through sophistical argument and fallacy (58). Despite a concern for rhetoric's ability to obscure divine truth, Ames exhibited a great faith in rhetoric's ability also to convey God's will in all its glory. He noticed that the Bible does not communicate through dry mathematical language but through rhetorical flourish in order to capture people's imaginations and draw them into the splendor of regenerate knowledge. Ames also recognized that the minister must promote the will of God through powerful rhetorical delivery, and though he eventually argued that the sermon must convince by "spirituall and powerful demonstration" not "perswading words," Ames fully acknowledged the necessity of the latter and never attempted to avoid their use. He even pronounced the first act of religion a rhetorical performance: hearing the word of God to receive His will (*Marrow* 170, 180, 271). And Ames himself consciously put rhetoric to use, claiming at one point in the *Marrow of Sacred Divinity* to arrange his work in a "Rhetoricall way" (A5 verso). Thus the British Ramists did not do away with rhetoric. Rather, they placed it into a larger apparatus of theology pointing toward obedience. Ames promoted a strictly deferential behavior. People should obey Christ and His appointed ministers.[3] From Yale's founding days, its students studied Ames's larger theological system and the place of rhetoric therein. The entire technologia and particularly its rhetorical theory were particularly well suited to early eighteenth-century Connecticut.

Samuel Johnson's experience provides a glimpse into Yale's curriculum, particularly into the Ramistic rhetorical theory that Yale students learned in the early eighteenth century. In 1710, Johnson enrolled in the Collegiate School at Saybrook, a predecessor to Yale University. He studied there for three years, leaving in 1713, his senior year, to become a master at the Guilford School. In 1716, he moved to New Haven to become a tutor at Yale. He remained in this capacity until 1720 when he was ordained minister of the West Haven Congregational Church. In 1714, as Johnson was finishing his fourth year at Saybrook and beginning to teach at the Guilford

School, he engaged in an exercise typical of Yale's graduates. In imitation of William Ames, he wrote a manuscript version of his own technologia, his own effort at describing and dividing divine art. Though not particularly remarkable for its philosophical content, Johnson's text does reflect a Ramistic vision of logic and rhetoric, focusing on topics and their division. Like Ames, Johnson collected rhetoric, along with grammar and logic, into the general *eupraxia,* which locate divine archetypes to guide beliefs and actions. Logic locates the principles of God's order. Rather than perceiving the topics as places where rhetors can invent arguments, in typical Ramistic fashion, Johnson treated them as divisible principles that underlie the universe's order. For instance, Johnson separated the topic of "cause" into "internal" and "external" subtopics, dividing external causes into effective and ineffective agents, and further dividing effective external causes into three modes, each itself subdivided: (1) creating or preserving, (2) alone or with others, (3) independent or secondary (*SJCW* 2: 71).[4] His logic proceeds thus—locating principal topics and dividing them without reflection on their use in argumentation. Johnson also discussed the formation of definitions, propositions, and syllogisms, ending with brief reflections on method, "arrangement of the various propositions [. . .] in order according to the clarity of their natures so that they may be held in memory" (*SJCW* 2: 95).

While logic finds divine truth, grammar and rhetoric—the arts of speaking correctly and with embellishment—present it. Again following the British Ramism that inspired him, Johnson placed grammar and rhetoric in the service of logic. His treatment of grammar mostly consists of rules about verb inflection and pronoun use. Rhetorical study consists of the knowledge and use of figures and tropes. Johnson's text demonstrates the rhetorical theory taught at Yale and the political implications thereof. In the preface, he claims that "art has reflected its rays into the intellect of intelligent creatures ever since the most ancient times." He even speculates that before the fall, Adam had available to him "illustrious wisdom" (*SJCW* 2: 59). Johnson believed that the technologia provided a map to divine knowledge and good action. Though he worried that original sin corrupts people's access to archetypes, in his last year as a student at Saybrook, he expressed a typical faith that certain elected people when following divine discursive paths can arrive at truth, which they can then deliver to other minds through rhetorical conduits. Johnson's technologia in effect justified the rule of religious elites by painting their rhetorical performances as reflections of God's law. Sovereignty lay in the Lord, not in the people. Political power flowed through human representatives of His order.

Democratic Populism and Authoritarian Backlash: Thomas Clap's Legacy, 1740–66

As Connecticut approached the midcentury, its citizens saw dark clouds approaching. Though the state's commercial economy was not growing at Boston's rate, minor trade centers like New Haven had developed. Though citizens did not demand universal suffrage or inclusion in the governing aristocracy, many clamored for less stringent church membership policies. In the 1730s, the first Great Awakening shook the established Congregational hierarchy by promising a more democratic distribution of political power. Charismatic ministers questioned the divinely granted authority of Yale- and Harvard-educated ministers, even going so far as to proclaim that unordained parishioners could have more grace, more divinely granted authority, than people like Samuel Johnson. Gilbert Tennent, a Presbyterian firebrand, argued vehemently that education did not necessarily grant access to divine truth. He warned people throughout the colonies about the dangers of unconverted ministers. People without formal credentials began to preach along itinerant circuits that traversed the colonies, passionately inciting agency among an elated public. Historians of early American culture commonly mark the Great Awakening as the first charge in a steady battle for democratic reform in American Protestantism (Hatch, *Democratization*).

Facing threats to their administration, Congregationalist ministers enacted the Saybrook Platform (1708), which placed greater authority in the hands of church elders and ministers, taking power away from congregation members and flirting with a more presbyterian system of church government (Bushman, *From Puritan* 151–62). Jonathan Edwards, preaching in Northampton in the 1730s, discovered lax membership, a disruptive young population, and a great unwillingness to succumb to church authority. This was all caused in part by the Great Awakening but also in part by the church's waning control over local resources (the Northampton government made its last land grants in 1703) and by commerce's increasingly enticing lure. Unable to distribute land and losing the centripetal momentum of their religiously founded communities, Congregationalist leaders blamed capitalism, its luxuries, its possessive individualism (Tracy 38–45; Bushman, *From Puritan* 191). They pursued authoritarian, anti-democratic politics. Yale, a defender of old-world authoritarianism, dug in its heels. In fact, Thomas Clap tried to create an even stricter culture after he ascended to the college's presidency in 1740.

Clap had studied at Harvard and sided with pedagogical conservatives there who resisted Boston's increasing cosmopolitanism. Before coming to Yale, he was a domineering minister who often drove out of town those who disagreed with or opposed his edicts (Tucker 42). Clap reformed the Yale administrative structure to establish himself as president, weakened the power of the trustees, wrote and implemented a long list of laws prescribing penalties for Yale students, and designed a strict daily routine for everyone to follow. He insisted that all judicial and pedagogical proceedings be written and then followed to the letter. He hierarchized the student body and the faculty into multiple levels. He even encouraged social practices, such as fagging, whereby the upperclassmen could abuse and order the freshmen however they pleased. These efforts were more than a sadistic power-grab. They were a conscious effort to reaffirm Puritan social order. In one historian's words, Clap's disciplinary reforms tried to "defend the college's identity as a religious society raised above all others to protect orthodox Calvinism and Connecticut's moral order" (Grasso 144). Clap's biographer, Louis Tucker, says that "with its system of gradation and rank, Yale was a microcosm of Connecticut society" (69).

Clap taught his students a strict brand of conservative Puritanism through William Ames's *Marrow of Sacred Divinity,* Jonathan Edwards's *Freedom of the Will* (1754), and William Wollaston's *The Nature of Religion Delineated* (1724).[5] Seniors recited all three under his care. Later in his career, Clap wrote his own textbook on theology and ethics, *An Essay on the Nature and Foundation of Moral Virtue and Obligation* (1765). In these theology classes and elsewhere, Clap continued and defended a curriculum built on the Puritan belief in a divinely scripted hierarchy of knowledge, a *paideia* of technologia.

The curriculum at Yale was consistent through the mid-eighteenth century. Students learned by reading and recitation exercises under the guidance of a tutor, and the president taught a capstone course (ethics, morality, or political science) in the senior year. The first year was dedicated to instruction in the learned languages (Latin, Greek, and perhaps Hebrew, depending on the tutor) and logic. Students continued to hone their skills in ancient languages through their sophomore and junior years. During the sophomore year, students recited geometry, geography, and rhetoric (out of Thomas Farnaby's Aristotelian primer, *Indexus Rhetoricus* [1625]) (Morgan 51). As juniors, they recited natural philosophy, astronomy, and other parts of mathematics; as seniors, they recited metaphysics and ethics. Every Saturday was spent studying divinity. The junior and senior classes engaged in Latin syllogistic disputation twice a week. Like most other colonial colleges, Yale introduced English forensic disputation in the mid-eighteenth century.[6] From then on, students engaged in both English forensic and Latin syllogistic disputations twice a week.

The broadsides published and distributed at commencement ceremonies clearly demonstrate Yale's heavy curricular dependence on the technologia. These documents publicly offered an outline of the entire Yale curriculum structured into headings and theses that students were supposed to know and, if necessary, publicly defend.[7] The broadsides present a topical-hierarchical organization of knowledge, reinforcing the hierarchization of mid-eighteenth-century Puritan society. The 1751 broadside, for instance, lists eight topics with defensible theses underneath each: *theses technologicae, theses logicae, theses grammaticae, theses rhetoricae, theses mathematicae, theses physicae, theses metaphysicae,* and *theses ethicae.* The first category, *theses technologicae,* is the most inclusive and provides a structure for understanding how all other knowledges fit into a hierarchized schema. At the 1765 commencement, technologia was defined as the general treatment of art and science (*technologia est generalis de artibus ac scientiis tractatus*). The *theses logicae* focus on method, a strict Ramistic construction for exploring, ordering, and understanding. If the *theses technologicae* show that a graduate understands knowledge's terrain, then the *theses logicae* show he can map and navigate that terrain. Logic is described in the 1751 commencement broadside as the art of investigating and communicating truth (*logica est ars investigandi et communicandi veritatem*). In each of these moments, logical method is presented as the student's ability to divide experience into knowable, mutually exclusive and exhaustive categories. Method stands in for invention, allowing the speaker to learn all there is to know about God's order before attempting to communicate with others.[8]

In the technologia's presumptive structure, method's rigorous examination located unquestionable, objectively determined, and divinely ordained verities. Grammar presented them in clear language, and rhetoric made the presentation appealing through proper use of figures. This hierarchy of knowledge is also a system of rhetorical invention. One begins with a dialectically derived map organized into polarized categories. One then uses logical method to discover how certain objective phenomena fit into that map (are manifestations of God's eternal order). Once methodically arranged, knowledge is translated into language along grammatical principles. At the 1765 commencement, grammar was described as the art of writing and speaking correctly by following rules (*grammatica recte scribendi ac loquendi regulas tradit*) and rhetoric as the art of speaking ornately and copiously (*rhetorica est ars ornate copioseque dicendi*).

The theses defended at commencement further illustrate the above hierarchy of knowledge and method of invention. In 1751, for example, students defended the following statements about logic: (1) "Method is the most useful part of logic[,]" and (2) "One cannot judge real knowledge of natural science without the existence of archetypes." The Puritan use of "typology" and notion of "archetype," as they appear in the theses above, are peculiar to this culture and rhetoric. Originally, typology was a hermeneutic used by biblical scholars to draw homologies between the New and the Old Testaments. In the hands of Renaissance Protestants, it became a way to interpret daily life and (more broadly) history by drawing homologies between daily experience and Bible narratives or characters. John Winthrop's biography and Cotton Mather's history of New England both compared biblical and New England events. To tell history without connection to biblical events or to the larger search for salvation is to engage in "secular history," but to identify "the individual, the community, or the event in question within the scheme of salvation" is to engage in "soteriology." Soteriology "eliminated the anxiety of process by elevating secular into sacred history" (Bercovitch 43, 120). The archetypes were eternal and unchanging patterns of existence, the types, daily manifestations of these patterns. At Yale in 1751, students learned that all logical inquiry (even inquiry into the physical sciences) must begin with knowledge of archetypes. Method draws connections between the archetypes and their manifestations in the secular world. Once these connections become clear, one has to translate them into language through grammatical rules. The 1751 *theses grammaticae* offer advice about clear pronunciation, such as, "Monosyllables take away from the smoothness of a dialect." The *theses rhetoricae* focus on gesture and style, positioning rhetoric as the handmaiden to truth methodically derived and grounded in divine archetypes: (1) "All oratory is tasteful not just by selection but also by construction of words[,]" (2) "The motion of every soul has its own gesture[,]" (3) "Clarity makes an oration emotional[,]" (4) "In poetry, one should express fertility in dactylic meter, but on the other hand should express pain with spondaic meter."

In Clap's rhetorical pedagogy, the residual culture of technologia and the rhetorical norms that it included were articulated to an authoritarian social order. But he also made a number of efforts to weave aspects of Enlightenment thinking into Yale's curriculum without sacrificing the political principles of hierarchy and divine authority. Though Clap was both a political and a pedagogical conservative, he respected the new science. His *paideia* included empirical methods of investigation that did not endanger the technologia's ability to reinforce Connecticut's religious order. The new philosophy first entered Yale in the 1720s when Samuel Johnson was still a tutor at the college. Johnson was affected by John Locke's epistemology, which he learned while reading books donated by Jeremy Dummer in 1714. Locke believed that human knowledge derives from sense perception of the natural world, not from methodically dividing and subdividing categories, certainly not from the divine light shining through the pinholes of complicated Ramistic categories. Locke's empiricism, of course, threatened the religious establishment in England by allotting everyone equal access to truth. Everyone, after all, has the same faculties of sensation. Locke's empiricism was also articulated to liberal democracy and to free-market capitalism in British circles. He famously argued for free speech and for a form of democratic government. He also argued against government intervention in economic affairs. His *Essay Concerning*

Human Understanding (1690) inspired backlash among Anglican ministers like Bishop George Berkeley, who attacked Locke's empiricism in order to undercut the political liberalism to which it was articulated. When Johnson taught Locke to Yale students in the 1720s, he encountered a similar resistance, and his resignation as tutor is often accredited to student recalcitrance. Yale was not ready for the new science.

In the 1750s, however, empiricism began to appear in Connecticut's most conservative intellectual havens. Even arch-Puritan divines like Jonathan Edwards and Thomas Clap appreciated science's explanatory power (P. Miller, *Jonathan Edwards* 54; Tucker 94–113). Of course, these thinkers managed to accept Lockean empiricism without threatening New England's social hierarchy. Early American religious leaders developed complicated methods of arguing that sense perception allows access to divine truth by monitoring one manifestation of God's perfection—nature. Jonathan Edwards reconciled Lockean empiricism with Ramistic rational argumentation, believing that what is empirically knowable will also be logically demonstrable. For Edwards, empirical and rational knowledge are necessarily reconcilable because both are manifestations of God's single archetypal and majestic arrangement (*"The Mind"*). Cotton Mather similarly claimed that the natural world is another manifestation of God's mind, pointing to homology between the book of God (Scripture) and the book of nature (empirical observation) (*Christian Philosopher*). Historians of philosophy are quick to notice that, by locating the knowable object outside the human mind, these Puritan divines paved the way for empiricism (Flower and Murphy 1: 30–31). Even more remarkable than their philosophical achievement, however, is their ability to disconnect empiricism from political liberalism and from laissez-faire capitalism. Locke's cluster of empirical philosophy, liberal democracy, and free-market capitalism shattered in the hands of New England divines who articulated the scientific method of careful observation into a very different constellation of technologia, authoritarian government, and sheltered subsistence agriculture.

In the Yale curriculum, Lockean empiricism began to replace Ramistic logic, but logic as a general *eupraxia* kept its place in the larger technologia. Instead of focusing on method as an analytical process of categorizing everything into binaries, the *theses logicae* began to focus on empirical observation as the foundation for logical inquiry. For example, the Lockean distinction between simple (empirically observed) and complex (analytically constructed) ideas appears in the 1759 *theses logicae.*[9] Yale students also defended many Lockean assumptions about language and its relation to empirically verified reality. Locke believed that words arbitrarily signal ideas. Words can clearly convey or utterly confuse (*Essay* 2: 149). Under the 1759 *theses logicae,* students defended a similar proposition about language: "Not nature but use connects a word and its ideas." Under the *theses rhetoricae,* students defended Lockean notions of language, always insisting on clarity and accuracy to the idea as principal rhetorical virtues: (1) "Defect of words in expressing ideas makes Rhetoric necessary[,]," (2) "No trope, exciting in the mind an impure idea, is appropriate[,]" (3) "No trope should be used unless it is clear and meaningful to the word used[,]," and (4) "The style of the orator should conform to the subject matter." The 1764 *theses rhetoricae* likewise show a Lockean empiricism and subjugation of language to the primacy of ideas: (1) "Loveliness of style in logic and rhetoric consists in perspicuity[,]" and (2) "The sum of rhetoric is the imitation of nature." Both Ramistic method and Lockean empiricism shared similar places in the Puritan technologia, and though the logic taught at Yale may have changed, the hierarchization of knowledge and the subordination of rhetoric and grammar remained. Lockean empiricism, as inserted into the Puritan technologia, became a way to investigate divine archetypes through their natural manifestations. In fact, at the 1766 commencement, Joseph Denison, then applying for his master's degree, had to argue affirmatively to the following proposition: "Are archetypes the divine perfection of ideas?"

While the appearance of Locke's empiricism certainly marks an important shift in Yale's rhetorical pedagogy, it did not manifest any major political change. Clap, the conservative, preserved a curricular structure that reinforced hierarchical social order. He even went so far as to teach from Isaac Watts's *Logick* (1725), a primer that built on Locke's epistemological suppositions. Watts's book begins with perception and spends a third of its pages offering directions for how to clearly apprehend empirical knowledge without the interference of words or superstitions. The remaining two-thirds of the book treats judgment (construction of propositions), argumentation (combining propositions), disposition (ordering propositions), and logical fallacies. Watts's text was a favorite among the dissenting academies in Great Britain in part because it allowed Protestant social climbers to claim epistemological and rhetorical authority. Anglican theologians like Berkeley sought a monopoly on truth and its presentation. While those at established English universities like Cambridge asserted their own Platonism against the potential threat of empiricism, dissenters like Watts developed new curricula suited for an aspiring commercial class and rooted in an empiricism that stripped the Anglican divine order of its epistemological right (J. Smith 30–36, 144–46). Like Locke, Watts articulated his empirical philosophy to developing capitalism in Great Britain, and he principally taught bourgeois aspirants in a British dissenting academy. In Connecticut, Thomas Clap tamed Watts's *Logick,* severing it from the British commercial class and inserting it into a conservative hierarchical order.

For the active minister, the chosen profession of many Yale graduates, the technologia (with either Ramistic method or Lockean empiricism in the logic slot) provided a working epistemological and ontological structure explaining Connecticut's social hierarchy. It also provided a way to understand discourse directed at an audience situated in that hierarchy. As other historians of Puritan rhetoric have noted, this was a rhetorical hermeneutic with political implications (Roberts-Miller, *Voices* 37). The minister begins with an understanding of God's plan (the technologia); he methodically discovers truth as ectypally manifested in a given moment, controversy, or Scripture passage; he grammatically translates that knowledge into a clear sermon; and finally he adorns that sermon with rhetorical figures to the congregation's delight. Some members of the congregation (presumably, the elders, the regenerate, and other elites) will understand the first two stages, but most will not. Most of the congregation is the silent majority, ignorant of method or technologia and needing a rhetorical midwife to deliver them. Implicit in this entire structure of knowledge, invention, and rhetoric is a principle of hierarchy that legitimized, perpetuated, and (re)constituted Puritan Connecticut.

Though the hierarchical principle served a social use, it had little practical rhetorical application. Recent studies of Puritan homiletics show that ministers did not follow this rhetorical approach. Among second-generation preachers, strict Ramistic division in sermons disappeared, and preachers adopted arrangement strategies depending on their audience's knowledge and their rhetorical aim (Stout 95). They did not begin with knowledge of God's plan and then discover/arrange it through Ramistic division. Typically, they began with a relevant theme, which they related to biblical passages, to common experiences, and to other forms of sermonic proof in order to argue their positions. In rhetorical practice, Puritan ministers behaved more like classical rhetors than Ramistic divines. The approach to rhetoric as taught at Yale had no widely accepted technical application, so its function was not to train orators but rather to justify a political order. Provided that Connecticut citizens widely accepted the technologia as an ontological/epistemological scaffolding, a full understanding of this knowledge hierarchy gave the Connecticut elite monopolistic control over meaning-making. Whether empiricism or Ramistic method appears in the logic slot is irrelevant to the curriculum's articulation to Connecticut's political economy. As long as the larger curricular structure remained, a new logical method posed no threat.

In Clap's classrooms, from 1745–65, Yale students learned always to reference a higher authority: either the Supreme Being or one of His chosen representatives. Students learned to directly consult God, to consult someone with organizational position granted by God, or to consult the empirical manifestations of God's archetypes. This is illustrated nowhere with greater force than in Clap's primer on ethics, as taught to Yale students: "*Moral Virtue* is a Conformity to the *moral perfections of God;* or it is an Imitation of God, in the moral Perfections of his Nature, so far as they are imitable by his Creatures. And the moral Perfections of God are the *sole* Foundation and Standard of all that Virtue, Goodness and Perfection which can exist in the Creature" (*Essay* 3). A similar deference to divine authority on all issues is evident in Yale's syllogistic and forensic debates. Two trends can be noticed in a close examination of these exercises. First, though students did argue by example and use other such inductive-empirical argumentative methods, they also tended to reference biblical verse as final authority or foundational axiom. Yale's curriculum may have imported scientific empiricism, but it did not import the challenge levied by such empiricism against religious dogma. Second, these debates did tend to circulate religious topics, but this does not mean that students did not learn to engage Connecticut's public sphere. Since religion was at the center of Puritan socioeconomic organization, religion was politics. Ability and authority at religious debate were part of a necessary rhetorical culture learned at Yale. Students engaged in debates in a sectarian public sphere where they learned its rhetorical practices, particularly the use of empirical evidence and biblical axiom to reinforce a belief in divine truth and social hierarchy.

Many of the Latin syllogistic debates referred to biblical authority. For instance, on June 19, 1750, Eleazer May syllogistically argued that animals could not reason, founding his claims on biblical axioms.

Si Bruto inter Bonum ac Malum distinguere possunt tum Morales
Agentes sunt
If animals can distinguish between good and bad, they are moral
agents
At Morales Agentes non sunt—
But they are not moral agents
Ergo non posunt distinguere inter Bonum ac Malum
Therefore they can't distinguish between good and bad.

The middle term in this syllogism is most interesting because it attempts to unite the major term and the conclusion with a religiously grounded assertion (animals are not moral agents).

The forensic debates, however, more liberally mixed inductive reasoning based on empirical observation with deductive argument founded on religious axiom. In November 1751, for example, May defended the Copernican conception of the solar system almost entirely by empirical observation, arguing primarily by ability to predict planetary motions and ease of explanation. He concluded by refuting biblical arguments, which, in his words, refer to "the Appearance of things and the Vulgar Notions and Opinions wich men have of them not according to there reality and Philosophical Verity." But May's argument is not entirely inductive, for he did begin with the assumption that there is a divinely ordained "harmony and agreement" among objects in the universe, leading him to believe that the earth rotates on an axis and travels in an orbit like all other objects in the solar system. May's skepticism about the "appearance of things" relied on a pre-empirical axiom asserting necessary order in the natural world, an archetype. On May 16, 1752, May defended the assertion that a promise extracted by force is obligatory, citing both divine authority and empirical observation. He initially said that "God who knows what is Right and fitting and best for us under all Circumstances has Commanded us to Keep all our Promises Without any Exception," but he then moved into a more elaborate discussion of human psychology and motive, concluding that, if people were allowed to break promises made under the threat of force, they would always do so, rending the fabric of trust in society and plunging the "World into Confusion and Tumult and distroy[ing] all Peace and Tranquility." Here, May coupled empirical observations about human psychology with axiomatic morality.

Finally, May's argument in favor of the lawful enslavement of Africans also uses both inductive observation and biblical axiom. May described Africa's social conditions as depraved and barbaric. He argued that Africans enslaved their own people, thereby exculpating whites who purchased African captives. A white slave owner "No More Deprives theme [Africans] of freedom and Liberty then if Man is Deprived of the Power of Walking who Willfully cuts of Both his own Legs." He even claimed that whites had introduced slaves to civilization and Christianity, thereby improving their lives. The last proof in this argument appears out of place among otherwise inductively-empirically derived claims. At the end, May turned to the biblical story about Ham, who was cursed by God to servitude; he argued that all Africans deserve their fate because they are Ham's descendants. In all, inductive-empirical argument is wedded to deductive use of biblical axiom to defend the most brutal political regime in U.S. history.

May was not the only student at Yale to argue forensically by empirical observation and biblical authority. Jeremiah Day, a sophomore in 1755, also engaged in forensic debates with similar argumentative structures. While defending despotic over monarchic or republican governments, for example, Day argued empirically-inductively that despotic governments are most efficient, using the Israelite kings as his example, and he also argued axiomatically that God, who allowed despotism among the chosen tribes of Israel, approves of these governments. A close look at both students' works reveals that they occupy different points on a spectrum of proof. Day, whose arguments are riddled with biblical citations, tended to rely much more heavily on biblical axiom than May. May relied more heavily on empirical observation, often inserting the biblical citation in the beginning or the end of his arguments. In these two students' works, Puritan technologia (and its deference to divine authority on all matters) combines with the empirical bent of the new science. At Yale disputation exercises, the two curricular formations came together in a religiously scientific rhetoric. Just as Clap articulated empirical science to the technologia, just as he positioned both observation and rational demonstration as avenues to divine truth, so did student debate exercises wed the two forms of evidence, thereby articulating Lockean empiricism to traditional Puritan epistemology and to the Puritan social hierarchy. Regardless of the argumentative foundation employed (be it empirically verified fact or biblical authority), divine intention was always at the ontological root of the argument, and rhetoric was always verity's handmaiden.

Historians have been quick to assume that before 1765, forensic and syllogistic debates were apolitical, focusing solely on religious issues or academic problems removed from common experience (Halloran; Morgan 395). Eleazor May's and Jeremiah Day's orations demonstrate that disputations did focus on sectarian topics with no apparent connection to political events. But one should not conclude that all topics were strictly religious or that all religious topics were apolitical. As evidenced by May's arguments, students were talking about important socioeconomic issues such as slavery or the right to (and obligation of) contract. Day also argued on several other topics, all having sociopolitical relevance. (See table 3.1.)

Furthermore, the religious topics debated had political relevance because a religiously driven government dominated Connecticut society. If Yale's graduates were to circulate among these people, they would have to traffic in the common religious discourse of the era, the rhetorical norms of the Puritan public sphere. When Day debated whether "it is consistent with the Perfections of God to elect Some and past by others," he began with the stated axiom that people were not spiritually regenerate "for their Good Works or any thing that they should do." By doing so, he clearly sided with Old Light Calvinists who believed in regeneration by the covenant of faith and not by the covenant of works. His allegiance to Old Light Calvinism engaged the most developed and inflamed dispute in pre–Seven Years' War Connecticut. Old and New Light Calvinists both

Table 3.1: Selected debate topics recorded in Yale student notebooks during Thomas Clap's tenure (Day and May)

Student	Question debated
Jeremiah Day	Is it Consistent with the Perfections of God to elect Some and past by others?
Jeremiah Day	Is Poligamy Lawful?
Jeremiah Day	Is the Eating of Blood Lawfull?
Jeremiah Day	Is Christ as the Mediator to be Worshipped?
Eleazor May	Whether All that Die in Infamy are Saved?
Eleazor May	Does the mind always think?
Jeremiah Day	Is dancing lawful?
Jeremiah Day	Is the marriage of children who are under the power of their parents valid without their Parents consent?
Jeremiah Day	Whether a private man may retain his right or property, by force or violence?

vied for control in the General Assembly and over Yale. Though these debate topics and the norms of this rhetorical culture might not jibe with contemporary emphasis on tolerant dialogue about secular-civic issues, there is no reason to paint Yale's rhetorical education as apolitical. The articulations between Connecticut's political economy and the Yale *paideia* of technologia made this rhetorical curriculum deeply political. The social implications of this entire *paideia* are underscored by the remarkable articulation of empiricism to the Ramistic rhetorical curriculum and to the larger political and economic interests of Connecticut's governing elders. In the 1760s, further social developments brought to Connecticut by capitalism's denizens would threaten the city on a hill. In particular, republicanism and a genteel variation of rhetorical education (belletrism) found their way to New Haven's harbor. Changes in Connecticut's political economy were also threatening the social formation that Clap so vehemently defended. The Connecticut hegemonic cluster was about to change dramatically, and Yale's rhetorical curriculum would reflect and participate in those changes.

Connecticut Political Economy after 1760

So far, this chapter has presented Connecticut as a quasi-medieval colony, preserving the political authority of a Puritan elite and interfering with economic developments whenever they threatened to change the colony's social structure. This story deserves a qualification. Connecticut's leaders did not distrust commerce wholly. In fact, some of the wealthiest and most successful colonial merchants in the northeast were Congregationalists. Also, the connection between Protestantism and successful capitalism has long been a mainstay in sociological theory. Connecticut's governing elders did not fear capitalism. They worried about its results. Particularly, they worried that prosperity and surplus would invoke a taste for luxury, a lazy moral character, and eventually a prurient existence. The Puritan, as Max Weber argued, did not fear money. S/he feared indolence and any labor not performed to further God's glory on this earth (157–58). Protestant asceticism, manifested in Congregationalists' unadorned, plain board meetinghouses, played a key role in the development of eighteenth-century commercialism in the northeast.

The Protestant resistance to commerce is a great historical irony, because Massachusetts and Connecticut settlers created the ideal breeding ground for an open commercial society. The eastern settlements in both New England and the middle colonies lay on a geography that discouraged agricultural production and encouraged a variety of economic pursuits, among them trade and manufacture. Mixed farming was nearly universal. Even in the Delaware Valley where the land was relatively flat and certainly arable, farmers grew a variety of crops to support themselves and their families, exporting surplus harvest only as a secondary means of subsistence. Ports, such as the Hudson and Delaware rivers and the Boston harbor, became manufacturing and trade hubs. Inland farmers traded surplus agricultural for manufactured goods on a regional circuit, and household manufacture in rural areas also contributed to a local carrying trade (Vickers 219–28). Finally, religious connections with the Old World developed into important commercial relationships. From these circumstances resulted a variegated economy most heavily striped by ribbons of manufacturing and commerce.

The social predilections in Connecticut also encouraged these developments. Connecticut Puritans encouraged industry to avoid immorality—idle hands are the Devil's playthings. Protestant industry, coupled with asceticism, accelerated economic growth in the area, while various factional efforts at education created a literate citizenry capable of working in a healthy commercial society. This combination of widespread education, industriousness, and asceticism, when placed in a geography that encouraged commerce, led eventually to a principally commercial society whose cosmopolitanism would finally threaten conservative settlements. During the 1760s, Connecticut's economy began more closely to resemble the capitalism already dominant in Boston and Philadelphia. Increased trade meant an influx of capital and an extension of people's desire for financial success. Changes in property structures between 1690 and 1740 also contributed to commercialization. As early as 1685, the colony began allowing private proprietorship of land. Property accumulated and stayed with families across generations. Private ownership drove up prices, encouraging more commercial-oriented agriculture and speculation, both of which allowed further accumulation of land among the privileged (Bushman, *From Puritan* 41–54). Increased trade and commercial agriculture allowed people to acquire status without participating in church life at all. Finally, an influx of financial capital allowed investment and growth in industries, such as shipbuilding, rum distilling, and craft manufacture.

The Awakening challenged Puritan hierarchy just as genteel British culture, already rampant in Boston, infected Connecticut. Economic changes, when paralleled with several cultural challenges and alternatives to Old Light Puritanism, opened a space for Connecticut's new aristocracy: the genteel Puritan. The movement away from Ramistic dialectic and toward Lockean empiricism in the Yale curriculum is one manifestation of a steady shift away from traditional Puritanism. Even New England's religious leaders grew more tolerant of cultural refinement. While second-generation ministers bemoaned commerce and its cosmopolitan trappings, third-generation ministers were more accepting. They were even willing to experiment with ornate speaking styles, turning away from the plain style that Yale graduates typically revered (Stout 76, 127–28). This newly ornate Puritan publicity articulated genteel rhetorical norms to a less strict variation of American Calvinism and to the cultural predilections of Connecticut's commercial class.

The new Connecticut capitalists were more tolerant of differing religions, less invested in church organization, less impressed by Puritan austerity, and more enthralled by baroque gentility. Clap was out of sync with the times. The college found itself at odds with its community. Initially, people fought Yale over religious toleration. Clap's strict policies requiring all students to attend the Old Light Congregationalist Church at Yale got him into trouble with Connecticut's elite. Clap and Benjamin Gale engaged in an extensive pamphlet war over the religious obligation of colleges and over how much money the General Assembly should give to Yale. Gale particularly objected to funding a professor of divinity and to Clap's system of discipline and student ranking (Gale, *The Present* and *A Letter;* Tucker 175–231). Eventually, the General Assembly refused to give any more public money to Yale. Clap was forced to resign in 1766, but public discontent over the Yale curriculum did not stop with his abdication. In fact, the battle between Connecticut's emerging commercial class and traditionalist Yale would continue long after Clap was gone, long after the Revolution was over. One of the last salvos was fired in 1783. A series of articles published in *The Connecticut Courant and Weekly Intelligencer* under the pseudonym "Parnassus" assaulted the Yale curriculum arguing many of the same points that Gale presented. There were twelve Parnassus articles in all, published between January 15 and May 27, 1783. Principally, Parnassus accused Yale of focusing on education of the clergy over education of the new professional bourgeoisie.

Clap's absence dominates the Yale tableau after 1766, when James Lockwood was president. Enrollment fell from 177 to 100. Student revolts came as regularly as the morning bells. When Lockwood died six years later, Napthali Daggett, then professor of divinity, assumed his post. Daggett made several efforts to articulate Yale's curriculum to the economic and cultural interests of Connecticut's bourgeoisie. He translated the college laws into English, introduced Newtonian physics to the curriculum, and stopped ranking students by their fathers' social positions. Students were now ranked alphabetically. Any one of these reforms is metonymically indicative of the larger changes negotiated at Yale among tutors, students, community, parents, and professors. All of these changes restructured the Yale curriculum to suit the nascent Connecticut commercial class. Daggett was not a strict disciplinarian like Clap nor was he so intrusively involved in the college's affairs. He trusted his tutors and professors to teach their classes however they wanted, and he monitored student behavior and performance less closely than Clap. During this time, a new generation of tutors reshaped the college curriculum, incorporating British culture and republican discourse into Yale's rhetorical pedagogy. These tutors' rhetorical education sutured together the economic interests of a developing economic class, the cultural pretensions of an increasingly cosmopolitan city, and the republicanism gaining favor among Connecticut's political leadership. Their curricular reforms helped to ensure that the reconstituted Connecticut hegemonic order would no longer favor the austere Puritan minister, though their rhetorical education was still articulated to key components in the earlier Puritan hegemony. The articulatory practice achieved in this newly bourgeois rhetorical education was still Puritan, still reliant on the technologia, for instance. But it also appealed to the cultural and economic interests of the nascent genteel Puritan capitalist.

Rhetorical Education at Yale, 1766–77

Both Timothy Dwight and John Trumbull were beginning students when Clap was leaving, and both men became tutors at the college while pursuing their master's degrees during the 1770s. Their experiences and their contributions epitomize student life at Yale under Daggett's tenure. Students living in New Haven had grown up in commercializing Connecticut. They had different tastes, were more tolerant, and were more professionally inclined. They lacked the patience to slog through lengthy tomes about the condition of one's soul, and they did not enjoy the austere Puritan rhetorical style. They did not even appreciate the gravity of ancient languages. Commercial traffic and cosmopolitan merchants exposed these young men to British genteel culture, and they responded favorably. They even found ways independently to study British rhetorical theory. In 1751, long before Clap left, distaste for his curriculum led students to form the secret Linonian Society, where they could read poetry, discuss literary texts, and practice English oratory. Timothy Dwight and John Trumbull

both belonged. At society meetings they secretly discovered a new rhetorical theory, developed among the British commercial class, that focused
on discursive cultivation of refinement and beauty. Historians of rhetoric
often refer to this brand of rhetorical theory as "belletrism."

British belletrism drew on seventeenth-century French aesthetic and
rhetorical theory that typically defined beauty as a natural phenomenon
triggering emotional and imaginative stimulation in the able observer. The
British belletristic tradition in the eighteenth century tended to focus on
psychology and the rhetorical forms capable of inciting aesthetic response
(Warnick chs. 1–2). In America, belletrism became one of the overriding
traditions in rhetorical theory for the next century.[10] British authors, like
Henry Home Lord Kames, developed a rich study of beauty in language.
Belletristic treatises typically focus on stylistic features of language (figures, tropes, and stylistic abstractions like order, harmony, clarity), and
they often include extensive taxonomies separating the beautiful from the
sublime. In effect, these texts codify and describe the rhetorical norms of
the eighteenth-century British cultural elite. For instance, Kames's *Elements of Criticism* (1762) avoids discussion of how to invent arguments
and offers no reflection on inventional topics, stasis theory, or evidence.
Kames instead spends the first fifteen chapters laying out an aesthetic
theory and the next ten chapters discussing taste and genres of literature,
and offering extensive advice about how to mirror certain human passions
in stylistic figures. He essentially wrote a manual to train the already
privileged in the rhetorical habits practiced among others of their class.
His elitism becomes painfully evident in chapter 25 when he says that taste
(an ability to appreciate beauty aesthetically) is not equally present in
all people. Nature only allots taste to the privileged few, because, if all
were able to appreciate beauty, no one would be satisfied as a worker (2:
489–90).

Among Scottish thinkers such as Adam Smith and Hugh Blair, belletrism caught on principally because a privileged class of moderate gentlemen enjoying the spoils of the Scotch commercial economy desired entrance into and the ability to participate in British high society. The
Scottish literati of the eighteenth century, mostly middle- and upper-
middle-class men, reacted against the Jacobite uprising of 1745 and
pressed for a moral regeneration to restore national order (Sher, *Church*

and University 38–45). Their crusade for cultural and national refinement conservatively followed the patterns set by English gentility, a reasonable course of action given that the Scottish parliament had been dissolved in 1707, putting their government in the hands of the English parliament, where Scottish officials held a minority of seats. Moderate Scotsmen ingratiated themselves with the English by imitating their culture. Hugh Blair, Regis Chair of Rhetoric and Belles Lettres at the University of Edinburgh (1762), produced the most developed belletristic rhetorical theory as it arose from Scottish moderate culture, and the printed version of his lectures would become the most popular rhetoric textbook in the early-national United States. Blair's *Lectures on Rhetoric and Belles Lettres* (1783), like Kames's *Elements of Criticism,* discusses literary style, criticism, beauty, the sublime, and the cultivation of taste, omitting completely any discussion of invention. Blair covered the different forms of argument, offering advice for eloquence at the bar, at the pulpit, and in "promiscuous assemblies" (lectures 27–29); giving classical advice about arrangement (lecture 31); and even mentioning the three types of proof (lecture 32); but he dedicated most of his lectures to style, even going so far as to closely analyze literary texts (the works of Joseph Addison and Jonathan Swift, especially in lectures 20–24). In fact, Blair spent more time lecturing on the nature of poetry and drama (lectures 38–47) than he did discussing more "practical" forms of address. While able to go on for pages about the difference between the beautiful and the sublime (lectures 3–5), he could only tell those interested in inventing arguments to "lay aside the common places, and to think closely of their subject" (2: 182).

Yale students in the Linonian Society recognized that by studying belletristic rhetoric, they could learn bourgeois rhetorical norms. They could become genteel citizens in Connecticut's emergent political economy. By candlelight, they read to one another belletristic and neoclassical rhetorical theory, like Kames's *Elements of Criticism* and John Ward's *System of Oratory* (1759). They debated in English about topics such as "what thing is most delightful to man in the world?" (April 13, 1773). They wrote and orally performed poems. They even wrote and enacted plays, with titles like *West Indian* and *Conscious Lovers* (April 9, 1776). (The students' enthusiasm for English drama is particularly noteworthy, especially when considering the long-standing Old Light Puritan disdain for the theater.) Latin performances did occur, but they were rare. The Linonian Society preferred English and consciously aimed at developing improved taste in English belles lettres. In 1764, another student society, the Brothers in Unity, was formed for similar purposes.

Comparing Clap's notion of taste with what students in the Linonian Society learned from Kames's *Elements of Criticism* provides a glimpse into the different rhetorical theories and pedagogies in circulation at Yale. When Clap talked about taste in his senior course on morality and ethics, he referenced many of the Scottish theorists that would influence Kames, men like Francis Hutcheson. Though Hutcheson was also Christian (Presbyterian), and though there were religious resonances to both men's notions of taste, Clap cleverly separated his rhetorical pedagogy from that of moderate Presbyterian clergymen. As Clap explained, Hutcheson's moderate notion of taste did not contribute to Puritan austerity nor to obedience. Clap did not stop with Hutcheson's construction of an "internal sense" or an ability to appreciate the beauties in nature through one's "capacity for receiving such pleasant Ideas" (Hutcheson 8). Clap claimed that self-love and self-interest led people like Hutcheson to focus on the beauty of nature without considering a higher cause. For Clap, true taste provided an internal sense of God's majesty and order, a sense that people lost when they fell from grace and that could only be recovered through the exercise of reason as guided by conscience and built upon the moral foundation of obedience (*Essay* 22–41). In his efforts to differentiate his notion of taste from that of moderate belletrists, Clap articulated his own rhetorical pedagogy to the Puritan social order that he defended throughout his career.

Young men like John Trumbull and Timothy Dwight, exposed to genteel culture in Connecticut, found more of interest in the belletristic notion of taste, since they had lived within and grown to enjoy imported British aristocratic culture. They had already internalized many of the habits and appreciations peculiar to gentility: love of linguistic embellishment and ornament, appreciation for arts without blunt moral messages, interest in polite conversation extending to topics beyond religion, moral order, and revelation. When the Yale curriculum did not offer a philosophical construction in line with the students' developing bourgeois sensibility, they looked elsewhere. They found what they wanted in Kames's genteel belletrism: "a just taste of the fine arts, derived from rational principles, furnishes elegant subjects for conversation, and prepares us for acting in the social state with dignity and propriety" (1: 9). Kames's Lockean description of human psychology appealed to minds less religiously and more empirically directed. It discouraged perception of natural events as types directly linked to eternal archetypes. Kames encouraged perception of the natural world as a manifold plenum ordered and made beautiful by a divine power along principles such as regularity, uniformity, proportion, order, and simplicity. His *Elements of Criticism* is an abstract, deistically inflected description of the qualities most eighteenth-century British gentry would find beautiful. While Clap's notion of taste promoted austerity and obedience, Kames's notion of taste reveled in beauty for its own sake, adoring eighteenth-century genteel culture for all its baubles and metaphors, all its ordered geometric lines and minute details, all its parlors and polite conversation. Connecticut social climbers interested in entering bourgeois society would find in Kames a guidebook for navigating the norms of its rhetorical culture.

In the early 1770s, Dwight and Trumbull became tutors at Yale and began to practice openly the genteel rhetorical norms they had developed in secret. Dwight and Trumbull readily articulated a Puritan genteel publicity, which sutured elements of British aristocratic culture to American Calvinism and to colonial bourgeois interests. What was once a surreptitious circulation of belletrism became an open resistance to Old Light Puritanism. Their rhetorical education articulated belletristic rhetorical theory to republican political discourse. British belletristic theory had within it a republican vocabulary, making it easy for the Yale tutors to incorporate the era's dominant political discourse into their efforts at good rhetorical instruction. Belletrists worried about civic virtue and saw literary study as a manner of cultivating it among the citizenry. Kames tied the cultivation of taste to the prevention of immoral activities (1: 9). Blair said, "The pleasures of taste refresh the mind [. . .] and prepare it for the enjoyments of virtue" (1: 12). Going back to Charles Rollin, who influenced belletrism in Scotland, England, and along the British Atlantic, one finds overt ties between virtue and the cultivation of taste (1: 11, 45). David Hume elaborated the most on the connection between belletrism and republicanism, arguing that eloquence was necessary to a healthy republic. Cultivation of polite style would contribute to a citizen's virtue. Hume even worried, in typical republican fashion, that excessive attention to stylistic refineries would corrupt. He found himself caught between the luxury of London's commercial culture and his own republican dispositions, between polite style and eloquence.[11]

Adam Smith likewise was caught in the same tension between republican politics and an affinity for free-market commercialism and bourgeois refinement. While Smith offered advice about appreciating literary style, he also said that in excess such flourish could corrupt one's discourse, making it "dark and perplex'd" (8). While discussing the value of appreciating Jonathan Swift's prose, he praised the "simple" orator who abjured the marks of "civility and breeding" (*Lectures on Rhetoric* 37). Smith assaulted Shaftesbury, whose work, he thought, exhibited the corrupting excesses of refinement, setting off "by the ornament of language what was deficient in matter" (59). In his brief history of rhetoric, Smith even touched on republican themes, such as the luxuries and refinements made available in commercial societies like Athens and their corrupting influence (137–38, 150–51). Smith's republicanism turned him away from the genteel culture of poetry and toward prose, which he characterized as "the Language of Business" (137). Trumbull's and Dwight's rhetorical pedagogy repeated these same connections between republicanism and belletristic rhetoric, articulating both to Connecticut's emerging commercial economy and to the bourgeois citizens favored therein.

In 1766, John Trumbull argued that education in polite letters benefits a republic, not by promoting obedience and austerity, but by "soften[ing] the Passions, sweeten[ing] the Mind, and correct[ing] the Morals of Mankind." Civic virtue was no longer embodied by Clap's silent majority but by a student body learning sympathy through literary exercise. Trumbull even argued that colleges should teach students to practice a belletristic rhetoric because "Literary Accomplishment [. . .] greatly assists the Attorney, furnishes him with Eloquence, adds Strength and Beauty to all his Reasonings, and makes him doubly Serviceable to the Publick and to Individuals" (*Letter* 6–7). A belletristic rhetorical *paideia* therefore benefits the commercial republic by making virtuous and professionally functional citizens. When receiving his master of arts degree in 1770, Trumbull told the graduating class of Yale, "No subject can be more important in itself, or better suited to the personal occasion and the exercises of this day, than the Use and Advantages of the Fine Arts, and especially those of Polite Literature." In his commencement address, he even defined taste in very Kamesian terms, saying that "the Divine Being, to raise us above these low desires, hath implanted in our minds a taste for more pure and intellectual pleasures" (*Essay* 3–4).

However, neither the students at Yale nor Connecticut's emerging commercial elite wholly accepted British gentility. There were still residual elements of Puritan belief within this rhetorical pedagogy. Just as Clap articulated Locke's epistemology to an authoritative Puritan social formation, the Yale tutors appropriated belletrism for commercially moderate but still Puritan political ends. The taste (re)constructed and circulated at Yale had two distinct differences from British belletrism, particularly Kames's version. First, it was much more religiously (Calvinistically) inflected. While Kames vaguely referenced God, an apparently Anglican and consummately rational deity, Dwight and Trumbull appealed to a Puritanical, patriarchal God. Dwight was influenced by Jonathan Edwards's theology, where he found a clear philosophical description of Puritan genteel taste. (Edwards, not coincidentally, was Dwight's grandfather.) Like Clap, Edwards thought that everyone has taste to appreciate the beauty described by British belletrists such as Kames and Hutcheson. He called this "natural beauty" and attributed to it many of the qualities Kames listed, such as "uniformity" and "quantity." Edwards also believed in "moral beauty," perceptible by the chosen few able to see the glory of God in nature. Only the regenerate can witness the latter. Natural beauty affects the mind, moral beauty, the soul. In *Religious Affections* (1746), Edwards listed regenerate taste as one sign that a person is saved: "a love to divine things for the beauty and sweetness of their moral excellence" (253–54). Needless to say, only a few can be regenerate. By articulating belletristic rhetorical norms to Puritan theology, Dwight managed to connect his rhetorical pedagogy to Connecticut's emerging commercial cosmopolitanism and also to a long-standing fear of direct democracy among Connecticut's leadership. While New Haven was certainly becoming more capitalist, its overseers were by no means more democratically minded. They might be commercially employed, but they were religiously governed. They might be genteel, but they were still Puritan. By all accounts, this was still a city on a hill led by a divinely privileged few who voiced God's commands.

Despite its articulation to Calvinist theology and New England authoritarian politics, Dwight's and Trumbull's Puritan belletrism still encouraged pleasure in many of the rhetorical artifacts that British gentility glorified. This Puritan belletrism also encouraged a deeper appreciation for a patriarchal God as manifested in nature and in language. Most importantly, Puritan genteel taste separated the regenerate from the unregenerate, thereby continuing the hierarchization of Connecticut society. The New Light focus on individual appreciation over ministerial mandate preserved the Puritan investedness in authority and obedience but shifted this authority from the church elders to Scripture and nature as experienced by the individual. Clap imposed his authority externally. He encouraged students to see the divine right in the minister's disciplinary directives. Dwight and Trumbull asked students to internalize and enact appreciation for divine authority. Puritan gentility, in effect, asked the individual to become both Lord and servant.

When he received his master's degree, Dwight delivered a speech at commencement that perfectly wedded Puritan theology to British genteel categories in rhetorical criticism. Dwight's *Dissertation on the History, Eloquence, and Poetry of the Bible* (1772) marshals Kamesian rhetorical criticism, including an affection for rhetorical tropes and figures, to argue that the Bible is beautiful. Dwight repeated many of Kames's criteria for beauty: novelty and sublime use of figures most particularly. But he also hinted at a deeper beauty that could reach the regenerate soul, saying that the authors of the Bible "snatched the grace which is beyond the reach of art, and which, being genuine offspring of elevated Genius, finds the shortest passage to the human soul" (4). In this passage, Dwight not only tied Puritan regeneration to a sense of rhetorical beauty but did so while echoing (nearly verbatim) Alexander Pope's *Essay on Criticism* (1711), another composition that lists belletristic guidelines for producing genteel verse. Pope said that sublime writers can eschew the rules of composition, because genius often finds direct rhetorical passage to the human heart.[12] The Popian allusion in Dwight's description of the biblical sublime shows his appreciation for British belletrism, his familiarity with contemporary British authors, but this passage also shows that Dwight articulated his notion of rhetorical beauty to a Puritan theology, something that neither Pope nor Kames would have imagined.

If the Puritan inflection is the first difference between eighteenth-century British and Connecticut genteel cultures, then the second is the employment of republican political discourse, particularly the corruption topic. As the Revolution approached, Connecticut's leaders and Yale's students differentiated themselves from the British in part by separating their Puritan gentility from its British predecessor. They labeled British culture debased, claiming that American Puritan belletrism avoided its excesses (Dowling 18). Dwight told the graduating class of 1776 that study of polite letters would disseminate uncorrupted taste, lead to the progress of God's empire, and help America triumph over sullied Britain. He ended with a nationalistic trumpet call to arms, but not to weapons of war. Rather, Dwight proposed that his students triumph through "learning and eloquence" (*Valedictory* 21). Dwight connected rhetorical performance, particularly his own brand of belletrism, to national virtue and success against a corrupt enemy.

Dwight and Trumbull also criticized education they considered inappropriate for the developing republic. Trumbull mounted a sustained assault on instruction strictly in classical languages and in overly refined culture, calling the former useless and the latter corrupt. In his three-part poem, "The Progress of Dulness" (1772), Trumbull proposed to replace traditional education in "the mere knowledge of ancient languages, of the abstruser parts of mathematics, and the dark researches of metaphysics" with instruction in "the elements of oratory, the grammar of the English tongue, and the elegancies of style and composition." Trumbull waged his satirical attack in three waves of mock character portraits. He recounted the educational experiences of Tom Brainless, schooled in a scholastic, classical curriculum, and taught to "learn the grave style [. . .] and shun [. . .] the infection of the modern style" (*Poetical Works* 2: 10, 27). Tom leaves college dumber than when he arrived and unable to function in any professional or useful capacity. Brainless's story is a direct attack on Clap's curriculum and also an effort to articulate Trumbull's rhetorical pedagogy to the interests of Connecticut's professional bourgeoisie. In the second section of his poem, Trumbull turned to foppish students who spent most of their time socializing, drinking, and gaming. This is a critique of excessive refinement, the kind of corrupting gentility that Trumbull located across the pond in British culture. Part two of "The Progress of Dulness" describes Dick Hairbrain, who learns to be a rake and a coxcomb, a result that could have been prevented by teaching him properly reserved, Puritan rhetorical taste. Hairbrain learns a good deal of his corrupting manners from British novels like *Tristram Shandy* ("soft simpering tales of amorous pain") and from magazines; he learns his religion from David Hume. In the end, he wastes his inheritance on a debauched voyage to Europe where he quickly lands in debtor's prison (*Poetical* 2: 44–45, 55–56). Part three recounts the experiences of a woman, Miss Harriet Simper, who does not receive any formal schooling and learns little more than coquetry and socializing. Trumbull opens this section with a prose prologue arguing that "[p]olite literature hath within a few years made very considerable advances in America [. . . yet f]emale education hath been most neglected" (*Poetical* 2: 60). Like Dick Brainless, Harriett Simper could have become a much better and more useful republican citizen had she learned polite letters. Instead, however, she reads British novels such as *Clarissa* and *Pamela,* "books that poison all the mind" (*Poetical* 2: 76). Harriett Simper's portrait makes a common statement about the importance of republican motherhood and the place of rhetorical pedagogy therein. The portraits of Dick Brainless and Harriet Simper were also assaults on British taste, showing how the rhetorical norms of this dandified and morally debased culture could lead to personal ruin.

Trumbull's criticisms in "The Progress of Dulness" were not limited to Great Britain's excessively refined belletrism. Trumbull also critiqued the Old Light Puritan rejection of all polite letters. He found virtue neither in the complete condemnation nor in the extreme adoption of gentility. While claiming that British literature, particularly novels and plays, was corrupting, he also claimed that Puritan objection to all polite literature was stultifying. He railed against "priests [who] drive poets to the lurch," ministers who "find heresies in double-rhymes / Charge tropes with damnable opinion, / And prove a metaphor Arminian" (*Poetical* 2: 75). Trumbull's ambivalent attitude toward polite letters, his Puritan gentility, his ascetic belletrism, was articulated to a common republican sense that too little cultural refinement could retard the nation's development and that too much could corrupt. He advocated a new type of belletrism, one suited to Puritan asceticism *and* to developing commercialism.

While he was a tutor at Yale, Trumbull wrote two series of essays, one published in the *Boston Chronicle* as "The Meddler" and the other published in the *Connecticut Journal* as "The Correspondent."[13] Evidence suggests that Timothy Dwight contributed to "The Meddler" essays (Howard 37–38). These are examples of the Puritan genteel publicity that Dwight and Trumbull encouraged among Yale students and of the uniquely Puritan belletrism that they thought appropriate to the virtuous republic. They are consummately genteel essays, comparable to Joseph Addison's and Richard Steele's *Spectator* and embodying many of the same rhetorical norms: direct address to the reader; lengthy ruminations on quotidian topics such as fashion or conduct; classical and at times pseudo-classical allusion; droll, offhanded remarks like "dying is certainly the most expedient way of gaining a reputation" ("Correspondent 11"); and finally an attempt to define genteel taste as different from lowbrow, popular taste and corrupt affection. "The Meddler 9," for instance, attacked the Connecticut education system with claims similar to those made in "The Progress of Dulness": country boys studying under ministers learned little more than obedience and did not learn to write well. "The Meddler" also claimed that town boys, educated by socialite mothers, learned little more than foppish behavior. When both country and town boys came to college, they ignored the boring, classical curriculum and behaved like "coxcombs," "rakes," and "gamesters." This form of gentility was morally depraved, just like the British culture that Dwight and Trumbull abhorred. In "The Correspondent 23," the speaker ridiculed affected, British taste through a mock myth about Theuth, the Egyptian God who gave people frivolity and gambling, thinking that these practices would be rejected outright. Instead, according to this myth, the people loved Theuth's gifts, and "the kingdom of Nonsense" was "erected [. . . to] triumph over the wisdom of the earth." Again, properly moral and reserved taste is not learned, so the whole of society putrefies.

In accord with their beliefs about properly virtuous rhetorical practice in the new republic, Trumbull and Dwight changed the Yale curriculum. They developed a new republican *paideia* that articulated both the political interests of Connecticut's Puritan leadership and the cosmopolitan taste of its commercial class. Trumbull and Dwight promoted more instruction in English rhetoric, grammar, and literature, directly rejecting Clap's focus on classical languages and also appealing to a practical bourgeois need for rhetorical acumen in the vernacular. Dwight even began teaching a senior course in English belles lettres. (In 1776 his students successfully petitioned the college to allow this course.) He taught out of Kames's *Elements of Criticism,* and he promoted the same Puritan, nationalistic, genteel writing style and literary taste Trumbull advocated and practiced in "The Correspondent" and "The Meddler" essays. At the 1772 commencement, Dwight delivered his *Essay on Education,* in which he advanced the liberal arts to hold off student corruption and depravity. He also argued that true, genteel taste, as circulated among students through polite rhetorical practice, would guide them away from lowbrow pursuits and toward greatness: "Animated with such principles, the youth will dare to take a higher aim in life, than the pursuits of the idle rabble; will reverence his nature, and be ashamed of those stains which degrade it" (8).

The particular changes made to the Yale rhetorical curriculum before 1776 are further exhibited through two phenomena: textbooks used in recitation and theses defended at graduation. The religious texts, such as Wollaston's *Religion of Nature* or Ames's *Marrow of Divinity* were replaced with Locke's *Essay Concerning Human Understanding.* In rhetoric instruction, scholastic texts were replaced in 1767 by John Ward's *System of Oratory.* Ward's text, mentioned earlier as a favorite among the Yale secret societies, is a neoclassical treatment of rhetoric, printed in English. This was the first time that sophomores at Yale would study rhetoric without a Ramistic bias and in their mother tongue. A few years later, Ward's text was replaced by John Holmes's *Art of Rhetoric* (1739), also a neoclassical treatment of rhetoric in English with a decidedly belletristic tilt. When placed against the belletristic rhetorical tradition, two things stand out in Holmes's text: his extensive treatment of style and his lengthy summary of Longinus's *On the Sublime.*

Holmes divided stylistic excellence into three virtues: composition, elegance, and dignity. Composition requires one to follow the rules of English grammar. Elegance consists of purity, perspicuity, and politeness, all of which relate to one's ability to write in a manner acceptable among genteel society. To become an elegant writer, Holmes recommended studying the "correctest" writers (27). Dignity, the ability to induce sublime thought with rhetorical flowers, gets the most extensive treatment, occupying more pages than are allotted to both invention and arrangement put together. This treatment of style promotes heavy use of figures and tropes, a baroque flourish that Thomas Clap would have found distasteful if not immoral. Holmes's recapitulation of Longinus's *On the Sublime* further promotes the ornate style common in belletristic rhetoric. Holmes did not find such sublimity in sermons or in the "plain" writing of Puritan elders. He found it in English poems by Thomson, Milton, and Shakespeare. In contrast to Holmes's unqualified celebration of discursive sublimity, Yale's tutors constantly warned students about the potential excesses in the rhetorical sublime, insisting that stylistic abstemiousness would more readily lead to divine wisdom and revelation. In doing so, they articulated Holmes's belletristic rhetorical theory to Puritan theology and to Connecticut's political order. Dwight told his students that the biblical sublime was rhetorically reserved, allowing God's majesty and prophecy more clearly to shine through. He said, "Nothing gives greater dignity to Poetry than Prophecy" (*Dissertation* 16).

Belletrism's dominance and its articulation to Puritan theology can be further illustrated by looking at Yale's commencement broadsides. In 1766, for instance, one of the *theses rhetoricae* was "sublimity consists in great ideas expressed in words" (*sublimitas, in ideis magis quam verbis consistit*). Instead of Ramistic advice to follow a strict hierarchy of logical categories, students defended more neoclassical advice about arrangement: "An argument should be arranged firmest at the beginning and end and weakest in the middle" (*argumenta firmissima in Initio et Fine, et imbecillima in Orationis Medio, collocari debent*). Many of the 1769 theses revealed a belletristic preoccupation with style and the sublime: "Many brief vowels and syllables are very necessary to anything expressed beautifully and delicately" (*ad aliquod belle et delicate exprimendum, multae vocales et syllabae breves sunt pernecessariae*). Still, sublime rhetoric, though a belletristic preoccupation, was defined in typically Puritan terms: "The dignity and sublimity of sentences demonstrates copiously their divine origin" (*dignitas et sublimitas sententarum, in saeris scripturis, divinas earum originem copiose demonstrat*).

Table 3.2: Selected *theses rhetoricae* defended at Yale during the early 1770s (see ch. 3, n. 7)

Year defended	Latin version of thesis	English translation of thesis
1772	Oratori, dispositio argumentorum quam inventio est majori operi.	Arrangement, along with invention, is most of the orator's work.
1772	Narratio sit simplicissima.	The narration should be as simple as possible.
1772	Sententiae quae vim sublimitatis maximam habent, oratione simplici optimi exprimuntur.	Sentences that have the most sublimity are expressed with optimal simplicity by the orator.
1772	Orationis sublimitas ex usu figurarum constat.	Sublimity in orations is constituted from the use of figures.
1774	Periphrasis in poesi, melius quam in oratione soluta locum habet.	Periphrasis has a better place in poetry than it does in oratory.

If this trace of Puritan theology is not enough to demonstrate that Yale's rhetorical pedagogy continued to promote obedience to political authority, one can find more convincing evidence in the places logic and rhetoric occupied in the entire curricular structure. Logic was still positioned as the discipline for finding truth, rhetoric as the discipline for making that truth presentable, and the *theses logicae* continued their focus on Lockean empiricism. In 1772, for instance, students defended theses like: "Abstract vocabularies are necessary towards reasoning in prose" (*vocabula abstracta, ad rationciandum sunt prorus necessaria*). The *theses logicae* offered no advice about how to form syllogisms and instead emphasized faculty psychology and the need to make language mirror empirical reality, both Lockean bugbears. While the technologia was preserved and while logic was still taught as a path to divine truth, rhetoric increasingly reflected John Ward's classicism and John Holmes's belletrism. (See table 3.2.)

The changes in textbooks, the shifts in theses defended at commencement, the tutors' assault on aspects of the old curriculum, all these local pedagogical efforts symbolically restructured taste. Dwight and Trumbull were more tolerant, even approved of, genteel culture, but their appreciation for belletrism did not necessarily lead to a less stratified society. Connecticut still had very rigid social classes, and it was still led by a Congregationalist government. The new Congregationalists were more tolerant of other religions, enjoyed genteel over austere Puritan cultural artifacts, and more intensely valued economic capital as a sign of social worth. Nevertheless, though Connecticut's ruling elite was becoming economically capitalist and culturally cosmopolitan, they were still Puritans, still politically authoritarian.

In fact, the belletrism taught at Yale contained vestiges of the traditional Puritan belief that excessive commerce should be restrained to preserve religious virtue. Trumbull and Dwight, while embracing belletrism, also worried over its corrupting effects and promoted a reserved rhetorical performance, better reflecting the social mores promoted in a Puritan social order. Of course, they found in belletristic rhetorical theory the means of accomplishing this end. As mentioned earlier, belletrists worried about rhetorical refinement's corrupting excess. But Dwight and Trumbull added to this a distinctly Puritan inflection, one peculiar to Connecticut's political elite, even echoing some of Clap's teachings. Neither Trumbull nor Dwight questioned the larger curricular structure of the technologia. Just as Clap imported Lockean empiricism without significantly jeopardizing the overall curricular structure or political upshot of Yale's curriculum, Dwight and Trumbull imported belletrism without threatening the privilege and political authority exercised by Connecticut's Puritan leaders. Dwight and Trumbull were still a religious speaking aristocracy standing before the silent majority, and they demanded a similar obedience from the lower classes, one grounded in similarly divine warrants. They taught their students likewise to follow divine orders as expressed in sublime rhetoric.

This new rhetorical pedagogy articulated republican discourse to bourgeois interests in practical education and in cultural refinement and to the Puritan political interest in maintaining an authoritarian order. The Yale tutors thus established their belletristic rhetorical theory and pedagogy in a new Connecticut hegemony, one undergirded by an emergent capitalist economic base, though still articulated to an authoritarian political order. This new articulatory constellation happened at the contested site of rhetorical education, and it incorporated several of the components sutured into the traditional Puritan hegemony that Dwight and Trumbull opposed. Thus, the articulatory efforts enacted by Yale's tutors were integral to the reconstruction of Connecticut's hegemony. These curricular developments were instrumental in the shift from one economic base to another, from one cultural constellation to another. Dwight and Trumbull engaged in cultural agon, occupying the important site of rhetorical education and rearticulating the components of both residual and emergent social and economic institutions. Their efforts were successful, demonstrating the political agency available to any educator in any democratic society.

Yale during and after the Revolution: Rhetoric under Ezra Stiles

Like all other colleges in the British North Atlantic, Yale was in turmoil during the Revolution. Ezra Stiles became president just as the war was beginning, and during the course of conflict Stiles lost most of his tutors to internal quarreling. Also, each remaining tutor took his respective class to a different town during the Revolution to prevent engagement with the British. But Stiles was a remarkable president. Despite the poor circumstances that he inherited, a waning faculty, a volatile political situation, no financial support from the General Assembly, and a scattered student body, Stiles managed to turn Yale into the most successful college along the British Atlantic by the end of the Revolution. In 1784, Yale had 270 students, over 100 more than Harvard (Morgan 359). Stiles's success as a president resulted from his ability to reconcile the curriculum with the social tenor of Connecticut's bourgeois Puritan elite. Stiles turned Yale into a genteel Puritan college, a transformation the Yale students and tutors had begun before the Revolution. Even the General Assembly, in 1792, voiced their open approval of reforms in Yale's rhetorical curriculum. Their report read, "[T]he literary exercises of the respective Classes have of late Years undergone considerable Alterations, so as the better to accommodate the Education of Undergraduates to the present State of Literature" (qtd. in

Morgan 419). For the first time since Clap was in office, the state appropriated public money for Yale's use.

To understand how mainstream Yale's genteel curriculum had become, one need only look at the altered status of the Linonian Society and the Brothers in Unity. The Yale secret societies, once havens for forbidden belletrism, openly appeared in student culture during the early 1770s, and they were college fixtures by the early 1780s. Their dramatic performances became increasingly elaborate, incorporating costumes, props, and even scenery. On April 13, 1773, for instance, the Linonian Society performed a comedy titled *West Indian*. One student's description of this event reveals its lavishness:

> Both the scenery and Action were on all hands allowed to be superior to any thing of the kind heretofore exhibited on the like Occasion. The whole received peculiar Beauty from the Officers appearing dress'd in Regimentals, & the Actresses appearing dress'd in full & elegant suits of Lady's apparel. The last scene was no sooner closed than the company testified their satisfaction by the clapping of hands. Between the third and fourth Acts a musical dialogue was sung between Fenn and Johnson in the characters of Damon and Elora, which met with deferr'd applause. An Epilogue made expressly on the occasion & delivered by Hale 2d was receiv'd with approbation. The musical Dialogue was then again repeated; A humerous Dissertation on Las was delivered by Mills; & at the request of several Gentlemen who were not present in the first part of the Day the first part of the Lecture on Heads was again exhibited. ("Linonian Society Records")

This is one example of the Linonian Society April anniversary celebrations, public events that became increasingly sophisticated throughout the last quarter of the eighteenth century. Plays, poems, lectures, dissertations, orations, and of course debates were all performed with great regularity before the college and the local community.

In addition to practicing literary genres, students continued to practice debate, often addressing relevant political topics. In the 1750s, students debated religion and local politics. In the 1780s topics still included local political concerns, but they also took on topics of national import. The

Table 3.3: Selected topics debated by the Brothers in Unity ("Brothers in Unity, Secretary's Records")

Date	Question Debated
February 21, 1788	Whether money ought to free a man from corporial punishment?
July 22, 1789	Whether a federal library would be beneficial?
July 24, 1788	Ought Vermont to pay her proportion of the publick debt, if she is admitted to the Union? Have the United States any right to oblige any one of the States to come into the Constitution?
February 28, 1788	Whether Ministry ought to be supported by taxes?
January 19, 1794	Whether a Sudden emancipation of slavery would be politic in the State of Connecticut?
June 18, 1789	Would it be beneficial for the United States to prohibit the Importation of Spiritous Liquors?
July 19, 1787	Whether a limited monarchy would be preferable to a republican government for these states?
March 4, 1790	Does justice and policy require the establishment of sumptuary Laws in the United States?

republican public sphere that the Brothers in Unity imagined in their debate exercises extended beyond Connecticut, including all thirteen of the newly formed states. (See table 3.3.) Of course, the national scene that the Brothers imagined resembled Connecticut. "Sumptuary laws" and a state-supported ministry were serious possibilities (if not achieved actualities) for the Connecticut legislature, but they were not so for the rest of the United States. In these debate exercises, Yale students were encouraged to imagine a republican public sphere where all citizens were equally invested in the religious autocracy that residually clung to Yale's home state.

By the late eighteenth century, rhetoric classes at Yale focused almost exclusively on English rhetorical theory and practice in English oratory. English textbooks like John Locke's *Essay* and William Paley's *Moral and*

Political Philosophy became the norm. In the late 1760s, students studied in Robert Lowth's *English Grammar* (1762). John Holmes's rhetoric textbook was used until 1785 when Hugh Blair's *Lectures on Rhetoric and Belles Lettres* replaced all other rhetoric and grammar texts. Students continued to defend belletristic theses at their graduations. In 1781, for instance, the following definition of rhetoric was offered at the top of the *theses rhetoricae:* "Rhetoric teaches polite letters and the art of ornately speaking" (*rhetorica literas politiores edocet artemque ornate dicendi*). The 1781 theses also show that students were learning to appreciate both Latin and vernacular authors: "Among all epic poets of clans, Homer, Virgil, Tasso, and Milton stand out before all; moreover they were the originals, all the rest, imitators" (*inter omnium gentium poetas epicos, Homerus, Virgilius, Tasso, et Miltones prae omnibus eminuerunt; horum antem prumus et ultimus originales fuerunt, caeteri imitators tantum*). In 1786, students defended the following thesis, relating the study of polite letters to national liberty: "Eloquence is always the master of and always flourishes among a free people" (*eloquentia in liberum populum semper floruit, semperque dominata est*). Under Stiles, rhetorical pedagogy and practice were tied directly to the construction of a stable republic. Following the lead of tutors who preceded him, Stiles articulated belletristic rhetorical theory to the new sense of national unity, the desire to build an American republic. Perhaps most remarkable is that by the early 1790s, the *theses* and *quaestiones* were published in English.

One can most clearly see the changes in Yale's curriculum by looking at the disputation exercises practiced under Stiles's tenure. In the 1750s, disputation topics focused on religion, dealt only with two genres (syllogism and argumentative oration), balanced instruction in both Latin and English, encouraged inductive argument by empirical observation or deductive argument from biblical axiom, and finally encouraged a plain style in line with Old Light Puritan taste. By the 1780s, disputation exercises had become something quite different. To begin with, syllogistic disputation in Latin was fast on its way out. When Stiles became president, students debated syllogistically every Monday. By 1782, Stiles had restricted it to the first Monday of every month, and in 1789 he did away with the exercise altogether (Morgan 395). Stiles still taught Hebrew, Greek, and Latin. Though he encouraged and presided over disputations in these languages, students were no longer required to dispute in anything but En-

Table 3.4: Selected topics debated at Yale during Ezra Stiles's tenure as president (Stiles 3: 63, 70, 197, 222, 261, 356)

Date	Question Debated
March 24, 1783	Whether a standing army would be dangerous in America?
March 25, 1783	Whether God is the author, and is as intentionally efficient in the production, of sin as holiness in His creatures?
April 28, 1783	Whether it would be best to establish a general Amnesty, and restore the Refugee Tories to their Estates and Franchises?
March 30, 1784	Whether depreciation ought in justice to be paid by the states or by public securities?
June 8, 1786	Whether paper money is a benefit?
June 19, 1787	Whether the States acted wisely in sending delegates to the general convention now sitting in Philadelphia?
April 23, 1787	Whether the public securities ought to be paid at their nominal value?
April 30, 1787	Whether an unregenerate man may go into the ministry?
June 9, 1789	Whether it would be right to compel unfederated states into the federal union?

glish. The topics for debate shifted away from the religiously political focus of 1750 and toward a more secularly national focus, paralleling the topics debated in student societies. Even still, several topics did have religious resonances. (See table 3.4.)

Roger Newton's student notebook recorded between December 1783 and December 1784 offers several examples of student forensic disputation under Stiles's presidency. Newton's notebook is interesting in comparison to student disputations in the 1750s, first because it includes more than disputations. Newton also wrote and presented poems, such as his "Ode for Bristol," his "Hymn for Newport," and his "Ode for Trumbull." Newton wrote orations situated outside of the debate format. He wrote an extended piece titled "On Brevity and Prolixity in Composition," which reads more like an essay than an oration or a disputation exercise. By learning to converse in these belletristic genres, Newton learned bourgeois rhetorical norms as they were gaining favor in Connecticut, especially in commercial centers like New Haven. Newton's notebooks also give evidence that Yale's students and faculty continually struggled to differentiate their genteel taste from what they read in the works of British writers like Blair and Kames. In his discussions of style, Newton defended Puritan, reserved gentility by championing brevity over prolixity. Truly tasteful composition, according to Newton, would not overindulge in "empty digression and futile prolixity." Tasteful writing would be "pleasing and the mode of escpression concise and comprehensive."

Newton did debate syllogistically in Latin, and he translated passages from classical works, such as Cicero's *De Oratore,* so one cannot conclude that education in the classical languages was erased from the curriculum. But the majority of his presentations were in English, demonstrating that he acquired skill in the vernacular, a skill that appealed to Connecticut's pragmatic bourgeoisie. The forensic disputations are the most interesting part of his notebook, in part because their topics reflect the national scope mentioned earlier. Newton debated topics such as "whether in a state of nature, one man has a right to impose law upon another" and "whether the state of America in Congress assembled ought to vote according to the number of inhabitants and property of each." These arguments are also interesting for their format and the kinds of proof that they employ. Appeal to biblical axiom so common in forensic disputations of the 1750s is completely absent from Newton's arguments. He argued by empirical observation, by commonplace construction of proper taste, and by logical consistency from deduction to deduction. Newton's reluctance to appeal to biblical axiom demonstrates that this rhetorical norm (once a feather of traditional Puritan public debate) was losing favor. Nevertheless, though he followed rhetorical norms more common among the newly cosmopolitan and capitalist Connecticut citizens, Newton articulated several residual elements from Puritan theology.

In his debate exercises, Newton articulated a newly Puritan publicity, one practicing both residual and emergent rhetorical norms and appealing to residual political authoritarianism as well as to emergent capitalism and gentility. On August 10, 1784, Newton argued affirmatively when asked the following question: "[W]hether more attention ought to be paid to the study of the solid parts of literature than to the belles letters?" His argument hinges on a positive valuation of Puritan, genteel taste favoring intellectual labor over purely aesthetic appreciation. He argued that taste is universally human, pointing to psychology and inductively reasoning from particular behaviors. Newton appealed to utility and to morality in his defense of "solid literature," further separating this study from polite literature, which might help the mind relax "when fatigued with the nobler studies of the natural and moral worlds" but which adds nothing to the construction of a properly moral taste. He even condemned excessive study of polite letters because "[n]othing renders the mind more vain and artfully intriguing than the accomplishment of elegance." This argument is built upon speculation about human psychology and professional endeavor, using empirical evidence (example), a belief in the split between truly virtuous and corrupted tastes (as illustrated in the division between solid and polite literatures), and consistency of deductive argument from one abstract claim to the next. When contrasting Newton's argument with those made by May and Day in the 1750s, the changes in rhetorical theory and pedagogy at Yale become evident. Lockean empiricism had fully taken hold as had belletrism. And all of these changes were articulated to a republican discourse labeling an ascetic gentility virtuous and an overly refined belletrism corrupting. All the same, Newton still defended a foundational notion of taste that would separate the elite from the rest, legitimizing the cultural authority of one group over another. His newly articulated publicity, therefore, presented no significant challenge to Connecticut's social hierarchy.

Timothy Dwight Returns to Yale: Belletrism, Puritanism, and Federalism

Dwight left his post as tutor at Yale to become a minister in the Revolutionary army. While Stiles was president, Dwight presided as minister over the wealthy parish of Greenfield Hill, developing, like many Congregationalist ministers at the time, an alliance with the Federalist Party. But Dwight did not at all favor Hamilton's industrial capitalism. Dwight wed-

ded Puritan hierarchical authoritarianism with eighteenth-century republicanism, conflated the American republic with John Winthrop's "city on
a hill," collapsed citizen virtue into Protestant piety. As discussed in the
first chapter, many of Dwight's writings, particularly his poem *Greenfield
Hill,* expressed a typical Puritan fear that capitalism could intrude on the
civic-religious mission of Connecticut's settlements. In Dwight's millennial republic, a strong authoritative federal government must curb commerce to protect citizen virtue. The greater public good is the good of the
church, citizen sacrifice often means asceticism, and democracy crumbles
before another iteration of authority. Nathan Hatch, a historian of early
American politics and religion, says Dwight's republicanism "evoked a decidedly reactionary pattern of thought, one which called upon the individual to govern himself by the premodern criteria of inequality, deference, subordination, and authority" (*Sacred* 114).

Dwight articulated this millennial republican vision to the politics of
the Federalist Party, which opposed direct democracy and even advocated governmental intervention in economic affairs. During the Federalist era (1789–1800), Dwight's republicanism reinforced the political
power that Connecticut's Puritan, predominantly Federalist bourgeoisie
enjoyed, but a new national hegemonic order was forming and would
ascend in 1800. From that point on, Dwight's millennial republicanism
sounded like a voice crying in the wilderness against the profligacy of
Democratic-Republican hegemony. As democratic reforms advanced in
Dwight's home state, his denunciations became more shrill. At Yale, in his
lectures on theology and on rhetoric, Dwight struggled to construct a
pedagogy that articulated belletristic rhetorical theory to republican discourse, Puritan social order, bourgeois capitalism, and Federalist political
principles. While he was pedagogically successful in his efforts to rearticu-
late hegemonic components in the 1770s, his efforts eventually failed in
the early nineteenth century. In 1819, Puritan Federalists watched in horror as the Democratic-Republican Party won a majority in the Connecticut assembly.

While president of Yale (1794–1817), Dwight delivered weekly lectures
on theology, which harmonized his politics and his religion into a single
hymn to Connecticut's social hierarchy. He also added republican lyrics:
"[P]ublic or common good [. . .] is more valuable and ought to be more

highly regarded, than the good of an individual" (*Theology* 3: 132). He argued that the family is the basic and most important social unit, the place where people develop good habits, where they learn religion, where they practice beneficence, and where they acquire the virtues of self-sacrifice, piety, and deference (*Theology* 3: 142–55). He defined virtue strictly in religious terms: "[C]onformity of the understanding and the heart to every doctrine of the Scriptures" (*Theology* 3: 314). "Disinterested benevolence," the kind learned by meditating on and following God's laws, is "the source of all good" (*Theology* 3: 420), and "[i]f the Benevolence of the Gospel governed men of all classes; this justice would be rendered cheerfully, and universally" (*Theology* 3: 427).

Indeed, for Dwight, proper republican government required obedience at all levels, obedience of children to parents, obedience of subjects to rulers, and obedience of rulers to God: "*The foundation of all government is, undoubtedly, the Will of God* [. . .] As God willed the existence of government for the happiness of mankind" (*Theology* 4: 133–37). This obedience, of course, did not mean elimination of electoral proceedings or democratic trappings. In fact, Dwight told students at Yale that a government of persuasion was preferable to a government of force since the latter could only bring about "the order [. . .] of a church yard; the stillness and quiet of death" (*Theology* 4: 139). Citizens were bound by duty to elect and then obey magistrates who embodied Christian virtues. When these magistrates demanded behavior contradictory to Scripture, citizens were bound by duty to follow the higher law (*Theology* 4: 148–53). Like the Puritans before him, Dwight believed and told his students at Yale that the "Christian Religion [. . .] the rule of all duty, and involving all moral obligation [. . .] is inseparably interwoven with every part of [politics]" (*Theology* 4: 161). The vita activa included a prayerful obedience. In his lectures on theology, he articulated these ideals, the product of a residual cultural and economic formation, to the discourse of republicanism, giving them a renewed life among students at Yale.

In a certain regard, Dwight's curriculum when he was a tutor and when he was president at Yale appealed to the Connecticut bourgeoisie. By offering a belletristic rhetoric and by teaching rhetorical norms of the bourgeois public sphere, Dwight's rhetorical education catered to the cultural interests of the emergent commercial class. He promised them social mobility by offering training in the refined markers of gentility. But in another regard, Dwight's rhetorical pedagogy was distinctly premodern and in direct opposition to the bourgeois culture that one would encounter at Harvard in the same era. While bourgeois Christian rhetoricians like John Quincy Adams located citizen virtue in a privately developed and cultivated Christian conscience, describing the moral, rhetorical agent as a private citizen voicing personal virtue in public circumstances, Dwight located citizen virtue in the rhetor's internalization of authoritarian dogma. The moral rhetorical agent did not enter the public sphere as an autonomous subject driven by a private Christian conscience. S/he was the obedient Protestant saint, voicing acquiescence to an established order founded in divine law. Dwight's rhetorical pedagogy, therefore, did not participate in the bourgeois civil society tradition that Hauser and Habermas recognize among eighteenth-century capitalist subjects. Though he might have offered training in the belletristic rhetorical norms of bourgeois culture, other norms, such as decorum and private conscience, made no appearance in his lectures. His students were therefore learning the norms of a culturally refined, though still decidedly Puritan, public sphere. Of course, Dwight's rhetorical pedagogy enacted this articulation of certain bourgeois rhetorical norms, republican discourse, Puritan theology, and authoritarian government.

Like all republicans before him, Dwight believed that education shapes citizen virtue, providing an essential service. He bragged about the plenitude of New England schoolhouses, all "contributing to the national character" (*Travels* 4: 524). Dwight also believed that development of national taste creates a virtuous citizenry. He said the "effects of Taste on our national character have already been happy and extensive" ("The Friend XI"), and he criticized the corrupt manners taught in Boston academies, saying "this educational system is expressly attempted with a view to superior refinement; but it is not a refinement of taste. It is merely a refinement of the imagination; of an imagination, already soft, and sickly; of a sensibility, already excessive; [. . .] already fastidious" (*Travels* 1: 429). Dwight's notion of taste was decidedly Puritan, recalling the austerity and simplicity that he promoted while working as a tutor at Yale. His was a Puritan gentility, not corrupted like the "soft and sickly" culture taught in commercial centers like Boston. Most importantly, Dwight's notion of taste was rooted in a Calvinist ideology of regeneration and obedience. Dwight, in effect, wove the Scotch philosophy of Hugh Blair and Frances Hutcheson together with the Calvinist theology of Jonathan Edwards to develop a uniquely belletristic rhetorical theory that promoted obedience to the divine order and the newly established federal government (Clark "Oratorical").

Dwight, like Edwards, divided taste into two categories: natural and regenerate. The former is available to all people and allows worldly enjoyment of art, literature, and polite company, while the latter is available only to saved souls, allowing knowledge and the joyous observance of divine beauty. Dwight, again following his grandfather, used the term "relish" to denote regenerate taste, saying that regeneration "merely communicates [. . .] the relish for Spiritual objects" (*Theology* 3: 63). In his definition of spiritual relish, Dwight invoked Edwardsean Calvinism, claiming that regenerate taste allows epistemic access to "the things themselves; as being in themselves delightful to the taste of the mind" (*Theology* 3: 283).

The rhetorical theory that Dwight taught at Yale hinged on his Calvinist-belletrist notion of taste, and it aimed at creating a pious citizenry able to function and promote the millennial republicanism to which Dwight and other Congregationalist ministers were committed. Virtuous rhetorical performance, following the mandates of regenerate taste and embodying properly reserved Puritan gentility, should contribute to a national rhetorical culture of citizen obedience. Rhetoric, the government of persuasion, could bring the divine kingdom to earth. Dwight repeatedly tied good rhetorical performance to his millennialism and to his nationalism. He wrote in his poem *America* (1771), "Eloquence, soft pity shall inspire, / Smooth the rough breast, or let the soul on fire; / Teach guilt to tremble at th' Almighty name, / Unsheath his sword and make his lightnings flame" (11). He told the Yale graduating class of 1796 that properly virtuous citizens should avoid a "florid," "slovenly" rhetorical style and should "*love* and *support* the *institutions of* [their] *country*" (*Sermons* 1: 303).

During Dwight's tenure as president, students at Yale read Blair's *Lectures* and attended sessions in which Dwight commented and expanded on the material. This commentary engaged a consistent effort to connect rhetorical performance to public virtue and to define virtuous citizens as

Table 3.5: Selected topics debated at Yale during Timothy Dwight's tenure as president (Theodore Dwight 7, 26, 67, 73, 83, 111, 135, 199, 259)

Date	Question Debated
November 2, 1813	Ought capital punishment ever to be inflicted?
November 9, 1813	Ought the liberty of the press to be restricted?
November 30, 1813	Ought the Poor to be supported by law?
December 1813	Would an extension of the union be politic?
December 8, 1813	Ought the clergy to be supported by the law?
December 22, 1813	Ought religious tests to be required of civil officers?
January 5, 1814	Is a party spirit beneficial?
March 1814	Which is more conducive to literature, a monarchical or a republican form of government?
March 22, 1814	Ought the judiciary to be independent?

those embodying Puritan gentility. Dwight told the class of 1807, for instance, that "moral objects [. . .] refine the taste." He even tied rhetorical success to Christian piety, saying "Probity and good morals [are] necessary to a high attainment in eloquence." He praised what he called the Attic simplicity of Cicero's oratory, saying that tasteful rhetoric avoids ornamental excesses. Holding Puritan gentility against rhetorical ostentation, Dwight said eloquence should be "artless, simple, and beautiful" (Freimarck 237, 248, 250).[14]

Students also met twice a day to dispute forensically. Debate exercises continued to address politically relevant topics, some of them generally applicable to all the states and many of them peculiar to Connecticut. (See table 3.5.) At the end of each exercise, Dwight offered comments, often resolving the debate by declaring the truth of the matter. In these resolutions, Dwight exerted his own authority over his students' rhetorical agency. Dwight's public sphere allowed open debate only to a certain point. In the final moment, a divine messenger revealed truth, and the participant-citizen had to accede, just as Dwight's students were expected to believe whatever opinion he offered.

Dwight's particular responses to these debates also revealed something interesting about his rhetorical pedagogy. He often offered lessons on pronunciation and style. For instance, he advised one student to pronounce "intrigue" properly, and he told another to include the definite article before words like "community" and "Deity" (Theodore Dwight 45, 8). Most often, however, Dwight simply commented on the issues rather than offering advice about how to argue more effectively. His pronouncements were finalizing, the expectation being that students would take his word as truth, which he said "is the same thing in all cases" (Theodore Dwight 136). In these moments, Dwight touched on themes central to his own millennial republicanism. He complained about party spirit and its divisiveness, typical Federalist kvetching. He told students that resistance to the government was justifiable when "perfectly agreeable to the will of God." He said that a stable republic should not be founded on a social compact but on the "law of God." He said the clergy should be federally funded since they perform a national service by promoting national morality. He even argued that tasteful rhetorical performance was an indication and a promoter of national virtue: "you will find that the periods when the people were purest, were those in which the national taste was best" (Theodore Dwight 135–40, 171, 238, 83–89, 249).

In the rare moments when Dwight actually discussed rhetorical technique, he typically accused students of using fallacious arguments to promote immoral positions. After two students debated the question, "are all mankind descended from one pair," Dwight said that the burden of proof lies with the objector, since it is common knowledge that all people descended from Adam and Eve (Theodore Dwight 117–28). After a debate on the topic, "does the mind always think," Dwight said the appeal to ignorance (because we do not know what the mind does while sleeping, it must not always think) "is no proof" just like the argument that the soul does not exist because we cannot perceive it. He told his student, "This argument is not worth a pinch of snuff" (Theodore Dwight 33). Dwight's comments, even when concentrating on rhetorical form, promoted a political agenda. The debate exercises at Yale, as he administered them, did not create a public space of equal exchange. They created a place where students could judge and alter their opinions against Dwight's model. In this, as in his rhetorical theory and its Calvinist-belletrist notion of taste,

Dwight advocated a brand of federalism in which citizens elect and then obey the divinely inspired representatives of God's order. Dwight told his students that "[u]neducated men can never be desirable citizens in a republic" (Theodore Dwight 16).

When looking at his rhetorical theory and pedagogy, it becomes obvious that Dwight's notion of civic education involved creation of obedient citizen-subjects. Once again, rhetorical pedagogy and theory at Yale changed while continuing to promote the established political agenda. Notably, however, Dwight's rhetorical pedagogy did import belletrism and did happen principally in English, two factors that would have appealed to the emergent Connecticut bourgeoisie. He tried to articulate the emerging economic base to Connecticut's Puritan social hierarchy, to the state's antidemocratic policy, and to the Federalist Party in part by teaching a particularly belletristic rhetorical theory and by having students engage in exercises that taught them the rhetorical norms of bourgeois gentility and of Puritan deference. For a while, at least, these articulations successfully reconstituted the Puritan bourgeois hegemony in Connecticut.

Of course, the politics of republicanism in Yale's curriculum continued after Timothy Dwight's tenure as president, as did the millennial slant in Connecticut's republican vision. Bourgeois gentility became a mainstay in Connecticut's rhetorical culture and in Yale's rhetorical education. And, of course, democratic reforms continued to threaten Connecticut's governing order as elite clergy cried in the wilderness. In 1819, when Connecticut's assembly passed a constitution that no longer allowed public money for a single church, Lyman Beecher predicted the end of the Puritan republican experiment. The decision to end this chapter in 1817, therefore, is a bit arbitrary, but continuing this analysis would belabor an already evident argument: as economic developments changed Connecticut's base, renewed struggles for hegemony were waged in cultural institutions like the rhetoric classroom. Yale's rhetorical curriculum shifted several times throughout the eighteenth century, each time opening opportunities for actors like Dwight to change the nature of political power by inhabiting important sites of hegemonic articulation. The various rhetorical pedagogies discussed in this chapter all made efforts at articulating their inherited and emergent circumstances. In each case, articulatory practice is aimed at and sometimes achieves hegemony. In each case, there is an important and contested site of rhetorical education in the struggle over power in eighteenth- and early nineteenth-century Connecticut. In the long history of one institution, then, one can see various rhetorical pedagogies, each articulating the specific historical circumstances, the cultural institutions, the rhetorical norms, the religious beliefs, and the economic interests of those engaged in the struggle over what the republic would become. The classroom was a principal site in which the early American political struggle over hegemony, a struggle that never ended, was always open for reconstitution.

4

King's College / Columbia and the College of Philadelphia / University of Pennsylvania, 1754–1800

T' inform young *Minds* and mold the ductile Heart
To worthiest Thoughts of GOD and social Deeds.
For *Education* the great Fountain is
From whence Life's Stream, must clear or turbid flow.

. . . .

Ah me! how long!
Shall *Party-Zeal,* and little sneaking *Views,*
of vile *Self-Interest,* our chief Thoughts engross,
And dim our Fires?

—William Smith

In 1794, Timothy Dwight looked at the small New England town of Greenfield Hill, its uniformity of manners, its austerity, its bucolic humility, and its abstemious commerce. This was his vision for a new republic, and it stands in stark contrast to what Jacob Duché witnessed through the panes of his Philadelphia window just twenty years prior: "Whilst I am writing this, three topsail vessels, wafted along by a gentle southern breeze are passing by my window. The voice of industry perpetually resounds along the shore; and every wharf within my view is surrounded by graves of masts, and heaped with commodities of every kind, from almost every quarter of the globe" (*Observations* 3–4).

The difference between Dwight's Greenfield Hill and Duché's Philadelphia is also the difference between Yale and the two colleges discussed in this chapter. The struggle for hegemony in New Haven was largely affected by tension between a residual Puritan social formation and an emerging capitalism and cosmopolitanism. In Philadelphia and New York, capitalism was dominant by the mid-eighteenth century. A thriving cosmopolitan culture had sprouted by the 1750s. Reserved Protestants readily threw off their plain clothes and their simple pleasures. Even once austere Quaker merchants traded their black coats fastened by hooks and eyes for colorfully embroidered waistcoats, lace, and powdered wigs. The desire to imitate British aristocracy led some urban inhabitants to build country houses for weekend excursions. The coach manufacturing industry blossomed in the colonies as estates appeared around Boston, Newport, and Philadelphia. Dancing and the theater, lascivious abominations in most Puritan imaginations, became not only common but also popular. Philadelphia's dancing assembly, the most successful in the colonies, began in 1740 and peaked in 1759. The most flourishing urban institution in the mid-eighteenth century was not the somber church but the promiscuous tavern. When that locale became too popularly attended, coffeehouses accommodated the exclusivity desired by exceptionally distinguished socialites (Bridenbaugh, *Cities in Revolt* 146–65).

Urban capitalists in New York and Philadelphia tended to favor British government because they benefited from its trade laws. These citizens were also typically social climbers. In order to distinguish themselves, they performed (an often clumsy) colonial imitation of British gentility. They also used their wealth and family connections to secure political power and to maintain economic dominance. In Philadelphia, as mentioned in chapter 1, the established commercial class formed the Proprietary Party and remained loyalists as the Revolution drew near. In New York, established genteel capitalists united under governors James Delancey and his son James Delancey Jr. In Philadelphia, other capitalists, those not yet enjoying social or economic security, formed the Anti-Proprietary Party, the chief opposition, under Benjamin Franklin. Likewise in New York, the principal opposition to the Delancey Party in the 1760s were the Sons of Liberty, lesser merchants, craftspeople, and shopkeepers who resented the elite's presence, their dominance in government, and their stranglehold on New York's trade (Tiedemann 32–40).

The tension between these two groups is reflected in various cultural developments. The established bourgeoisie adopted gentility, the culture of European aristocracy, and held the social high ground through the early nineteenth century. Even elected leaders in the early republic sought the veneer of cultural refinement. The first two Federalist administrations kept the center of American government in the gentrified city of Philadelphia. Only the austere Democratic-Republican Thomas Jefferson was willing to move the nation's capital to Washington, D.C., where there were no dancing halls. Yet the new capital was not devoid of aristocratic pretense. The city was designed by Pierre Charles l'Enfant to resemble, in its general layout and wide streets, the baroque courtly city of Versailles; it was built, like Versailles, principally by slave labor. The city's architecture, however, was austere, and the streets were unpaved. The buildings had simple facades, reflecting clean Roman simplicity more than French courtly majesty (Elkins and McKitrick 46–47, 179–82). Early Americans might not have had Europe's ancien regime, but "[t]he spread of gentility reminds us that the *ancien regime* still had a grip on the social imagination of Americans" (Bushman, *Refinement* 408). This sometimes led to comical episodes. For instance, the first House of Representatives engaged in a somewhat absurd debate over whether or not elected officials should be allowed titles or ceremonious address. But early American urban capitalists were not totally enamored of genteel culture. Economic tensions between established and emergent capitalists affected early American cultural inclinations. These tensions and their affiliated cultural differences were often negotiated through the republican topics discussed in chapter 1. Ostensibly guided by fears of corruption, many emergent capitalists like Benjamin Franklin shed gentility's exaggerated artifices while imitating some of its habits and mores. Just as Puritan nationalists in Connecticut defined British culture as corrupt, urban emergent capitalists saw luxuriant putrescence among the very wealthy. This cultural warfare among capitalists was evident even in home architecture. Early nineteenth-century homes often had elaborate parlors but were occupied by families that preferred to spend their time in the less refined and more comfortable kitchen. Eventually, as emergent capitalists gained dominance, the parlor would disappear from American home architecture altogether.[1] Shunning the parlor was one tactical maneuver in a larger fight over cultural hegemony in early republican cities.

Just as a seemingly innocuous development in home architecture can participate in a hegemonic struggle, so also did higher education in both Philadelphia and New York participate in the battles between established and emergent capitalists. Both the College of Philadelphia and King's College were founded in commercial cities whose political leadership before the Revolution was dominated by loyalist Anglican merchants. These same merchants wanted to acquire a genteel burnish, so they established institutions where their sons could learn to be gentlemen. King's College remained elite through the Revolution, but the College of Philadelphia received support from locals like Benjamin Franklin who desired a more practical education to prepare their children for commercial climbing. Both institutions were shaped by competing views of education. Established merchants saw education as a means of demonstrating and reaffirming their status. In their minds, a college should provide cultural polish for already privileged citizens. Emergent capitalists, on the other hand, saw education as a means of acquiring social status. They wanted professional training. And these economically inflected views of education were not the only forces at play. Political allegiances were also key factors. Prior to 1776, at King's and at the College of Philadelphia, rhetorical pedagogies articulated various theories of good oratory to decidedly loyalist politics. Thereafter, these same rhetorical theories were articulated to a genteel republicanism. The established bourgeoisie, though never without contest, managed to maintain its hegemonic control over higher education by articulating its view of education's purpose to the political interests of both pre- and post-revolutionary America. It did this largely through instruction in rhetoric.

Though the preceding discussion and the following analysis will focus on how this tension between two economic classes played out in conflicting *paideiai,* I do not mean to imply that economic factors determined the curricular struggles in New York or in Philadelphia. In fact, though economic factors were central to the formation of and the contest over rhetorical education at both Columbia and the University of Pennsylvania, these interests were connected to religious traditions, methods of philosophical and scientific inquiry, local political affiliations, and of course republican political discourse. These various economic, political, cultural, and social threads were woven together in the practice of rhetorical education.

At King's College before the Revolution, Samuel Johnson constructed a curriculum suited for the Anglican commercial elite in New York. Principally, rhetorical education at King's provided the student an elegant sheen and a lesson in obedience to the crown and scepter. Johnson's rhetorical pedagogy, however, depended on more than an effort to accommodate the cultural predilections of an established economic class. In Johnson's rhetorical instruction, an economic interest was articulated to British Anglicanism, to the local loyalist party, to an idealist epistemology, and to a set of inherited cultural markers. At the College of Philadelphia, in a political environment where emergent capitalists were more influential, William Smith constructed a curriculum that would appeal, at least initially, to both the emergent and the established bourgeoisie. Like Franklin, he advocated vernacular education with a pragmatic tilt, but he also taught a belletristic rhetoric, thereby appealing to established merchants who desired the kind of instruction offered by Samuel Johnson. Woven into Smith's rhetorical pedagogy was an allegiance to British imperialism and an appreciation for belletrism, but Smith managed this quite differently from Johnson. Also like Johnson, Smith constructed a program of rhetorical education that articulated economic interests to a religious tradition (Anglicanism), a method of scientific inquiry (natural science), an epistemology (common-sense realism), and a local partisan affiliation (the Proprietary Party). After the Revolution, both colleges were overhauled, but a central element remained in their curricula. At both Columbia and the University of Pennsylvania from 1780–1800, instruction in rhetoric was principally belletristic, though no longer loyalist. Instead, rhetorical pedagogies articulated belletrism to republicanism and to the Federalist Party. The articulations to Anglicanism, to idealism, to common-sense realism, and to natural science all fell away, while the affinity for polite letters persisted.

Belletrism's continuity demonstrates the dominant and persistent commercial interest in both cities—established merchants continued to hold the field, though they were continually challenged by pragmatic upstarts like Benjamin Franklin and Samuel Adams. And, of course, the hegemony of bourgeois culture would not remain without its (re)articulation to various cultural and social developments throughout the eighteenth century. Nevertheless, despite the shifting constellation of cultural appreciations, religious beliefs, and philosophical concerns, pre-revolutionary loyalists and post-revolutionary republicans in New York and Philadelphia shared an economic interest: they were all and always members of the established bourgeoisie. Though the articulations to religious traditions, to philosophical traditions, and to local parties might change, rhetorical education at both colleges was continually tied to the interests of wealthy capitalists.

King's College, 1754–77

Divisions between the conservative established bourgeoisie and the revolutionary emergent bourgeoisie can be seen in local government. In New York, the assembly was dominated by emergent capitalists, while the governor represented the established bourgeoisie. This opposition between governmental branches resulted in an extended struggle over the governor's salary, which the assembly controlled and often refused to pay. In both Philadelphia and New York, emergent capitalists, interested in widening commercial access and supported by proletarian radicals, spearheaded the revolutionary effort. They met resistance against a deteriorating wall of Anglican merchants loyal to the church, the crown, and the mercantile order. As the revolutionary engine gained steam, those fighting wealthy loyalists coupled their efforts to republican discourse. Just as Benjamin Franklin couched the economic interests of Philadelphia's craftspeople, shopkeepers, and small traders in a republican argument about liberty, so the Sons of Liberty and the Livingstonites articulated their concerns about loss of trade and fear of taxes to a republican fear of tyranny (Tiedemann 65).

Given New York's political strife, it should come as no surprise that the city's first college was founded in a hail of controversy over whose interests the curriculum would serve. The King's College controversy in the early 1750s featured Livingstonite republicans arguing for a curriculum that would benefit social climbers and William Smith representing the established bourgeois Anglican loyalists who wanted a patrician luster. Controversy also erupted over the college's religious affiliation. Though the board of governors was comprised principally of laymen, over half of whom were not Anglican, the college charter was drafted by Anglican trustees who inserted two very controversial clauses: (1) the president always had to be Anglican, and (2) the daily liturgy must be Anglican in nature. This raised such consternation that the charter was not ratified immediately and was never ratified by the assembly. Also the college was denied money raised in a public lottery. (This money was eventually split between the college and the city.) Two other groups, the Livingstonites and the Dutch Reformed Church, tried to found their own colleges, a free school, and an academy to train Dutch Reformed ministers. (The latter were eventually successful, establishing Queens College [Rutgers] in 1766.)

Though the Anglican Church never had a great deal of direct influence over the college or its curriculum, the first president, Samuel Johnson, was an Anglican minister. (Johnson converted shortly after leaving his post as tutor at Yale.) The controversy, the college's acceptance of a land grant from the local Anglican Church, and the provisions inserted into the charter led many city inhabitants to distrust their college for the next twenty-five years. Curiously enough, the curriculum did more to serve the bourgeois gentry than it did the Church of England. While only twenty pre-1776 King's graduates became Anglican ministers, more than half of its students during the first six years were the sons of governors. The college also cost 50 percent more than its nearest rival, Princeton, and more than half the students left before the end of the second year (Humphrey 73, 91–95). Most students, including Alexander Hamilton, never completed their degrees, showing a typically patrician disregard for certification. Unlike the emergent bourgeoisie, these young men, born into wealthy capitalist families, did not need education to acquire social or economic status. William Smith, writing in the midst of the controversy, outlined the college's genteel mission: "unifying the Gentleman and the Scholar, or ever arriving at Politeness which is the Bond of Social Life—the Ornament of human Nature" (*Some Thoughts* 14). King's College before the Revolution remained a small, expensive institution principally training the New York bourgeois elite for their participation in genteel society. It stands to reason that the rhetorical education offered there would involve a heavy dose of belletrism. This was certainly the case. However, Samuel Johnson's political inclinations led him to articulate belletristic rhetorical theory to a loyalist, antidemocratic politics that would support the Anglican commercial leadership in New York. In William Smith's terms, the college should carry "Empire and Liberty" across the continent in the liberal arts carriage (*Some Thoughts* 23–24).

Johnson was influenced by the famous British philosopher George Berkeley, with whom he maintained an active correspondence while drafting his own philosophical text, the *Elementa Philosophica* (1752). Berkeley was a political conservative in England and a staunch supporter of (bishop in) the Anglican Church. He argued that there is no material world, only souls receiving and transmitting ideas. His classic formulation of this epistemology is "*esse* is *percipi*" (54). Instead of a material world, Berkeley claimed, there is only a divine mind communicating ideas to other spirits who can transmit copies of these ideas among themselves. In his *Three Dialogues Between Hylas and Philonous* (1713), an effort to clarify the arguments originally sketched in the *Principles of Human Knowledge* (1710), Berkeley used the vocabulary of archetype and ectype, common to the British Ramists and to John Locke, positioning archetypal knowledge in the divine intellect and ectypal knowledge in the human copy of divine ideas (200). Berkeley worried that language distorts thought by encouraging people to treat words as things.

Berkeley, like Locke, was skeptical of language, and he tried to proceed without its pernicious distortions (Walmsley 10; Ulman 52, 55). In the introduction to his *Principles of Human Knowledge,* he vowed to avoid all rhetorical affectation so that he could "take [ideas . . .] bare and naked into [. . .] view" (49). Berkeley also articulated his philosophy to British imperialism and Anglican authority. If all knowledge derives from the divine mind, then people must endeavor to learn and obey higher moral mandates. He said at the end of his *Principles* that his philosophical system should "fill our hearts with an awful circumspection and holy fear, which is the strongest incentive to virtue." Berkeley's principal concern was "the consideration of God, and our *duty,*" leading people away from vain, secular philosophy and toward "the salutary truths of the Gospel, which to know and to practice is the highest perfection of human nature" (112–13). Johnson, also a political conservative, found a great deal of value in Berkeley's idealist epistemology and especially in its articulation to British mercantilism and to Anglican authority.

Like most presidents at early American colleges, Johnson taught senior courses in both rhetoric and moral philosophy. Students in these classes read the *Elementa Philosophica* from which they learned a basic curricular framework, representing, according to Johnson, an integrated order of knowledge while also offering insights into the various disciplines, particularly logic and moral philosophy. Influenced by the Ramistic curriculum that he learned at Yale, Johnson created his own disciplinary structure, one that presumptively enabled the learner to access divine knowledge. However, this was not a simple repetition of the Puritan technologia. Johnson completely rethought the hierarchy of knowledge, and he articulated his overall curriculum not to the semifeudalistic social formation of rural Connecticut but rather to the mercantile social formation of Anglican New York. Johnson divided all knowledge and the King's curriculum into philology and philosophy. The latter treats what people know absolutely, including logic and moral and natural philosophy. The former treats how people transmit knowledge, including grammar and rhetoric. Like Berkeley, Johnson believed in a knowable divine truth, and he wanted to instruct students in both the order of things and the task of learning this order without distortion. Through moral philosophy and logic, he taught moral and ethical verities. Through rhetoric and grammar, he taught the path thereto.

The second part of Johnson's *Elementa Philosophica* is a system of morals built upon his metaphysics. Johnson's conclusions echo Berkeley's: all human endeavor aims toward happiness, a condition realized when one fully understands and obeys God's will, which can be perceived through critical and rhetorical acumen as learned in philological study. Norman Fiering noticed that in his later work Samuel Johnson placed moral philosophy at the center of his encyclopedia. For Fiering, the overall concern with human happiness and the subordination of logic to the achievement of said happiness make Johnson more of a moralist than a metaphysician (232). By theorizing and then teaching this system, Johnson encouraged colonials generally and King's College students particularly to obey the Anglican scepter and the British crown.

The first part of the *Elementa Philosophica* opens with a declared allegiance to a Berkeleyan idealist epistemology, claiming that there is no substance outside the mind, nothing beyond perception, that all human ideas are ectypes of celestial archetypes, and that by way of a divinely awarded intellectual light, people have the capacity to see universal principles (archetypes) in many particular ideas (ectypes) (*SJCW* 2: 372–80). Johnson professed a representational notion of truth, which he located in sensation of God's ideas, but he veered sharply from Berkeley's skepticism about rhetoric. In fact, Johnson defended the rhetorical capacity, the necessity of certain rhetorical functions, in the search for and transmission of knowledge. The effort to achieve happiness requires both philology and philosophy. Students reading Johnson's work learned that language could help one to perceive and demonstrate truth. They learned the epistemic and moral value of rhetoric. Like other philological studies—history, poetry, and oratory—rhetoric and grammar became paths to moral philosophy, manners of knowing and doing the good. Fiering has called them all "propadeutic studies" (227).

While Johnson clung to the Berkeleyan notion of divine archetypes and also maintained that language should strive to accurately represent these archetypes, he did not hold so strictly to representationalism. He admitted that some things were known not by direct witnessing (not by induction of any stripe) but through rational demonstration or by following a preponderance of convincing evidence. Judgment and reasoning lay in logic's province and philosophy's kingdom. Students recited William Duncan's *Elements of Logick* (1748), a primer that mixes Lockean empiricism and Cartesian rationalism by discussing both the accurate representation of empirical phenomena in language and the proper construction of propositions and syllogisms. Duncan's text even reinforced Johnson's faith in language's ability to represent truth, saying that God gave people language so they could communicate what they learned of His majesty in nature (88–94).

Johnson's curricular focus on logic was important because it revealed his belief that divine knowledge could be acquired both through observation and through discursive demonstration. By accepting that people could not perfectly know some propositions' certainty and must string probable propositions together into coherent, however contestable, arguments, Johnson allowed rational mapping of divine moral archetypes without the possibility of ever reaching complete cartographic accuracy. Moral conclusions rely on contingent propositions and are therefore closer to rhetorical than to empirical certainty. Johnson taught that science is the province of things known absolutely. Though he never used the term *rheto-ric* to describe the contingent realm, he certainly imagined the non-scientific landscape as a rhetorical topography:

> And when any proposition is supported with all the reasons it is, in the nature of it, capable of, and there remains no sufficient reason to doubt of the truth of it, we are then said to have a moral certainty, and our assent to it is called persuasion, which implies a settled ac-quiescence of the mind in the truth of it [. . .] If the reasons for the probability or moral certainty of any proposition are taken for the nature of the things considered in themselves, our assent to it is called opinion (*SJCW* 2: 409–10).

Johnson allotted to discourse a distinctly epistemic function and permit-ted the use of argument to establish understanding of the world so that people could manage moral issues. He claimed a space for discursive ar-rival at moral certainty to construct real political institutions. If these moral arguments can be trusted as representations of archetypes, then they can form the basis for an authoritarian politics. By defending a ra-tionalist notion of truth, Johnson also defended the exclusive claim that Anglican ministers made about epistemic access—only those properly trained in argumentation could cut a path to divine wisdom. The congre-gation (and the colonists), lacking philological acumen, should passively listen.

The epistemology and rhetorical theory that students learned from Johnson's *Elementa Philosophica* reasserted a faith in moral certainty and a hope for language's ability to represent divine moral archetypes. This hope infected the rest of Johnson's rhetorical pedagogy. Even debate exercises were cast as efforts to discursively arrive at archetypal knowledge. John-son hoped disputation would help King's College students to arrive at divine certainty through dialectic. Though he disparaged syllogistic and celebrated forensic debate, he did not articulate the latter to a tolerant public sphere. Rather than encouraging widespread democratic participa-tion by teaching forensic disputation, Johnson hoped to get his students closer to divine archetypes by having them argue on various topics. He adulated Plato's dialogues, which he imagined as efforts to arrive dialec-tically at an ideal truth (*SJWC* 2: 242–43). As a result of Johnson's authoritarian political moorings, his speaking exercises embodied a ponderous formality (Roach 15). In the end, debates did not teach students the rhetorical norms of the bourgeois public sphere. Toleration and individual liberty were not permitted in Johnson's ideal public discourse. Rather, students learned to be publicly and rhetorically obedient.

Exercises performed at commencement reveal that Johnson's students did discuss several politically relevant topics, though they did so by tending to general propositions, not specific issues. In 1763, for instance, a student gave a Latin oration on Thomas Hobbes titled "*Utrum status naturae sit status belli*" (is the state of nature a state of war). In 1764 two students, Jay and Harison, debated in English "on the subject of national Poverty, opposed to that of national riches." In 1767, at the end of the Stamp Act crisis, Jay and Harison debated this question: "Whether a Man ought to engage in War without being persuaded of the Justness of the Cause." There were also at least three moments when students discoursed on republican topics (liberty [1765], luxury [1770], and virtue [1771]). However, most often, the forensic and syllogistic disputation topics at King's College commencements reflected two preoccupations, neither of them overtly articulated to the Whiggish republicanism in circulation among New York's Livingstonites: a belief that divine truth could be apprehended and a belletristic pursuit of beauty in language.[2] (See table 4.1.) These two topical threads running through the commencement exercises suited Johnson's political exegesis. The belief in discursive apprehension of truth suited British imperialism, and the belletristic preoccupation suited the cultural pretenses of the established bourgeoisie who were themselves largely loyal to the crown. Johnson wedded an authoritative understanding of language and truth to a belletristic concern for discursive beauty and sublimity. In fact, Johnson taught that rhetorical allure reflected divine resplendence.

Though Johnson appealed to the colonial bourgeoisie by teaching the rhetorical norms of bourgeois gentility, he articulated this belletrism not to a public sphere of decorum and open interaction among equals but rather to the public practice of locating and following veracity in discursive flourish. Twice in the *Elementa Philosophica,* Johnson described stylistic form as indication of divine knowledge. He discussed beauty and harmony in all of nature as the marks of divine influence. Harmony, an assemblage

Table 4.1: Selected debate and oration topics from King's College commencements, 1762-73 ("King's College Commencement")

Date	Latin (if applicable)	English
1762	An datur vacuum in Natura? Et an sine libero Arbitrio possint esse virtus et vitium?	Can a vacuum exist in nature? And without free witness, can virtue and vice exist?
1765	Vestigia atque sapientia dei ex shedio physicarum evidentissime patent?	Does physical reality most clearly reveal the mark and wisdom of God?
1766	An sensibus fidendum sit?	Why is there confidence in sense perception?
1766		On the propriety and elegance of language.
1770	An omnes ideae oriantur a sensibus?	Do all ideas come from the senses?
1771		Whether a lively imagination is conducive to happiness?
1771		On delicacy.
1772		On the beauties of poetry.
1773		On the pleasure of refined conversation.

of language to please the ear, appears in artistic expression and is most appreciated by those with proper critical training, a philological art (*SJWC* 2: 392–93). Criticism, far from being a handmaiden to philosophical truth, became a divining rod capable of pointing to celestial fountains. Johnson also described two stylistic figures, metaphor and analogy, as necessary epistemic devices for understanding spirits. Since spirits are not ideas, they cannot be apprehended through sense perception, but Johnson held, like Berkeley, that people have experience of spirits nonetheless. (Without this experience, one would have no apprehension of God or other people.) In order to communicate this experience, said Johnson, people must resort to the language of ideas, talking of spirits as if they

were ideas, putting "spiritual things" into "material terms" (*SJWC* 2: 403).
Like the art of criticism, the study of rhetorical figures, a philological pursuit, became necessary to apprehend truth. The rhetorician found the
deity in the stylistic details.

Johnson taught rhetoric by having students recite from two books, John
Sterling's *System of Rhetoric* (1733) and Anthony Blackwell's *The Sacred
Classics Defended and Illustrated* (1727) (Humphrey 166). Sterling's book,
quite popular in Great Britain and the colonies, was little more than a list
of ninety-four tropes and figures presented in abstract description and
example. Blackwell's book was a study of stylistic figuration in Scripture.
The presence of these textbooks demonstrates that Johnson clearly sub-
ordinated rhetoric to philosophy by positioning the former as a study
of stylistic presentation. Blackwell's book, however, also reinforced the
epistemic value that Johnson afforded to beautiful language. Blackwell argued that the Old Testament's apt and often sublime rhetorical figures
indicate the presence of divine wisdom and help people to appreciate
Scripture. Blackwell said at one point, "[A] good opinion of the [Bible's]
style would bring [. . . readers] to consider the soundness of the moral,
and the majesty and purity of the mysteries of the Gospel" (197). Johnson's
use of Blackwell's text, when set in the context of his comments about
discursive beauty, clearly points to a rhetorical curriculum that offered
more than a sugarcoating of truth. Rhetoric, in this pedagogy, was the path
to scriptural certainty. Public rhetorical performance was an effort to embody authoritative knowledge and moral directives apprehended in philosophical endeavor.

Johnson was president and professor of rhetoric and moral philosophy
from the college's beginning in 1754 till 1763. Between his retirement and
his death (1772), he watched with horror as colonial ties to Great Britain
strained and began to snap. He argued for extension of royal power to
actuate religious control. He read political events as a reflection of a cos-
mic disorder (Ellis, *New England Mind* 249–64). The unpublished Raphael
dialogue is his last completed manuscript. In it, Johnson offered an extended argument for the necessity of public subordination to religious
(Anglican) order. The dialogue ends with a plea for British Empire and the
extension of Anglican Christianity further west to benefit all people. Most
interesting is the importance Johnson afforded education in this imperial-

Anglican effort. He wrote that education was the most important business available to legislators, for proper education created good citizens of the commonwealth, obedient people willing to put the good of the whole before their own self-interest. In this document, Johnson articulated his authoritarian, Anglican-imperialist political allegiances to a republican rhetoric of citizen sacrifice and to a rhetorical pedagogy similar to what he offered at King's College.

In his last days, Johnson believed that commercialized self-interest would rend the British Empire by putting aside a greater religious mission in favor of individual wealth accumulation. In effect, he feared that capitalism would stall the Anglican Church's imperial-mercantile engine. Ironically, after the Seven Years' War, the capitalist class that Johnson had empowered by teaching British genteel culture now threatened the imperial commonwealth that they had once supported. In New York, economic depression after 1763 led to an alliance between equally affected established merchants and emergent shopkeepers, craftspeople, merchants, and professionals. All colonial capitalists united to fight British mercantilist policies. Johnson's solution to this dilemma was largely pedagogical. He hoped that civic education would create good citizens of the British Empire, loyal to the scepter and the crown. He even saw rhetorical education as a vital component in this imperial *paideia* (*SJWC* 2: 564–65, 571–72, 568).

Johnson was replaced by Myles Cooper (1763), an English-born Anglican educated at Queen's College, Oxford. Cooper changed some of the curriculum. Principally, he stopped teaching John Locke and focused exclusively on pre-Enlightenment scholasticism. Under Cooper, students recited Robert Sanderson's *Logicae Artis Compendium* (1618), an extensive Aristotelian primer covering the square of opposition, the syllogism, the logical topics, and the fallacies. Also, Cooper did away with any pretension to teach rhetoric as a manner of attaining divine truth. Nevertheless, he continued to offer instruction in genteel belletrism. Johnson was a pious, Cooper a cosmopolitan, Anglican, a difference reflected in their curricula. Cooper pushed classical texts less than Johnson, and he increased students' exposure to English literature, introducing modern poetry and history to the curriculum and awarding copies of Milton's *Paradise Lost* for excellence in these pursuits. He also encouraged students to write verses along with their declamations. In one historian's words, "the education of a Christian gentleman under Cooper was less a matter of piety and more a matter of refinement" (Humphrey 180–83). Debate topics under Cooper also reflected an increased concern with rhetorical style and with typical belletristic issues such as taste. (See table 4.1.) Of course, this increased gentrification of an already belletristic curriculum suited the interests of the established New York bourgeoisie. But Cooper would eventually lose his post at the university, not because of the belletrism that he taught but because of the imperial politics that he openly espoused in public documents.

As the Revolution approached, Cooper spread a great deal of loyalist vitriol and thereby attracted copious animosity. His biographer says that, by 1775, "he was probably the most hated loyalist in all of New York." Cooper was among the initial recipients of the "Three Millions" letter, which recommended that he save his life by fleeing the colonies on the British warship *Kingfisher.* On the evening of May 10, 1775, a mob persuaded him to follow the letter's good counsel (Vance 278–79). The college remained open till 1777 under Rev. Benjamin Moore's direction, but waning matriculation finally closed the doors. The college reopened in 1787 as Columbia University, no longer an Anglican nor an imperial institution, now led by William Samuel Johnson, the former president's son.

The College of Philadelphia, 1755–79

William Smith emigrated from Scotland and was working in New York as a private tutor during the King's College controversy. An Anglican educator himself, Smith tried to gain a position at the new college by publishing his thoughts on civic, particularly rhetorical, education. These writings did not win him sufficient favor among King's trustees, but they did interest Benjamin Franklin, who invited Smith to visit the newly founded Philadelphia Academy. Smith found that he and the academy trustees had a great deal in common. Among other things, he was an Anglican and a supporter of the Proprietary Party. In 1754, the trustees hired Smith to teach logic, rhetoric, ethics, and natural philosophy. In 1755, he helped to write a new charter that included provisions for a college. When the charter was granted, he was named provost of the newly founded College of Philadelphia (Gegenheimer 1–43). Smith discovered that he was nurturing a college among social tensions very similar to those in New York. Though austere Quakers dominated early eighteenth-century Philadelphia, by midcentury, commerce had brought gentility and a bourgeois elite to its harbor.[3] Wealthy Anglicans and a group of emergent capitalists struggled over control of the city. The College of Philadelphia garnered support from both groups by offering a curriculum that featured both professional training and cultural refinement. This happy alliance did not last, however. The Anglican Proprietary influence not only encouraged Franklin to distance himself from the college, but it also garnered a great deal of public distrust.[4] The College of Philadelphia was not always popular among Philadelphia's social climbers. Their discontent aired in 1758 when the *Journal,* an opposition newspaper, published a series of articles signed "Pennsylvanius" arguing that the college was an instrument of Proprietary tyranny (Cheyney 110–11). In 1756, popular sentiment against the college, particularly Smith, raged so feverishly that the trustees conducted a public investigation to determine whether or not Smith was promoting his own politics in the classroom (Montgomery 270–73).

Given the similarities between Philadelphia and New York and the remarkably similar allegiances at King's and the College of Philadelphia, it should come as little surprise that Smith's rhetorical pedagogy also featured belletrism to serve the mercantile elite and the British effort at empire. But there are also notable differences between Smith's and Johnson's curricula. Smith, for instance, pushed rhetorical instruction in the vernacular much more than Johnson, arguing that education largely serves to prepare students for their lives as functional professionals. Doubtless, Johnson himself made similar overtures, but they were muted and halfheartedly pursued in the King's curriculum. Smith, on the other hand, appealed to emergent capitalists like Franklin by verbalizing these principles and by putting them into practice. His curriculum included subjects like government, trade and commerce, optics, astronomy, chemistry, fossils, and agriculture. In addition, Smith promised to remove any overt religious references from the college's curriculum. The College of Philadelphia was a theologically diverse institution, including Presbyterians, Baptists, Deists, and Anglicans among its faculty and its board of trustees.

It could not afford to lay bare its religious affiliations. The solution—Franklin's solution—was to keep religion out of the curriculum. In the classroom Smith could safely appear an imperialist but not an Anglican.

Smith was influenced by the Scottish common-sense school of philosophy, an intellectual camp that opposed Berkeley's idealist epistemology (Diamond). Rather than imagining human knowledge as a reflection of divine archetypes that exist only in the mind of God and are transmitted as ectypes to human intellects, Smith taught that people apprehend nature empirically and notice, through a common sense, the divine order. While Johnson was busy hanging his curriculum on strictly theological preoccupations, Smith hung his on natural philosophy. While Johnson's students read the book of Scripture to find God's order, Smith's read the book of nature to find the same. In fact, in a letter to Richard Peters (10 Aug. 1754), a local minister and founder of the college, Smith remarked that Johnson's students did not learn enough about natural philosophy (Wemyss Smith 1: 49–50). Throughout his time as provost, Smith supported the study of natural philosophy, which he tied to religion and rhetoric, and which he emphasized above all else.[5] Though Smith and Johnson developed rhetorical pedagogies that articulated a common belletrism to differing philosophical presuppositions, they did not differ in their political allegiances. In the end, Smith's instruction in common-sense realism and natural philosophy was just as authoritarian, just as antidemocratic, as Johnson's instruction in Berkeleyan idealism. Also, both Smith and Johnson articulated their rhetorical-philosophical systems to British mercantilism and to Anglican political dominance.

Students under Smith's care learned moral and natural philosophy before anything else, especially before rhetoric, which Smith depicted as a vehicle to express knowledge acquired elsewhere. He insisted that students first become "philosophers" and that they attain "a taste for polite letters [. . . and] moral virtues" before conveying anything through language (WWS 1.2: 203).[6] As Smith said in a 1761 graduation sermon, rhetoric teaches students "how to cloath our wisdom in the most amiable and inviting garb; how to give life and spirit to our ideas; and to make our knowledge of the greatest benefit to ourselves and others." He placed language in service of natural philosophy, describing rhetoric as "an Instrument [. . .] of Science" (WWS 1.2: 344).

Smith advocated a common-sense realism with roots in the Aberdeen school, particularly the works of Francis Hutcheson, Alexander Gerard, David Fordyce, and George Turnbull. He "assumed the existence of a rational moral sense, justified by God's providential ordering of man and nature" (Diamond 124). He pointed his students to the natural world, where they could holistically perceive divine order. He said that people should not "bewilder" themselves "in the search of truth, in the vast tomes of ancient schoolmen; nor in the more refined speculations of modern metaphysicians, nor yet in the polemical writings of subtle casuists." Instead, he appealed to the "senses in the constitution of our nature, and the constitution and harmony of the material universe, to see God's 'revealed will' to guide the college" (*WWS* 1.2: 176–77). Smith taught his students that in earthly manifestations they could find indications of a benevolent, beautiful, and magisterial God. In his lectures on natural philosophy, he said, "This Earth rolls round with various seasons of the year, that, in all her changes and appearances, she may speak Thee [God] the original of all beauty" (*WWS* 1.2: 160).[7]

Not only did the book of nature reveal God's kingdom, but its proper study also spread this kingdom throughout people's contingent and fallen worlds. Smith saw science education as a missionary effort. In a sermon preached before the Anglican clergy of Pennsylvania in 1760, he proclaimed science the best instrument for "spreading the rays of heavenly knowledge far over this untutored continent" (*WWS* 2: 328). Smith's science education pointed his students toward appreciation of the whole, love of God, and awe of the ever-growing empire. One student's compendium of metaphysics, compiled during the summer of 1759, includes the following statement about God's majesty as revealed in the book of nature: "He, I say, that views the wide extended Heavens, and considers the immense magnitude, the certain Revolutions, the order, beauty, and usefulness of the sun, moon, and stars must proclaim the wisdom and power of the creator to the ends of the earth" (Yeates, "Brief Compen." 65).

The differences between Johnson's epistemological idealism and Smith's common-sense realism are remarkable, and they deserve notice. But the politics of each, as articulated in the two curricula, are far more similar than this comparative exercise indicates. Surely, Smith took his students down a different path than did Johnson, and surely students at the College of Philadelphia learned more of natural science than did Johnson's (though students at King's College got a substantial dose as well). But in the end, students at both institutions were taught to seek out and obey a higher authority learned through some epistemological exercise conducted prior to any rhetorical effort. Through logic and Scripture, Johnson's students learned to respect and obey the British crown because they saw that imperialism and mercantilism followed the divine plan to spread Christianity westward. Through natural philosophy, Smith's students learned the same. Though unable to mention the church explicitly, Smith obviously thought that his pedagogy would advance Anglican interests. In two companion sermons, one preached before the Anglican congregation in Philadelphia and another preached before the college at its 1761 commencement, Smith declared his mission to spread "science" westward so that this wave of knowledge could carry the Anglican faith and the British culture along its crest (*WWS* 2: 308–50). Smith told graduates of the college that British, Anglican knowledge would tell people "what we are, and whither destined; what our constitution and connexions; and what our duties in consequence thereof" (*WWS* 2: 326). Though Smith was no epistemological idealist, in the end, his common-sense realism pointed to the same political and economic interests articulated to Johnson's idealism. Both men also folded their differing belletristic rhetorical theories into Great Britain's imperial efforts. Both taught their students genteel culture through belletristic rhetoric, and both taught their students to find in beautiful language the majesty of a divinely ordained empire.

In *The General Idea of the College of Miriana,* a text that he wrote to impress the King's College trustees, Smith advocated a belletristic rhetorical pedagogy where students would learn oratory largely through the aesthetic analysis of great speeches. While natural philosophy would teach students to witness God's majesty and empire in the natural world, rhetoric would reveal the same in language. Students would read Cicero and Demosthenes to analyze and appreciate their "conformity to the laws of rhetoric" (*WWS* 1.2: 186). Smith imagined that students would write and deliver compositions, which a tutor could hold to the standards of great oratory, correcting them and helping students to learn rhetoric's rules. This curriculum centered on the rules of beautiful writing and on cultivating students' taste and understanding. Smith even said that cultivation of taste, the ability to see the sublime beauty of the divine whole in language, was a primary goal of education in rhetoric: "[W]e have reason to think a few months properly spent in forming this taste a very essential part of education [. . . T]his taste for polite letters, not only teaches us to write well, and renders life comfortable to ourselves, but also contributes highly to the cement of society, and the tranquility of the state" (*WWS* 1.2: 192).

Smith's rhetorical pedagogy hinged on the common-sense notion of taste, a divinely granted faculty tied to British aristocratic culture and imparted through instruction in rhetoric. To improve their taste, students rigorously dissected great orations. In 1754, Smith described these analytic exercises, which he took to be the "true way of Learning Rhetoric": "From October till February or March we shall be employ'd in reading some ancient Compositions critically, in applying the rules of Rhetoric and in attempting some Imitations of those most finished Models in our own Language" (Wemyss Smith 1: 49–50). Smith's belletristic pedagogy appealed to the cultural pretenses among Philadelphia's established bourgeoisie. This pedagogy articulated these cultural factors to Smith's beliefs about natural philosophy, his support of the divine British imperial mission, and his declared effort to create the order of an obedient commonwealth. Smith opened his lectures on rhetoric by reflecting on the importance of empirical, scientific knowledge to be gotten through moral and natural philosophy:

> Those Sciences, therefore, which inquire first, into the Nature of our Constitution and how to conduct our intellectual Powers best in searching after Truth; and secondly point out to us the Duties incumbent on Creatures as constituted, must be the Supreme Wisdom, the Philosophia Prima, or that grand System of Knowledge which can only lead a rational Being to its supreme Felicity, and the highest Improvement of its Nature (Yeates, "The Substance" 5).

After explaining the importance of science and its ability to reveal divine laws, Smith contended that language holds society together, allowing for communication of just sentiments and observations about God's kingdom. Beautiful language leads to recognition of and obedience to God's order. Without rhetoric, "[m]an would be but an unsociable Creature, ignorant, savage, solitary and wretched" (Yeates, "The Substance" 8–9). Rhetoric not only maintains civic converse, it also expresses divine wisdom by transforming beautiful ideas about God's creation into beautiful words about His kingdom. Like Johnson, Smith taught certain genteel rhetorical norms without encouraging a public sphere of freely debating citizens. Like Johnson, Smith encouraged rhetorical obedience and public recognition of imperial authority in beautiful rhetorical performances that reflect the empire's splendor.

Though this belletristic rhetorical pedagogy is interesting and certainly parallels Johnson's curriculum, Smith also had to accommodate the emergent Philadelphian capitalists, a task he accomplished by incorporating pragmatic instruction in professionally useful vernacular rhetorical performance. He lectured in English and promoted practice in the mother tongue. Smith also incorporated classical rhetorical theory to teach students the tools of persuasive performance in promiscuous assemblies. While Johnson's belletristic rhetorical pedagogy largely trained students to display and to appreciate genteel rhetorical norms, Smith's appropriation of classical rhetoric taught students to be persuasive, to invent arguments, to accommodate their audiences, and to recognize and appropriately respond to different rhetorical situations.

He repeated four of the ancient canons of rhetoric: invention, disposition, elocution, and pronunciation. He told his students about the topics of argumentation, though Smith's topics were hardly classical categories (deliberative, juridical, conjectural). He likewise discussed the kinds of argument (finitive, quantitative, and qualitative), and he informed students that good arguments come from good observations and good moral sentiments. In his lectures on disposition, Smith laid out a five-part, Ciceronian arrangement and explained how the poetic oration must differ from the prosaic. He defined elocution as the "proper, graceful and beautiful Manner of cloathing and adorning our Thoughts" and pronunciation as proper adornment with "Emphasis, Feeling, and Action" (Yeates, "The Substance" 24–25). He subdivided elocution into composition, elegance, and dignity. Composition insures the clarity of one's writing, while elegance and dignity add color. Dignity is paramount, for it adds sublimity. It is "the Heart and Passion for its Object" (Yeates "The Substance" 26). Like the classical sources on which he drew, Smith's lectures had a practical face, offering sound advice for inventing, arranging, and polishing arguments. To suit emergent bourgeois pragmatism and established bourgeois cultural elitism, Smith taught rhetoric as a productive and as an interpretive art.

So far, this review has considered only one-third of Smith's lectures on rhetoric. The remaining two-thirds summarized Longinus's treatise *On the Sublime*. In these lectures, Smith's interpretive belletrism trumped his pragmatic emphasis on classical rhetoric and vernacular performance. Smith's focus on the rhetorical sublime demonstrates that his allegiances lay with the established Philadelphian bourgeoisie and their desire for instruction in cultural refinement. His lectures on the sublime strictly offered a vocabulary for critical analysis, stressing the importance of taste. He listed sublimity's primary components ("Boldness of thought," "vehement and fine Pathos," "proper Use of Figures," "graceful Manner of Expression," and "Dignity and Grandeur in the Structure of the Periods"). He also provided many examples from English poets, particularly Thomson, Milton, and Shakespeare (Yeates, "The Substance" 46–48). Smith notably excluded what is perhaps the most practical section of Longinus's treatise: the detailed categorization, description, and instruction for arranging figures to maximum rhetorical effect. Though Smith discussed the sublime a great deal and though he had many examples and manners of identifying it, in the end, his lectures mystified the sublime. In this regard, Smith did the same violence to Longinus that Nicolas Boileau did in his famous 1674 translation, which Smith knew and referenced in his lectures. While Longinus worked to "demystify" the sublime, Boileau described rhetorical sublimity as a mysterious quality with transcendental origins. Boileau located sublime beauty outside of language. He saw the sublime as an effect on the hearer, rather than as a product of language (Warnick 75–80).[8] Smith's vague and extensive descriptions of the sublime and his focus on taste as one's ability to recognize sublimity did little to exactly explain the rhetorical quality. However, he did not equivocate when explaining that the culturally privileged would know sublime oratory when they heard it. In Smith's hands, rhetorical sublimity became a genteel marker displaying one's status rather than a pragmatic persuasive tool.

Smith's treatment of the sublime focused on acquisition of taste and its proper, critical application. He told his students that "the true Sublime and it's Effects" were only evident to "an exact critical Taste [. . .] only to be acquir'd by long Experience [. . . and the] Improvement of much Study and Observation [. . . through] Converse with Men and Writings of acknowledged Politeness" (Yeates, "The Substance" 40–41). Judging by Smith's lectures, one could easily conclude that students wrote very little, that they fretted over their own genius and taste, struggling constantly to improve by sitting in uncomfortable desks, poring over Greek and Latin orations, and trying desperately to critically wrest sublimity from these documents through rigorous application of the rhetorical rules. And this might not be too far from the mark. As evidenced by many of his own accounts, Smith's students did spend a lot of time pondering the sublime, finding it in great orations, and improving their critical faculties of taste. But they also wrote and performed orations.

Second-year students wrote imitations of the great orations studied, while third-year students spent their whole afternoons performing. In fact, as mentioned in chapter 2, in the college's early years, public performances occurred frequently and with much success. The first of these performances (14 Nov. 1754) included orations on education, logic, method, and moral philosophy. One presentation in particular brought Smith a great deal of pride: a performance of the *Masque of Alfred* before the Earl of London and several others. The *Pennsylvania Gazette* (20 Jan. 1757) recorded the event and praised the college for teaching its students the art of public speaking. Social climbers, like Franklin, supported these performances because they wanted students to learn the practical-professional skills of oral communication. These public performances, however, fell away in the late 1750s, disappearing by 1789. Philadelphia's wealthy favored polite over pragmatic education. Public speaking exercises did not refine one's sense of taste.

Like almost any college in the colonial period, the College of Philadelphia held public performances at graduation—usually a few student orations, some forensic and syllogistic disputations both in English and in Latin, and sundry poems. A description in the *Pennsylvania Gazette* (27 May 1762) recounts a typical commencement performance, which included a salutatory oration in Latin, a forensic disputation, a Latin syllogistic disputation, two English orations, a valedictory oration, a dialogue, and an ode set to music. Topics addressed in these exercises reflect Smith's politics. From the first orations given in 1754 to those given at commencement, May 17, 1775, most of the students' vernacular performances approached rather abstract topics or discussed politics in England. The same can be said of the poetic odes. At commencement in 1761, the ode performed was about King George III's ascension to the English throne (*An Exercise*). In 1763, the ode celebrated the peace (the Seven Years' War had just ended), but peace in Britain, not peace in America (*Pennsylvania Gazette* 26 May 1763). At the May 17, 1775, commencement, with revolution hanging in the air, just thirty-two days after the battles at Lexington and Concord, a reporter chronicling the event remarked that most of the English performances had little to do with "the present state of affairs." In fact, he refused to register any but one of the orations, which did take a pro-revolutionary stance by claiming that oratory had declined in the colonies because British tyranny suppressed colonial liberty (Ennals 3). With this 1775 speech as a notable exception, public performances at the college generally did not deal with colonial events. Most often, Smith's students discursively adopted loyalist political postures or at minimum parroted Smith's political allegiances and his lessons in natural or moral philosophy.

Perhaps the most famous moment combining student rhetorical performance and loyalism occurred on May 20, 1766. John Sargeant, an alumnus of the college, offered an award (a medal) for the best student or alumnus oration written and delivered "on the Reciprocal Advantages of a Perpetual Union Between Great Britain and her American Colonies" (*Four Dissertations*). But there were many other, similar moments. At the first public performance (1754), Francis Hopkinson defended education as a colonizing force, arguing that British colonials should "take Care that the Stream of Education be diffused thro' the Land, and directed impartially to every Denomination of Men." Immediately following Hopkinson's oration, Samuel Magaw argued for moral and natural philosophy as Christian inquiry, even repeating Smith's vision of rhetoric as "only [a] Means" by which a person should express the divine beauty witnessed through scientific investigation. Josiah Martin followed Magaw, describing rhetoric as a "means" of expressing or learning about Christian science. Martin claimed that "we are by Nature *communicative*," positioning rhetoric as the commonality unifying various peoples under a single culture. At later public performances, students continued to repeat Smith's ideas about empire, education, science, religion, and rhetoric. In 1765, for instance, Nathaniel Evans publicly delivered his "Oration on Science," in which he described scientific investigation's ability to reveal and spread Christianity. "By Science youthful Minds are taught to know / What to their *God,* their *Country, Friends* they owe" (Evans 115–17).

Though students were certainly regurgitating Smith's loyalist politics, his common-sense realism, and his lessons on rhetoric and natural philosophy, they were also learning genteel culture, which the established Philadelphia bourgeoisie would have particularly appreciated. Smith encouraged students to compose in literary genres. He even helped them to write and publish poetry. He edited the *American Magazine and Monthly Chronicle for the British Colonies,* where he printed several of Francis Hopkinson's student poems. In 1754, Smith also published a sermon on the death of a student, to which he appended student poems by Francis Hopkinson, Jacob Duché, Thomas Barton, and Paul Jackson (*A Sermon*). Nathaniel Evans wrote poems while attending the college, many printed in the *Pennsylvania Gazette* (7 Aug. 1760, 11 Feb. 1762). After Evans died, Smith collected and edited his poetry, publishing them as *Poems on Several Occasions* (1772). He even introduced several of these budding collegiate poets to one another, encouraging their interaction (Gegenheimer, ch. 4).

Like the students' orations, most of their poems dealt with subjects removed from American economics or politics. Many directly espoused loyalist beliefs. In the October 1757 edition of the *American Magazine,* Hopkinson published an ode on music, and in the November edition he published imitations of John Milton's "l'Allegro" and "Il Penseroso." In fact, none of the poems that Hopkinson published in the *American Magazine* have anything to do with current events in the colonies, nor do they illustrate the professionally direct prose of Franklin's bourgeois republic. They are all quite ornamented, entirely aesthetic endeavors, attempts to improve and demonstrate taste. Evans's poetry is similarly detached from colonial life. One notable exception to this trend is Jacob Duché's poem (1756) about violence in the western counties (*A Poem*). None of these texts embodies the practical discourse of the emergent Philadelphian bourgeoisie. Though he made overtures and some concessions to rhetorical pragmatism, Smith principally taught students to write for genteel culture.

As this review of the speaking exercises at the College of Philadelphia demonstrates, Smith did not encourage the norms of rhetorical culture suitable to the civil society tradition as described by Habermas and Hauser and as often articulated to political liberalism, nor did Smith's rhetorical education connect to the civic virtue tradition as described by Arendt and Hauser and as often articulated to republicanism. In fact, though they relied on different philosophical and epistemological suppositions, both Smith and Johnson promoted similar norms of rhetorical culture. Both promoted belletristic practices in line with the urban cosmopolitan culture typically encountered in colonial cities. Both also promoted a public sphere where citizens would testify to the dogmatic truths and the moral and political imperatives of British imperialism and to its affiliated mercantilist economic policies. Smith's and Johnson's students practiced this effort in oratorical performances that parroted the wisdom of their teachers, in debates that revealed divine wisdom, and in poetic compositions that praised British government and its expansive empire. These rhetorical norms bear similarities to what one would find in the Puritan public sphere described in chapter 3. In both cases, an antidemocratic, intolerant rhetorical culture was promoted in the interest of maintaining a deferential political order. But Smith and Johnson were by no means Puritans, and their ideal public spaces were not inhabited by praying saints. They were inhabited by loyal British colonists and by devout Anglicans. As the Revolution approached, this articulation to Anglicanism and to British government led local citizens to oppose the rhetorical education offered at King's College and at the College of Philadelphia. That both curricula eventually gave short shrift to the economic interests of emerging capitalists had little to do with the widespread opposition among Philadelphia's and New York's inhabitants. Some, like Franklin and William Livingston, faulted the colleges for not catering to the emergent professional class, but most established capitalists voiced no such concerns. As a result, rhetorical education at both colleges continued to function largely as a marker indicating, rather than as a means of achieving, social status.

Smith's gentility and his belletristic rhetoric won him approval among

Philadelphia's established bourgeoisie, while his pragmatic classical/vernacular rhetorical pedagogy, at least for a time, won the approval of emergent bourgeois citizens such as Benjamin Franklin. But as these two groups found unity in their desire to split from British mercantilism, Smith's loyalism became a liability. When the British captured Philadelphia in September 1777, the college closed. Smith found himself in a very difficult position. Though he did not oppose the revolutionary cause, he did oppose separation from the mother country as he declared on a number of occasions.[9] He was investigated during the Revolution. Though no charges were officially levied, he did lose his position at the college. The men who eventually took power in Philadelphia after the Revolution were of the same economic and social cut as the earlier Proprietary Party, but they were revolutionaries. The new Constitutional Party established a committee in 1779 to inquire into the college. Their report was unfavorable. The legislature reappointed many of the trustees and the faculty. It also renamed the college the University of Pennsylvania. Like their predecessors, the new trustees were Anglican gentry, but they were not loyalists. They removed Smith from the faculty.

Columbia University, 1787–1800

In 1784, Columbia University opened without a president. The trustees worried that if they appointed an Anglican, they would invoke local suspicion. If they appointed someone of another denomination, they would lose the campus, which had been donated by Trinity Church under the provision that an Anglican always be president. In 1784, they decided on William Samuel Johnson, a lax Anglican layman, one-time loyalist turned revolutionary turned Federalist, who, during the 1760s, openly criticized both colonial radicals and British conservatives. He exhibited antidemocratic sympathies as Connecticut's representative at the Continental Congress and the Constitutional Convention. These political leanings appealed to New York's commercial elite who felt threatened by emergent capitalists spouting radical republican platitudes, men like William Livingston, flush from their victories over the Delancey Party and the British army. W. S. Johnson's desire to restrict national leadership to a natural aristocracy won over the trustees, who were largely established bourgeois merchants in support of the Federalist hegemony. (W. S. Johnson also represented Connecticut in the U.S. Senate, 1789–91, as an avid Federalist, shaping the 1789 Judiciary Act [1789] and fighting for Hamiltonian proposals to strengthen the executive branch.) Additionally, the appointments of Dutch Reformer John Daniel Gross as professor of moral philosophy and John Ewing as provost (1780) helped to allay fears of Anglican dominance. W. S. Johnson taught rhetoric and belles lettres for the duration of his presidency excepting four years (1795–99) when funds permitted him to hire John Bissit for that post (McCaughey 244–60).

W. S. Johnson continued to teach the norms of belletristic rhetoric. His *paideia* articulated rhetorical belletrism to an authoritarian and elitist version of Federalist republicanism. David Humphrey, the premier historian of Columbia's early years, says of this period, "Despite the flowering of republican sentiment, subordination to political authority remained a crucial value in the moral code inculcated by the Columbia College faculty" (303). Samuel Johnson had already drawn connections among rhetorical pedagogy, citizen virtue, and belletrism, so it was no great innovation for his son to shift from coaching imperial to coaching republican citizen-subjects through a belletristic *paideia*. W. S. Johnson shed most of the philosophical presuppositions underlying his father's curriculum. Students no longer learned the larger order of human knowledge, no longer worried about philology and philosophy, nor were they preoccupied with divine knowledge reflected in human ideas. In effect, though he left behind the larger philosophical apparatus, W. S. Johnson's pedagogy continued along a political trajectory established by his father with a crucial exception: loyalism was no longer the authoritarian politics du jour.

Initially, students studied out of classical texts like Cicero's orations and Longinus's *On the Sublime*. New York's commercial elite, however, were more interested in genteel trappings than they were in classical rhetoric, and their continued demand for gentrification spurred the regents in 1788 to insist on a new curriculum (McCaughey 250). W. S. Johnson responded by downplaying the classics and increasing the belletristic component of his rhetorical pedagogy. Though other textbooks remained in the curriculum (Lowth's *Grammar,* Sterling's *Rhetoric,* Holmes's *The Art of Rhetoric*), W. S. Johnson began using Hugh Blair's *Lectures* almost exclusively, and he had students study literary texts such as the novels of Oliver Goldsmith, Laurence Sterne, and the essays of the English Samuel Johnson (Humphrey 297). Samuel Latham Mitchill described this curriculum in 1794, stressing its belletristic components:

> In Rhetoric, on the plan of Holmes' and Stirling's Rhetoric; and in Belles Lettres on the plan of Blair's Lectures [. . .] so as to comprehend, as far as possible, a complete course of instruction in the Origin, Nature, and Progress of Language in general, and of the English Language in particular; in the art of writing and speaking with propriety, elegance and force—the rules and principles of every species of eloquence—the principles of true taste and the rules of just criticism, whereby the students may be enabled to judge properly of each species of composition in every branch of literature. (2–3)

Mitchill's description demonstrates that this curriculum continued to glut the wealthy merchant's appetite for cultural distinction.

Other aspects of Columbia's *paideia* also demonstrate the university's continuing belletristic tilt. Student literary societies began appearing almost immediately. In 1784, students formed the Columbia College Society, which withered in the mid-1790s. The Belles Lettres Association and the Uranian Society were both founded in 1788 under the president's auspices and guidance. Students wrote and presented pieces for critique by other society members. Though these exercises often degenerated into cruel correction and (in one student's words) "*carping,*" they were directed largely at genteel rhetorical contrivances such as "sentiment and stile" (Tompkins 39). None of these societies survived for long. Nevertheless, their existence indicates a continuing student preoccupation with polite letters.

Official collegiate exercises also demonstrate the genteel nature of Columbia's curriculum. Syllogistic disputation disappeared from commencement exercises entirely, and speeches in Latin were rare. Forensic disputation in English continued, and stand-alone orations flourished. Belletristic rhetorical genres and norms certainly dominated rhetorical education at Columbia, but they were articulated to a particularly authoritarian republicanism then associated with the Federalist Party in New York, a political institution allowing established merchants to continue suppressing popular sovereignty and to maintain their grip on political and

Table 4.2: Selected topics of student presentations at Columbia commencements, 1786–1800 (Roach 27)

Date	Topic
1786	The impolicy and imprudence of a republic's aiming at being a conquering nation
1789	On the necessity and usefulness of eloquence for preserving the liberty of a country
1791	That the necessity of a liberal education is not confined to the learned professions
1793	On the impropriety of capital punishments
1793	On the inhumanity of the slave trade
1796	On the rights of women
1800	On imprisonment for debt

economic policy. The topics debated at student commencement exercises demonstrate that W. S. Johnson's rhetorical pedagogy articulated belletristic rhetorical theory to the norms of bourgeois rhetorical culture and also to republican discourse. (See table 4.2.) Though they engaged republicanism in student speaking exercises, Columbia faculty did not tolerate student dissent or open inquiry. This public sphere did not tolerate agonistic deliberation, nor did it encourage the liberties of thought and expression that Whiggish Livingstonite republicans advocated. Columbia's forum was a space for students to demonstrate their allegiance to Federalist hegemony. Faculty vetted student presentations for "style and sentiment," often refusing anything that smacked of dissent. In one famous incident (1811), John B. Stevenson refused to alter his presentation and was consequently denied his degree. Students rioted (Roach 123–26).

Daniel D. Tompkins (class of 1795; governor of New York, 1807–17; vice president of the United States, 1817–25) left a valuable record of the compositions and orations he produced while under W. S. Johnson's tutelage. In these, Tompkins articulates a publicity that brings together a Federalist republicanism, a belletristic rhetoric, and the norms of a genteel public sphere. In his disputation exercises and his stand-alone ora-

tions, Tompkins treated a variety of subjects including idleness, the theater, drunkenness, slavery, novels, prejudice, relations with Amerindian
peoples, government, and education. In his discourses on government,
Tompkins repeated a host of republican ideas. He said monarchy leads to
luxury, which threatens republican virtue (34). He also worried about
excessive democratic influence and equality, which could "reduce all to a
promiscuous level" (35). In these passages, Tompkins voiced typical Federalist concerns about mob rule and the need to foster a virtuous natural
aristocracy to lead the republic away from its own excesses. He even made
backhanded comments about "strict democrats" who would promote radical equality, clearly a reference to leveling sentiments among some in the
Democratic-Republican Party (37). In one composition on choosing public officials, Tompkins said that power belongs in the hands of a natural and
virtuous elite (1–2). He made explicit connections between rhetorical
education and the virtue necessary for his proposed natural aristocracy.
Like his professor at Columbia, Tompkins believed that rhetorical refinement shapes virtuous republican leaders.

Tompkins voiced a typical impatience with education in Latin and the
classics, saying that familiarity with modern languages better prepared
students for their lives as citizens and professionals (6). In this regard, he
appealed to the economic interests of New York's emergent professional
bourgeoisie. He wrote that oratory is "one of the greatest and most useful
acquisitions that a man is capable of" (12). He even channeled Livingstonite Whiggism when he claimed that a proper liberal arts education could
prepare young men for republican leadership to check "the oppression of
aspiring Governments" (17). Nevertheless, despite these ostensibly democratic declarations, Tompkins had no intention of including all voices and
rhetorical contrivances in the Federalist public sphere. He favored the rhetorical culture of New York's established commercial elite. Education in
rhetoric, particularly practice in the composition of a clear, vivid style like
that found in Blair's *Lectures,* was a key component in Tompkins's proposed republican *paideia*. Notably, however, though Tompkins worried
that overly ornate writing could corrupt discourse and citizen virtue, he
did not level charges of corruption at popular genteel genres such as the
novel. (Timothy Dwight, driven by his Puritan austerity, did commonly
claim that novels corrupted citizen virtue.) In fact, Tompkins defended the

novel as an important place where young republican leaders could learn the "love of virtue and the detestation of vice" (25). Even when he claimed that poetry did not suit the rhetorical norms of Federalist publicity, he avoided appeal to the corruption topic. Poetry was not appropriate because it was not useful in political affairs (27–28). Republican utility, not virtue, was at issue.

By vouchsafing a place in the Federalist public sphere for belletristic genres such as the novel, Tompkins articulated the cultural aspirations of New York's established bourgeoisie to the dominant political discourse of the era. By insisting that the healthy republic put power in the hands of a natural aristocracy, Tompkins articulated Federalist fears of democracy to republicanism and to the rhetorical norms practiced at Columbia. Columbia's program of rhetorical education for a healthy republic justified the privilege of an economic and political elite by reaffirming their cultural gentility, by excusing their exclusionary public sphere, and by advocating their political elitism. Tompkins concluded his valedictory oration (6 May 1795) with high praise for W. S. Johnson's Federalist republican *paideia,* where he had learned all of the above lessons: "May the citizens of our Republic be ever persuaded that the interests of science are nearly connected with the liberty and happiness of their Country. General Knowledge must be the basis of our glory and independence; cherish, therefore, institutions of learning, as the ornaments and blessings of our land" (63). W. S. Johnson made some remarkable changes to the rhetorical education at Columbia. Most notably, he abandoned the philosophical idealism that was central to his father's curriculum, expanded the belletristic component of rhetorical practice and theory, sutured republicanism to his pedagogical musings and to disputation exercises, and scrubbed all vestiges of loyalism from the college's curriculum. But the norms of rhetorical culture at Columbia remained largely the same.

W. S. Johnson no more engaged the civic virtue tradition than did his father. At Columbia, students still learned that the public sphere was a place where citizens testified their allegiance to the hegemonic order. Those who did not were silenced. Those lacking economic and social privilege were never invited to the conversation. W. S. Johnson's rhetorical pedagogy, therefore, abandoned certain philosophical components that were vital to his father's *paideia,* but he maintained the crucial articulations of bourgeois rhetorical norms, belletristic rhetorical practice and theory, and antidemocratic politics. The effects of W. S. Johnson's pedagogical articulatory practice are illustrated nowhere better than in the Federalist publicity that his student Tompkins articulated in his orations. By looking at W. S. Johnson's pedagogy and Daniel Tompkins's publicity, one can see that the articulatory efforts at rhetorical education and the students' rhetorical practice were directly related. Students learned to be republican citizens in one constellation of rhetorical theory, politics, culture, religion, and economics: students repeated this hegemonic order in their public performances, thereby reaffirming the connections on which Federalist hegemony depended.

The University of Pennsylvania, 1795–1813

From William Smith's removal in 1779 until the end of the century, circumstances at the College of Philadelphia were tumultuous. Smith fought the decision to fire him, and in 1789 he won. The board restored the colonial college with Smith as provost. The University of Pennsylvania still existed, even though it had to cede its campus to the reinstated College of Philadelphia. For a while, the university took shelter in a Mason lodge, and the public expressed great dissatisfaction with the college's curriculum. The principal critique reflected and was repeated by Franklin: Smith's curriculum was not practical enough; it did not suit the needs of a professional bourgeoisie who sought training for industry and commerce. In 1791, the college and the university united, and the new board named Dr. Davidson provost. Smith left Philadelphia and returned to Washington College (which he founded in 1782) in Kent County, Maryland, where he presumably continued to teach his unique rhetorical pedagogy but without the articulation to loyalist politics that had cost him so dearly. The University of Pennsylvania struggled financially for years, in part because its curriculum never fit the bourgeois pragmatism that Franklin promoted in higher education. This dissatisfaction led to decreased enrollment and paltry financial and political support from a populace leaning toward the inclusive republicanism popular among Philadelphia's less established capitalists.

After 1795, rhetorical education at the newly constituted university largely became the province of John Andrews, a former loyalist, an Anglican, and a graduate of the college under William Smith. Andrews moved into education when his political sympathies forced him to flee a parish over which he presided in Maryland. He taught in Yorktown, became principal of the Philadelphia Episcopal Academy, and was then appointed to the chair of moral philosophy (which included teaching rhetoric) at the new university. Andrews stayed in this post, serving as vice provost and then as provost, for three years before his death in 1813. His lectures on logic and rhetoric reveal that the established bourgeois interest in Philadelphia continued to trump Franklin's pragmatic vision. At the University of Pennsylvania, rhetorical pedagogy continued to be more an exercise in cultural polish than pragmatic training for professional and public performance.

Andrews's lectures on logic repeated the four-part structure and much of the actual advice in William Duncan's *Elements of Logick*. The first lectures treated simple apprehension and repeated a great deal of Locke's epistemology, particularly the separation of simple and complex ideas. Andrews further divided complex ideas into two subcategories: compound and relative, the former of which was divided again into universal, general, and abstract ideas. Andrews also gave directive advice about conveying empirically acquired information. He explored two types of definition, each relating to the two types of ideas (simple and complex). Like both Smith and Johnson, Andrews positioned language as a handmaiden to some truth acquired beyond discursive exercise, but unlike his loyalist Anglican predecessors, Andrews did not articulate his epistemology to any political authority. This notable absence of political posturing demonstrates that the university's curricula could permissibly continue and would meet approval by the established bourgeoisie provided that it made no overt connection to British loyalism.

Andrews repeated many of the lessons that both Smith and Johnson taught. He reiterated the common-sense realism that Smith espoused, particularly in the lectures on simple apprehension and judgment. Though Andrews did not employ the common-sense vocabulary, he did explain that people are disposed to certain types of evidence by the "law of our nature" (*Elements of Logick* 159). His lectures on acquiring information and dividing it into types of evidence continually repeated a vocabulary of "natural" inclination, reflecting an underlying belief in a universal common sense about matters of fact. In his lectures on propositions (*Elements of Logick* 70–82) and syllogisms (*Elements of Logick* 109–55), Andrews adopted a rationalism not unlike Johnson's. These lectures encouraged students to find truth by following rational form rather than sticking to the mandates of common sense. It would be wrong to say that Andrews's lectures on logic repeated verbatim the epistemological lessons taught by the two most influential pre-revolutionary Anglican educators. Andrews presented an amalgam of material acquired from a number of sources. However, his curriculum's principal elements certainly reflect what Smith and Johnson taught prior to 1776.

When looking at his lectures on rhetoric, the same thing becomes evident. Other historians have noted the common belletristic tilt shared by both Andrews and Smith, a commonality pointing to their shared bourgeois culture (Barone, "Before"). But the political differences merit attention as well. Andrews taught a belletristic rhetorical theory just like his predecessors, just like his mentor, but he removed the nettling preoccupations with Anglican authority and British Empire, making his rhetorical pedagogy entirely palatable to an established bourgeoisie interested in learning the cultural trappings of gentility. Andrews also inserted typically genteel republican assertions about the moral value of literary genres.

The rhetoric lectures were divided into four sections, two on style, a third on genres, and a final section on poetics. The lectures on style listed desirable properties, such as perspicuity, strength, and harmony, and gave advice about using tropes and figures. Andrews counseled students on how to achieve stylistic effects, and he presented examples, typically from English literature. His lectures were clear and useful both for those interested in analyzing and for those interested in producing genteel prose. His eight rules on the use of figures and tropes are particularly sensible, recommending attention to audience, subject matter, intelligibility, and coordination of stylistic flourish in an essay (*Elements of Rhetorick* 95–100). Like Smith, Andrews demonstrated a pragmatism that suited the emergent bourgeois interest in professional training. Also, like Smith, Andrews focused his lectures on the interpretive uses of rhetorical theory. This becomes especially evident in the lectures covering thirteen kinds of style with illustrative literary examples. He discussed everything from the concise to the vehement to the sublime styles, in each instance providing a definition and a bevy of examples from English writers like Archbishop Tillotson, William Temple, John Dryden, Alexander Pope, Jonathan Swift, and of course Joseph Addison. Needless to say, he spent more time discussing the sublime than he did any other single kind of style, but his lectures on the sublime made no reference to the majesty of empire or even to the glory of God's works. Andrews stuck to the technical components of sublimity without rhapsodizing about its political implications. The closest he came to Smith's imperial sublimity was an offhanded remark that descriptions of God commonly produced sublime rhetoric (*Elements of Rhetorick* 139).

At the end of his lectures on style, Andrews offered some pragmatic counsel. He told his students that, though he could not teach the art of writing through mechanical rules, he could offer seven "directions." Three of these detailed how to study and imitate great authors, while the other four gave advice about adapting the style to the subject and to the audience's inclinations, the necessity of frequent practice, and the importance of not allowing style to completely dominate one's attention. In all, Andrews's lectures on style reveal the tension between Philadelphia's established bourgeoisie and her newly empowered capitalists. Like Smith, Andrews catered his rhetorical pedagogy to both interests by presenting instruction in genteel rhetorical norms and by presenting pragmatic advice for producing persuasive prose. Also like Smith, Andrews's lectures were heavily weighted to the former purpose, demonstrating, in the end, an allegiance to Philadelphia's wealthy merchants.

After this exhaustive treatment of style, Andrews delivered several lectures on prose genres: history, philosophy, dialogue, epistles, fiction, essays, and orations. Excepting the lectures on orations, he focused exclusively on written genres, lending some credence to Franklin's observation that students did not learn to speak publicly. Rather, they learned to write and to analyze genteel genres. To be fair, the lectures on orations were extensive, far more developed than his treatment of any other single genre, and they repeated a great deal of useful classical advice about inventing and arranging arguments. This was the sort of thing that Franklin would have appreciated. Students learned a variation on the five-part arrangement (exordium, narration, argument, pathetic appeal, peroration). They were taught the possible emotional proofs, and they even received detailed advice about pronunciation and gesture in delivery. These lectures showed a striking familiarity with Cicero and Quintilian, but they also showed Hugh Blair's influence, particularly in the declaration that invention is "beyond the power of art to give any real assistance" (*Elements of Rhetorick* 202).

While Andrews was at his most pragmatic when discussing orations, he was at his most belletristic when discussing the remaining genres. These lectures typically described the genre's stylistic properties, offered fleeting advice about how to address the appropriate audience, and presented the students with examples. When discussing "fictitious history," Andrews voiced a genteel republican belief that novels positively affect a citizenry's virtue. He praised authors like Henry Fielding and Daniel Defoe for their lively styles, their humor, and their portrayal of people overcoming adversity, but he had particularly kind words for Samuel Richardson, whose novels offer moral lessons (*Elements of Rhetorick* 187–88). Of both the French and the English novel, Andrews said, "Imitations of life and character have been their principal object. Relations have been professed to be given of the behaviour of persons in particular interesting situations, such as may occur in life; by means of which, what is laudable or defective in character or conduct, may be pointed out, and placed in a useful light" (*Elements of Rhetorick* 186). Andrews's appreciation for the virtuous potential of the novel, set alongside similar sentiments expressed by Daniel Tompkins at Columbia, demonstrates that early American Federalists were not all opposed to belletristic literature. The novel was not necessarily a threatening democratic institution, nor was belletrism an apolitical rhetorical pedagogy, as some have suggested (Davidson 41–52; T. Miller, "Where"). The genteel republicanism of Philadelphia's established bourgeoisie clearly located political value in literary study. Belletristic rhetorical education under John Andrews prepared students for conversations in the polite salons where wealthy Federalists discussed the fine points of beautiful literature.

The remaining lectures simultaneously arrived at a belletristic zenith and a pragmatic nadir. Here, Andrews treated poetry, describing its general nature, its arrangement, and styles of and rules for versification, and providing a laundry list of poetic genres. He also connected poetry to the spread of citizen virtue, saying that verses promoting vice were typically bad and would usually fail to gain popular appreciation (*Elements of Rhetorick* 233–34). Good poetry is good for the republic. These lectures offered no applicative potential. They were entirely interpretive instruments, valuable to those wanting fluency in an aspect of privileged culture. Andrews's lectures, like the curriculum at Columbia University, demonstrates that the established bourgeois interest still dominated higher education in Philadelphia. Belletrism's presence was the only constant in rhetorical pedagogy from the mid-eighteenth to the early nineteenth centuries, though it was articulated to two very different political positions: an Anglican loyalism and a genteel, Federalist republicanism.

Since I began this chapter with Jacob Duché, I will end with him as well, to sharpen an argument dulled by repetition: a rhetorical pedagogy has no necessary impact until articulated concretely by actors (both students and teachers) in history. If a curriculum had necessary ties to a given politics, then one would expect all of William Smith's students to become genteel loyalists, but in most cases the outcome was quite different. Francis Hopkinson became an avid supporter of the Revolution, writing songs for American soldiers (Hastings 212–64). Jasper Yeates served as a soldier in the Revolution and later became a Federalist judge on the Pennsylvania Supreme Court (Landis). Isaac Hunt published several attacks on the Proprietary Party and the college he believed served it. He accused the Pennsylvania governor and the college faculty of conspiring with "*British* America" to "burthen us with Taxes," a direct reference to Grenville's Stamp Act (1765) (iv). Yet in 1775 Hunt turned loyalist (Bailyn, *Ideological* 311). The public arguments that these students made after their college careers include a variety of articulations to differing political programs, many of them at odds with the allegiances central to Smith's rhetorical pedagogy. Unlike Daniel Tompkins, who practiced a publicity fully in line with the rhetorical pedagogy that he encountered under W. S. Johnson's tutelage, many of Smith's students developed public arguments that opposed their professor's political leanings.

Among the Smith alumni, Jacob Duché cuts the most tragic figure. He became a minister in the Anglican Church and was a political conservative before the Revolution. He even praised the college for its genteel *paideia* and for Smith's efforts to teach obedience to the Anglican order, saying that a proper liberal education should happen "under the direction of a heaven-taught mind" (*Observations* 15–22, 55). Like Smith, he bowed to the scepter and the crown. He conflated the two while observing that the king should be considered a "minister of heaven." For a time, he developed a publicity whose political agenda mimicked what he had encountered under Smith's tutelage. Despite these sympathies, in 1776, Duché supported the Revolution, even preached before the Continental Congress (4 Sept. 1774, 11 May 1775) (*Observations* 166–74, 233–41). As the Revolution drew near, Duché practiced a new publicity that articulated the bourgeois rhetorical norms that he learned under Smith to a separatist political platform. But when the British entered Philadelphia, he lost heart and wrote a letter to General George Washington recommending surrender. Embarrassed by the letter and shunned by society, Duché moved to England shortly thereafter.

Just as William Smith's rhetorical pedagogy had no necessary political impact until it was taken up by its students, it had no necessary political connection until taken up by someone like Duché. Smith's student John Andrews developed a similar rhetorical pedagogy, articulating belletrism to yet another politics. Belletrism variously served the interests of a loyalist and a republican established bourgeoisie as it continually stroked this group's cultural preoccupations. Also, the republicanism to which this rhetorical pedagogy was articulated differed remarkably from what Timothy Dwight promoted at Yale largely because this was the established bourgeois vision of the genteel republic, the bustling commercial center that Duché saw out his center-city window, not the millennial republic that Dwight saw nestled among Connecticut's verdant hills. When comparing Dwight's system of rhetorical education with W. S. Johnson's and John Andrews's *paideiai,* one cannot help but notice that all three men articulated their pedagogical energies to the Federalist Party, but clearly they had differing visions of Federalist republicanism.

They agreed, at least, that the Federalist public sphere should not be a tolerant space of agonistic deliberation or of free speech. But they disagreed about the cultural mores that the federal republic should promote,

and they disagreed about economic policy as well. Dwight favored restrictions on capitalism to protect the millennial republic from its corrupting luxuries. Urban Federalists tended to favor laissez-faire capitalism unless advocating duties to protect the local manufacturing interest, as did
Alexander Hamilton, Myles Cooper's student. Though they shared a common republican vocabulary and a common affiliation with the hegemonic
political party, these men disagreed about what a good republic should
look like, and their various systems of rhetorical education tried to realize
these conflicting visions, even tried to serve conflicting economic interests. Of course, these two visions of the republic do not exhaust its available mutations. Benjamin Franklin in Philadelphia and William Livingston
in New York sustained an emergent bourgeois hope for a republic of pragmatic capitalists speaking a plain, respectable rhetoric in professional circumstances. Though this (equally capitalist) set of rhetorical norms never
gained hegemonic dominance, it continued in both cities, resisting the
rhetorical education offered by Smith, Andrews, Samuel Johnson, and
W. S. Johnson.

Juxtaposing Smith's and Samuel Johnson's very closed systems of verity
against the openness of their own hegemonic order—the availability for
new rhetorical articulations, new pedagogies, new political and economic
configurations—one has to wonder about the proper purpose of rhetorical education. Should we be teaching students to locate and convey a
single "truth," as did the rhetoricians discussed in this chapter? If there is
no guarantee that they will follow the mandates of a given order, should
we become ideologues in its defense? However much we might believe in
the rightness of a (counter)hegemonic articulation of rhetorical practice
to any social formation, should we expect our students to repeat these
connections? The differing publicities articulated by Smith's and Johnson's
students tell us that such an effort may not only be theoretically questionable but also practically futile. If hegemony is an open process, if rhetorical
pedagogy and publicity are key sites of struggle in any hegemonic order,
then perhaps the most effective course of action for rhetorical education
is to help students to parse the varying positions at play in a given historical
moment, the articulations among political discourses, policies, economic
interests, partisan alliances, and rhetorical norms of public exchange. We

should also teach them the rhetorical art of forging new articulations both in public discourse (publicity) and in civic education (pedagogy). Robert Scholes extols this position eloquently when he says

> We must prepare our students not just to accept change but to participate in bringing it about with the most enlightened sense of their interests—and larger interests—that we can help them to develop. We are not artisans shaping the impressionable minds of our students. We are—or should be—masters of our craft helping others to master it, and human beings of integrity helping others to achieve it in their own ways in their own lives. (67)

To achieve this pedagogical end in the present, we must become critical of our own efforts at rhetorical education. This requires the kind of historical inquiry that I have practiced so far.

As a capstone to this historical study, in one more effort to demonstrate the open quality of any hegemonic order, the next chapter considers a third vision of the ideal republic, as manifested in John Witherspoon's *paideia* at the College of New Jersey, a rhetorical pedagogy suited particularly to commercial farmers in the middle colonies/states. Of course, Witherspoon's vision was at odds with the elite genteel republicanism taught at both Columbia and at the College of Philadelphia and with Timothy Dwight's millennial republicanism. In their efforts to shape citizens through various rhetorical pedagogies, therefore, all of these men engaged in a struggle over what America would become, just as politicos in the late eighteenth century argued in public spaces over what the ideal republic should look like. Representing the various economic interests of their era, speaking a common political discourse, all of these people, educators and politicians alike, fought over what would become of their society. Their students did likewise, in new and interesting ways.

5

The College of New Jersey,
1746–1822

The moral causes of the prosperity of a country, are almost infinitely more powerful than those that are only occasional [. . .] The moral causes arise from the nature of the government, including the administration of justice, liberty of conscience, the partition of property.

. . . .

Suffer me to recommend to you an attention to the public interest of religion, or in other words, zeal for the glory of God and the good of others.

—John Witherspoon

Contemporary scholars dedicated to reviving a republican tradition in rhetoric have found their historical hero in John Witherspoon, once president and professor of rhetoric and moral philosophy at the College of New Jersey (1767–95) (T. Miller, "Witherspoon"; Clark and Halloran). In their narratives, Witherspoon appears as a laudable ancestor who championed the tradition of an active, educated citizenry. His republican *paideia* is held favorably against the liberal tradition that "left the community behind," eroding the bedrock of shared values on which a republican polity could stand, replacing communally established discursive terra firma with the shifting silt "of individual conscience" (Clark and Halloran 11, 13). On close examination, however, things appear more complicated. Recent revisionist historical accounts have stressed, for instance, that Witherspoon's rhetorical pedagogy appealed to the bourgeois desire for pragmatic education allowing social mobility in a commercial republic (Scott). Witherspoon's republican *paideia* was articulated to an economic interest. Witherspoon also saw the *vir bonus bene dicendi* in Christian, particularly Calvinist, terms. His rhetorical pedagogy included not only economic but also religious threads.

This last chapter presents one final demonstration of early American civic education as complicated terrain where actors struggled over hegemonic articulations to a common republican vocabulary. Witherspoon's saga is the final act because, in present historical scholarship, he appears as the great forefather of an American republican rhetorical education. Yet his republican pedigree is not so pure. In fact, Witherspoon's republican *paideia* articulated the economic interests of New Jersey's commercial farmers to the political interests of New Side Calvinist Presbyterians. In doing so, he often directly undercut certain principles of republican democracy (such as the privileging of public over private virtue) and of republican rhetorical exchange (such as agonistic deliberation). Witherspoon lived in a predominantly rural middle colony/state where commercial agriculture catapulted many into very comfortable lives. In New Jersey, he witnessed and participated in the struggle between proprietary landowners who tried to preserve their privilege and emergent capitalist farmers who fought the semifeudal institutions left over from New Jersey's early days as a proprietary colony. While New Jersey's proprietary class tried to instate economic circumstances whereby a few royally appointed landowners could live from the quitrents paid by their tenants, commercial farmers favored a laissez-faire model where land and goods were traded equally and where no particular class would have any special claim to ownership of any commodity. Witherspoon also lived in a state torn by division between New and Old Side Calvinists, and his own allegiances in this religious schism affected both his efforts to teach rhetoric and his definition of the good citizen. He imagined the virtuous republican as a particularly orthodox Calvinist and as a commercial farmer. Like Smith, Johnson, Dwight, and Andrews, Witherspoon articulated a rhetorical pedagogy whose components included an economic interest and a host of other factors such as a religious tradition.

Witherspoon's economic allegiances led him toward certain tenets of political liberalism, which he repeated to students in his lectures on moral philosophy. As the analysis below demonstrates, Witherspoon's melding of liberal and republican discourses places him in a transitional position not unlike that occupied by John Quincy Adams before him. Jacksonian liberalism did not materialize out of thin air in the early nineteenth century. Early American rhetorical educators prepared a space for this political discourse by suturing it to commonly held republican beliefs. While Witherspoon's economic interests led him to liberalism, his religious beliefs led him away from the public and open rhetorical exchange often championed by liberals and republicans alike. His religious allegiances led him to favor a restricted and somewhat authoritarian public sphere.

Though he certainly appropriated the vocabulary of republican political theory, Witherspoon's historical circumstances led him to articulate this republicanism to two other traditions. Rogers M. Smith, in a penetrating analysis of American civic ideals from the seventeenth through the early twentieth centuries, finds that three discourses have simultaneously shaped Americans' vision of a good democratic citizenry. Two of these have already been explored here, liberalism and republicanism, but the third deserves mention: ascriptivism. Smith argues that in addition to imagining citizens as equal possessors of rights and privileges or as equally active participants in political affairs, Americans have also imagined citizens in ascriptive terms that tend to exclude nonwhite, non-Protestant, nonmale peoples from the public sphere. This ascriptive tradition, actuated in complex and often contradictory ways, has persisted throughout American history and has resulted in some of its more regrettable effects, such as the systemic exclusion of Amerindians, the continual enslavement and then disenfranchisement of African Americans, the refusal of anything but a crippled political agency to women, and the cruel suspicions pasted onto Catholic immigrants at their arrival. (See Smith's introduction and ch. 1 particularly.) Smith finds that Americans in the revolutionary and early national periods blended republicanism and ascriptivism "without any sense of disjuncture" (83). What he notices in legal statutes and court decisions about who gets to vote or own property can also be illustrated in John Witherspoon's rhetorical education: a mixed tradition of liberalism, ascriptivism, and republicanism. Despite Witherspoon's use of republican political discourse, one cannot, without qualification, label him a republican. Like every other figure discussed so far, he appropriated a common vocabulary, articulating it to economic and political interests, to the historical environment in New Jersey.

Of course, though this chapter focuses on one person, he was not the sole cause of eighteenth-century New Jersey's version of democratic republicanism. Rather, this analysis demonstrates that certain economic circumstances articulated to a political discourse made possible and even probable Witherspoon's existence and his popularity. One lone Scotsman did not make New Jersey into a liberal, ascriptive republic. Rather, Witherspoon dialectically interacted with New Jersey, a region inhabited principally by Protestant commercial farmers. In this interaction, both the circumstances and the actor changed. From this interaction developed a version of republicanism peculiar to the area. To understand how these economic, cultural, and political circumstances favored his rhetorical pedagogy, one should look at two projections that also affected the college's geography: the tension between New and Old Side Presbyterians and the remarkable economic and political equality among freeholding farmers who comprised a substantial capitalist class. Each of these contributed significantly to Witherspoon's politics and made possible his rhetorical pedagogy.

Presbyterianism and the New Jersey Bourgeoisie

While the colony was home to a diverse number of religious groups—including Baptists, Quakers, Congregationalists, and Anglicans—Presbyterians exerted the most influence on the College of New Jersey. Presbyterians, like Congregationalists, split during the Great Awakening, with New Side ministers taking up charismatic delivery, populist appeals to salvation, and religious zeal. The New Side Presbyterians, many of them Harvard and Yale alumni, founded their own academies where they could train ministers. William Tennent's Log College (1727 in Neshaminy, Pennsylvania) and the Shepherd's Tent (mid to late 1740s in New London, Connecticut) were among the most famous places where evangelicals like Samuel Finley, James Davenport, and Gilbert Tennent (William's son) trained (Sloan 35–72; McClean 1: 57–59). Old Side ministers also founded academies such as Francis Alison's school in New London (1744). When flaring tempers stoked by the Great Awakening burned out, a concerted effort toward founding a chartered Presbyterian college arose from the ashes.

New Side evangelicals like Gilbert Tennent joined the effort, but the charter application downplayed their role for fear of political reprisal from conservative Anglicans in Britain. Nevertheless, New Side ministers did have a big impact. They particularly contributed an inclusive approach to religion and education, a belief that everyone should be welcomed into the college. This inclusivity appealed not only to the evangelical Protestants but also to New Jersey's commercial farmers who desired to be included in the developing capitalist economy and who had become fond of the Lockean belief that everyone should have the same rights and privileges. New Side ministers advocated full church membership and proclaimed that anyone who had been saved should be allowed to preach the gospel. This open policy dovetailed nicely with the New Side belief in equal and full education for all church participants. They wanted knowledge to be a common possession among church members, not a "clerical monopoly" (Sloan 53). This inclusive theology rested on a catholic government and educational system, and New Side ministers took public education as one of their chief duties. They wanted to create an informed citizenry, capable of debating theology and participating in civic life through both religious and secular institutions. The New Side academies, therefore, did not focus strictly on sectarian education. They offered religious instruction as well as instruction in the arts and sciences in order to educate both ministers and an informed public leadership of religious professionals. In New Jersey, the economic aspirations of the eighteenth-century bourgeoisie found expression in a Presbyterian demand for open church membership and congregational agency. The bourgeois belief that everyone should compete equally on a commercial field found support in the New Light dream of an educated and empowered flock.

The College of New Jersey's initial charter took up many of the New Side educational goals, including an inclusive posture, a commitment to educating an informed leadership (ministerial or professional), and equal attention to theological as well as to secular education. One New Side minister and trustee who participated actively in the initial establishment and design, Samuel Blair, reflected that the college was founded "on a free and catholic bottom" (7). Though this inclusivity suited certain bourgeois interests, its presence should not occlude another feature of the college's political countenance. Presbyterian founders did not open their public sphere to non-Protestant Christians. They wanted the college to cut citizens from a Calvinist cloth. During the early years (1742–67) the college produced more ministers than lay professionals. Five of the six students included in the first graduating class were ordained (McClean 1: 116).

The struggle between Presbyterian factions over control of the College of New Jersey also indicated Protestantism's ascriptive influence. New Side ministers maintained control through the early 1760s and managed to appoint presidents sympathetic to their theological proclivities, men like Samuel Davies, Aaron Burr, and Jonathan Edwards, but the Old Side gained power, and by the late 1760s they exerted considerable influence over the presidential appointment. Witherspoon was chosen as a compromise candidate between the two groups, since he professed a staunch Old Side Calvinism but allied himself politically with the Scottish version of New Side equalitarian theology (Butterfield). Witherspoon's appointment and the attention paid to his theological leanings reflected the trustees' generally Presbyterian desire to create a Christian republic.

While the Presbyterian influence affected the college's civic mission, New Jersey's economy also created an environment particularly conducive to a bourgeois version of civic education. The college was founded and operated in the midst of a struggle between New Jersey proprietors and emergent commercial farmers. Like its neighbor to the west, New Jersey was a proprietary colony, but the period of proprietary rule was tumultuous, ending in 1701 when the crown took over. Proprietors still existed and tried to live off the rent from their lands. They exerted great influence over the New Jersey assembly, pushing for legislation that worked in their economic favor, such as the consistent denial of specie or easy credit that would have promoted inflation and allowed more popular land distribution. Unlike Pennsylvania, New Jersey had no large commercial hubs where a merchant bourgeoisie could grow large or strong before the Revolution. Genteel culture, therefore, only found a reception among the dwindling proprietors. Most of the Jersey colonists were farmers (landowning or renting) who shared a common, respectable culture and common economic interests. They wanted a commercialized agricultural order in which individual farmers could prosper by selling a surplus of their staple crops on an open, unregulated market.

While the wealthiest 10 percent of New Jersey's citizens owned one-third of the land, and 30 percent of families in the colony owned no land, cultural tensions between the classes were low (Pomfret 217). Proprietary gentry lived in towns like Perth Amboy and Cape May but comprised a small portion of the colony's population, so the agrarian austerity of farming towns dominated New Jersey's cultural landscape (Purvis 24–49). Political tensions, however, did exist. The proprietors were constantly at odds with freeholding citizens, and these two groups projected very different visions of what New Jersey society should look like. In the words of one recent historian, "the proprietors wished to create a hierarchical society dominated by large estates, with the land-tenure system firmly under their control; the yeomen wanted to live in self-governing communities with a broad distribution of freehold property among white men" (McConville 11). Freeholders consistently defended their position with appeals to liberal tenets, particularly John Locke's classic contention that the right to property belongs to anyone capable of investing labor into natural resources. Also, the Great Awakening in New Jersey found traction among freeholders, who were particularly interested in condemning the proprietary gentility's cultural excesses (McConville 28–46, 81). In both their political liberalism and their religious cultural warfare, freeholders fought the proprietary gentry. When proprietary efforts to exert authority became too overbearing, violence erupted. Freeholders often rioted to resist proprietary strong-arming in the assembly or to vindicate those arrested for imposing on proprietary land claims.

Proprietors consistently lost economic ground to freeholders throughout the eighteenth century, and after the Revolution they ceased to exist as a political or cultural force. Freeholding republicanism, its agrarian commercialism, and its respectable culture eventually dominated the Jersey-scape. The New Jersey bourgeoisie, their laissez-faire economic sympathies along with their adherence to New Side condemnation of genteel corruption, provided a friendly environment for a college offering pragmatic education for a Christian republic of social climbers. The bourgeois influence on the college is best demonstrated in the steady drift away from strictly religious and toward professional education, though professional pragmatism never wholly took possession of the curriculum. Rather, education at the College of New Jersey became preparation for both a liberal commercial and an ascriptive Christian republic.

Though the College of New Jersey was originally founded as a primarily religious institution, though most early graduates entered the ministry, and though New Side religious leaders like Aaron Burr, Jonathan Edwards, and Samuel Finley served as presidents, the curriculum, prior to Witherspoon's arrival, was never theocentric. The first year continued students' instruction in Latin and Greek. In the original languages, students read Horace, Cicero, the Greek Testaments, and Lucian's dialogues. In the second year, they continued to study languages, reading Longinus and Homer, and they also took up geography, rhetoric, logic, and mathematics. Juniors continued study in mathematics while learning natural and moral philosophy, metaphysics, and history. Seniors reviewed the whole course of study and continued syllogistic and forensic disputation exercises in Latin and English respectively. Juniors and seniors also delivered stand-alone orations in English and publicly performed passages from Cicero, Demosthenes, Livy, Shakespeare, Milton, and Addison on a rotating schedule. Sundays were spent disputing religion (S. Blair 24–26; McClean 1: 268). The College of New Jersey always stressed secular subjects and contemporary texts alongside religion and the ancients.

New Jersey's freeholding bourgeoisie certainly favored a pragmatic education to prepare their children for equal participation in the capitalist British Atlantic economy, but they rejected the gentrified culture that they saw developing in port cities like Perth Amboy. They instead championed a respectable, Protestant virtue. In John Witherspoon, they found a presidential candidate able to do all this. Witherspoon had his political schooling in Scotland, where he learned to value civic inclusivity and popular rule through alliance with the Popular Party of orthodox Calvinist ministers and officials. As a Presbyterian minister in Scotland, he opposed genteel political moderates whose leading figures (including Hugh Blair) were also faculty at the University of Edinburgh. Witherspoon, acting against the moderate literati, joined popular party ministers and propounded an evangelical theology very similar to New Side Presbyterianism. He often engaged in debates against moderate political and religious principles, his most famous contribution being a satirical pamphlet, *Ecclesiastical Characteristics* (1753), which lambasted the Moderate Party and its aristocratic approach to religion, manners, and public life. He promoted an orthodox Calvinism and a strong republican belief that political sovereignty lay with the people, actuated through public debate and resulting in moral consensus. He disdainfully and facetiously insisted, "the political opinions of the moderate man must disagree with that of the people" (*WJW* 1: 240).[1] In his insistence on popular sovereignty, Witherspoon espoused a republican politics, and in his claim that all people deserve equal say, he espoused a liberal ideal, but "the people" in *Ecclesiastical Characteristics* were specifically defined as a Protestant lot clamoring for more religion and less refinery. Even in his pre-American writings, Witherspoon blended ascriptive and liberal elements into his republicanism.

In 1766, the College of New Jersey was without a president, and the trustees disagreed about its future direction. New Side leaders, who had dominated the administration since the 1740s, insisted on another New Side evangelical, while moderates and Old Side proponents demanded a more orthodox leader. Witherspoon seemed to represent the best of all possible candidates: he had allegiances with Scottish evangelicals very similar to American New Side theologians, yet his religious views were very orthodox, and he had openly criticized certain evangelical tenets, such as the necessity of zeal or the opposition to any established church government. Also, Witherspoon trained at Scottish universities (he studied alongside Hugh Blair), so he knew the secular curriculum and had commitments to a program that would prepare young men for both religious and secular lives. He was perfectly capable of offering a curriculum to train young capitalists for professional pursuits. As a compromise candidate between feuding Old and New Side trustees, as a political leader with liberal, republican, and ascriptive sympathies, as an educator able to offer pragmatic professional training for the commercial economy, Witherspoon appealed to the trustees and was hired as president in 1768. In his rhetorical pedagogy at the college, he articulated a program of civic education to the cultural and economic interests in New Jersey, thereby directly participating in the hegemonic struggles between freeholding capitalist farmers and feudal proprietors, between New and Old Side Presbyterians, between genteel and respectable cultures.

John Witherspoon's Republican Rhetorical Education

During his time as president of the college (1768–94), Witherspoon incorporated many republican principles in his *paideia* and specifically in his rhetorical pedagogy. When he arrived, the college had a professor of mathematics and natural philosophy, but no one to fill the chairs in moral philosophy or in divinity, so Witherspoon assumed these responsibilities in addition to his duties as president. He delivered lectures on moral philosophy, eloquence, and divinity to juniors and seniors. He also stressed education in the natural sciences by purchasing a number of apparatuses, like an orrery made by David Rittenhouse and globes to teach geography.[2] He believed rhetoric to be the cornerstone of a republican education, so he advocated education in English grammar, composition, and oratory across the curriculum. He personally administered the grammar school on campus, added reading and writing in English to the entrance requirements (1769), promoted speaking societies where students practiced public debate in English, and instituted a graduate program to prepare students "for serving their Country in public Stations" in part by teaching them to become eloquent orators in their native language (qtd. in T. Miller, "Introduction" 21). (James Madison was the first to graduate from this program and also the college's first graduate student who did not study divinity.)

Not only did Witherspoon teach his students that the good republican citizen is a rhetorically active member of the public sphere, but he also embodied that ideal both in Scotland and New Jersey. In America, Witherspoon advocated political separation from the British Empire, distinguishing himself as the only clergyman to sign the Declaration of Independence. He also served in Congress from 1776–79 and again from 1780–81. He invited the Continental Congress to hold session at the college when disgruntled soldiers staged a mutiny and ran them out of Philadelphia in the summer of 1783 (Collins, *The Continental*). His system of education not only appealed to the republican ideal of active citizenship but also to the bourgeois hope for professional education. During Witherspoon's tenure, many attended the college for professional, not ministerial, accreditation. The number of students entering the ministry decreased significantly (Collins, *President* 2: 1–55).

His lectures on moral philosophy showed a particular concern with citizen virtue, which he discussed in terms adopted from Scottish common-sense philosophy, as propounded by figures like Francis Hutcheson and Thomas Reid. Though Witherspoon opposed Scottish moderates, he adopted much of their common-sense creed, and he articulated this moral philosophy not to a possessive individualism of personal conscience as often attributed to Hutcheson (T. Miller, *Formation* 187), but rather to a belief in divinely ordained and implanted common sentiment, a shared, divinely rooted *sensus communis* that could form the basis for republican rhetorical exchange. Surely, Witherspoon's common-sense philosophy put him at odds with idealists like Samuel Johnson.[3] By emphasizing the divine origins of common sense, he also differed from Scottish moderate individualism. In fact, it would be unfair to paint all of the common-sense tradition with possessive-individualist colors. Thomas Reid, after all, often described common sense as an understanding of one's place in a hierarchical, divinely established social order. For Reid, to have divinely implanted common sense was "to be suited to our state and rank in [God's] creation" (76). Witherspoon also placed a divine element in common-sense tradition, and he articulated this entire psychological system to a hierarchical social order. Common sense, for Witherspoon, did not isolate the individual conscience from all social circumstances. It shackled the individual conscience to God's word and to the moral mandates delivered by His messengers. This common sense also provided a common ground of republican consensus.

While citing Hutcheson, he taught students that "a sense of moral good and evil is as really a principle of our nature, as either the gross external or reflex senses," but unlike Hutcheson he separated the moral from the aesthetic senses (*WJW* 3: 379). This separation points to an important deviation from the genteel Scots. For Hutcheson and Blair, the public sphere was a vital place where people could discuss shared political concerns in a common vocabulary, but this was not the Roman agora or the colonial town square. Scottish gentry imagined the public sphere as a group of genteel literati discussing aesthetic issues among British aristocracy. By collapsing moral into aesthetic taste, theorists like Hutcheson imagined and helped to construct a parlor of polite conversation whose participants avoided overt political discussion and thereby absented themselves from their own government. The political absenteeism implicit in this rhetorical practice permitted British rule of Scotland at a time when British parliament effectively controlled Scottish affairs by dissolving their government and allowing only a token few seats in the British assembly.

By splitting the moral and aesthetic senses, Witherspoon imagined and invited his students to participate in another public sphere, one separate from the parlor, where political agents could discuss current events and influence government (T. Miller, "Witherspoon"). In the 1760s, Witherspoon invited his students to enter the public sphere of American politics and to discuss British political platforms in the common vocabulary provided by their shared moral sense. These same lectures delivered throughout the eighteenth century continually invited students to participate in a public arena where they could influence their government. Like Hutcheson, Blair, and others, Witherspoon promoted a particular moral character among his students, a character in line with his ideal version of the "good man skilled in speaking": politically engaged and guided by a common, divinely granted moral sense. His notion of civic virtue and his dedication to the politically active republican citizen led to a continual focus on public debate about politically relevant issues. Witherspoon's students at commencement exercises often repeated the vocabulary of republicanism, debating issues of citizen virtue, national prosperity, luxury, and corruption. They also demonstrated a remarkable knowledge of contemporary political and economic policy before the Revolution, often directly addressing the merits of specific policies. (See table 5.1.) After the Revolution, students continued to engage in nuanced debates about public policy. They cut their oratorical teeth on topics like free trade, patriotism, king's rights, and whether or not manufacturing deserved federal backing.

Probably the college's most famous politically charged public debate was held on July 4, 1783, before the Continental Congress (then holding session at Princeton). Ashbel Green and Gilbert Tennent Snowden debated the superiority of republican government. At the commencement celebration that same year, students debated the merits of "cool and dispassionate" eloquence in a democratic society. George Washington and several other congressional celebrities attended and remarked on the patriotism displayed. One attendant, an eavesdropping British officer, later recalled that "the orations of the younger boys were full of the coarsest invectives against British tyranny" (Collins, *Continental* 77–80, 156–63). Of course, by encouraging rhetorical norms of an engaged republican democracy, Witherspoon upset those arguing for an authoritarian curriculum in support of British imperial policy. One citizen writing in the *New York Gazette and Weekly Mercury* (24 Nov. 1772) complained that Witherspoon's curricu-

Table 5.1: Selected topics debated at commencement exercises during John Witherspoon's tenure as president

Date	Topic Debated
September 28, 1768	It is in the interest of any nation, to have the trade of its new countries as free from embarrassments as possible. (*Documents* 26:287)
September 26, 1770	The non-importation agreement reflects a glory on the American merchants and is a noble exertion of self denial and public spirit. (*Documents* 27:268)
September 30, 1773	The corruption of state is not hastened by the improvement of taste and literature; but by the introduction of wealth. (*Documents* 29:51)
October 24, 1774	Whether a state which derives all the necessaries and conveniences of life from its own territories, is preferable to a state which, by means of foreign commerce, is supplied with all the elegancies of different climates. (*Documents* 29:497)
September 28, 1775	A retired and solitary life has no tendency to promote knowledge, happiness, or virtue. (*Documents* 31:205)

lum promoted faction and dissent, unlike the more admirable imperial *paideiai* found at the College of Philadelphia and at King's College (*Documents* 28: 345–59).

Students practiced their public speaking skills outside of the official college curriculum in debating societies, where they continued to make use of republican topics. When Witherspoon arrived in 1768, two clubs were already present, the Plain-Dealing and the Well-Meaning, both founded in 1765, but their rancorous disagreements disrupted college affairs and eventually the faculty dissolved the clubs (1769). A year later, a new society was founded under the politically charged name *Whig*. The Well-Meaning Club renamed itself the Cliosophic Society. Like the literary societies at other colleges, these organizations provided a forum where students could practice public speaking, debate, and writing and where they could become acquainted with literature.[4] Though no records exist of disputations in either society prior to 1792, judging by the minutes after this date, the groups appear to have debated politically charged topics much like the college's required exercises.[5] (See table 5.2.) Debate, however, was not the only thing that went on in these societies. The paper wars were also a vital part of students' rhetorical training in the early 1770s.

During paper wars, the societies lobbed satiric ad-hominem verses at one another. Whenever a verse was completed, members would call the faculty and students to hear it. This would go on for days until a winner was declared or until the faculty tired of having their schedules and their classes interrupted (Beam 59–67). Though less apparently politically motivated than the societies' disputation topics, the paper wars did help students to learn an important literary vehicle operative in the republican agora: satire. Poems from the paper war of 1771, for example, written by Whig Society members Hugh Henry Brackenridge, Philip Freneau, and James Madison, all demonstrate verse patterns and literary postures very similar to those used by eighteenth-century political pamphleteers who published satiric works in newspapers, on broadsides, and in stand-alone pamphlets. Like the Connecticut Wits (Timothy Dwight and John Trumbull) who trained themselves to write political satire at Yale during the 1770s, these Whig poets sharpened their satiric axes on literary society stones. They even titled their collection of poems against the Cliosophic Society "Satires Against the Tories," implying that Whig members defended republican liberty against Clio tyranny. The poems themselves are less than remarkable, mostly exercises in crude derision. One poem, for instance, ridicules a student's delivery during declamation exercises, while another ridicules a young man for being the son of a lowly tailor.

Set in concert with Witherspoon's emphasis on civic virtue, and with the politically charged topics debated at commencement and in the literary societies, these paper wars completed the framework of a republican rhetorical pedagogy at the College of New Jersey. Contemporary historians of rhetoric wanting to find a democratic republican ancestor in John Witherspoon have done so in good faith and with ample evidence. But when one looks closely at other aspects of Witherspoon's *paideia,* it becomes evident that like all other civic educators of this time, his republi-

Table 5.2: Selected topics debated at the Whig and the Cliosophic societies

Date	Topic Debated
Whig Society ("Whig Society Archives")	
May 3, 1802	Will the cessation of hostilities between France and Great Britain be of disadvantage to the United States?
June 21, 1802	Would a standing army be of advantage to the United States?
August 16, 1802	Is it requisite to the liberty of a nation that the bulk of the people be enlightened?
August 30, 1802	Which ought most to be attended to, manufacturing or commerce?
Cliosophic Society ("Cliosophic Society Archives")	
July 12, 1792	Whether was it political or not in Congress to grant the lands over the Ohio to the soldiery, or would it not have been better to have paid in specie?
August 22, 1792	Are not factions serviceable to the state?
November 21, 1792	Whether in the present state of affairs in Europe would the establishment of a republican form of government in France be beneficial or not?
December 12, 1792	Does refinement of manners add to national happiness?

canism was articulated to specific economic and cultural elements in early American society. Particularly, Witherspoon advocated a professional pragmatism and a liberalism that suited New Jersey's freeholding bourgeoisie. His rhetorical education was also articulated to an ascriptivism that limited citizenship to Calvinist Protestants.

Witherspoon's Bourgeois Liberal Republican *Paideia*

The bourgeois quality of Witherspoon's republican *paideia* manifests itself in his lectures on eloquence, which encouraged an open and inclusive space of debate by tendering oratorical acumen to all. In this regard, Witherspoon participated in the civil-society tradition of rhetorical deliberation, one often articulated to liberalism. In the first few lectures, Witherspoon promised an inclusive public sphere by proclaiming that anyone could improve with diligent practice and adherence to the rules of study. He consistently placed his advice on the side of pragmatic use rather than aesthetic appreciation, always assuring his students that anyone could improve. These two aspects of Witherspoon's lectures, their pragmatism and the inclusive public space that they projected, made them perfectly suitable to the economic interests of New Jersey commercial farmers who saw education as a means of professional advancement. Like Benjamin Franklin, Witherspoon promoted practical training in public address, something that contenders in a capitalist order would need. Unlike William Smith or John Andrews, he spent little time teaching rhetoric as an interpretive art, preferring to trim the corrupting excesses of genteel culture and to preserve its more respectable center. Unlike William Samuel Johnson, he promised an open political arena where everyone, not just the "natural aristocracy," could participate in public debate. Though he certainly articulated his rhetorical pedagogy to bourgeois mores, he never lost sight of certain republican principles, such as a continuing concern for civic virtue and a desire to create a like-minded community of discoursing subjects.

Both Hugh Blair and Witherspoon studied rhetoric under John Stevenson, professor of logic and metaphysics, so it should come as no surprise to find commonalities among their lectures. For instance, Witherspoon, like Blair, offered little advice about inventing arguments, saying "it exceeds the power of man to teach it with effect" (*WJW* 3: 541). Like Blair, Witherspoon spent most of his time discussing style, and he also divided oratory into three categories: the pulpit, the bar, and promiscuous assemblies. While Blair and Witherspoon may resemble one another in many regards, their political allegiances differed dramatically. Blair trained his students to rhetorically function among British aristocracy, focusing on stylistic traits and cultivation of literary taste that would facilitate circulation in British high society. Witherspoon trained his students to function rhetorically in an agonistic arena of political debate. The principal difference between the two is the amount of time dedicated to appreciation of great literary works and examination of literary genres. Blair dedicated several lectures to closely reading and pointing out the aesthetic beauty in great writing, and he also taught his students to recognize and examine literary genres popular in polite society.[6] Witherspoon never taught his students aesthetic appreciation for its own purpose, and he never discussed genteel genres. In fact, like many orthodox Calvinists, he rejected drama altogether, even disapproved of the stage, thinking it morally depraved.

His first five lectures discussed eloquence in general, giving rules for its study and practical advice for those wanting to improve their abilities. Like Blair, he dedicated lectures to taste, criticism, and composition, but, unlike Blair, he spent little time on the former two. In fact, taste disappears altogether until the last lecture (lecture 16). After telling his students that great orators possess both natural talent and extensive training, he chose to focus on the latter, saying that anyone can improve the talent s/he possesses. He offered five practices for studying eloquence: study and imitation of great speakers, exercise in pronunciation, acquaintance with the rules of eloquence, avoidance of bad habits, and following one's nature. These five practices stretched over two lectures that also gave advice about which authors to study (Addison, Steele, Pope, and Swift) and which phrases and rhetorical habits to avoid. Lecture 4 defined effective eloquence as both informative and persuasive. Witherspoon said that the rhetor informs the audience by clearly providing information and persuades the audience by appealing to commonly held sentiments. Unlike William Smith and Samuel Johnson, Witherspoon's notion of informing the audience did not depend on any ideal of clear or proper reasoning. Witherspoon defined language as a communally constructed system of arbitrarily agreed upon signs and claimed that the orator uses figures to persuade people by forming communities of commonly felt emotions and commonly imagined ideas. This treatment of description and persuasion points to the communicative (community forming) capacity of language central to Witherspoon's republican rhetorical pedagogy. The pragmatic advice that he offered and his emphasis on education in the vernacular appealed to New Jersey's bourgeois citizens, to their interest in education for professional advancement.

The fifth lecture stressed the practice of eloquence by offering a history of effective oratory. Witherspoon told his students that "those who have given the history of oratory have rather given us the history of the teachers of the art than its progress and effects. It must be observed, however, that in this, as well as in poetry, criticism is the child and not the father of genius" (*WJW* 3: 507). He offered as examples of great orators George Whitefield and William Pitt, two civically active figures, a far cry from the prim poets and aesthetic essayists that Blair exalted as paragons of eloquence. Witherspoon also claimed that rhetoric has the most power in "promiscuous assemblies," like the town square or the political stump, thereby avoiding the parlors and the ballrooms of corrupting gentility. Throughout these lectures, Witherspoon carefully differentiated respectable rhetorical norms and spaces from corrupt, genteel genres and overly refined parlors. In doing so, he participated in a cultural warfare waged against New Jersey's genteel proprietary class. Witherspoon's rhetorical education appropriated the republican discourse of corruption, articulating it to the respectable culture in circulation among New Jersey's freeholding capitalists.

In lectures 6 through 12, Witherspoon offered advice about using figures and tropes and the types of rhetorical style. He mentioned three types of style—simple, sublime, and mixed—discussing the simple and the sublime in detail. Witherspoon argued that sublimity was a quality only perceptible to those with "taste," but he did not dwell on aesthetic appreciation. Rather, he taught students to produce sublime oratory. After recapitulating Longinus, he gave concrete advice about inciting emotion through language and writing descriptive passages to fire the audience's imagination. He even provided guidelines for rhetorically raising the passions: learn about the world; feel the emotion incited; never raise the emotion higher than the subject admits; and pay attention to gesture and posture. Other lectures on style continued this pragmatism. Lectures 7 and 8, for instance, presented figures and tropes with advice about how to create and use them in sublime oratory.

Lectures 9 and 10 discussed the simple manner of composition, differentiating it from "low" or "mean" writing and pointing to its uses. (Witherspoon mentioned that a person of true taste would know the difference between the vulgar and simple styles.) Lecture 10 covered several stylistic virtues that Witherspoon attributed to good writing and several that he thought could produce nothing but oratorical bombast and vulgarity. After advising against sententious writing, Witherspoon argued that a style could be described as simple, smooth, sweet, concise, elegant, ornate, just, nervous, chaste, and severe. In this taxonomy of stylistic variety, he offered his students significant possibility. He also demonstrated a respectable republican concern that excessively ornate prose could corrupt virtuous display. Simplicity, said Witherspoon, rots in an excess of "sentiment" or "too great refinement" (*WJW* 3: 530). He concluded his discussion of civic virtue and stylistic simplicity by claiming that a community's discourse both reflects and affects its virtue: "not only the circumstances which appear in a language, but several others that have also been attributed to climate, owe very little to it, but to the state of mankind and the progress of society" (*WJW* 3: 535).

Lectures 11 and 12 covered the five canons of rhetoric. Though he offered no practical advice for inventing arguments, he did discuss arrangement, saying that good order does five things to a discourse: makes it easily understood, gives it force, makes it memorable, makes it beautiful, and makes it brief. He also gave three pieces of practical advice about ordering arguments: pay attention to the arrangement of the entire argument; subdivide the main argument into smaller points that can be treated individually (he offered lots of advice about how individual points should be subdivided and related to the larger argument); order emotional appeals so that they ascend in pathetic effect. Lecture 12 on style and pronunciation focused mainly on harmony and cadence in composition and delivery. Witherspoon also advised that students appear sincere, practice distinct articulation, practice a conversational tone, follow the manners of decent company, and learn their vocal ranges. As with the rest of his lectures, Witherspoon's treatment of the rhetorical canons, excepting his treatment of invention, taught students how to create effective arguments. His pragmatism appealed to the bourgeois belief that anyone with proper training can enter and prosper in civil society—in the market as well as the public sphere.

Lecture 13 discussed the ends of rhetoric, which Witherspoon divided into information, demonstration, persuasion, and entertainment. He offered descriptions of model orations aimed at each end and advice for attaining each ideal. He concluded the lecture by distinguishing between wit and drollness, saying that the latter lowly invites the audience to laugh at the rhetor, while the former admirably directs satire toward an object. As his earlier writings show, Witherspoon was an apt political satirist. By teaching his students to deploy this style of writing, he taught them one of the rhetorical norms common in early American public discourse. Many of Witherspoon's students would go on to write their own satiric pieces. The most famous is Hugh Henry Brackenridge, who wrote *Modern Chivalry* (1792–1815) while pursuing a political career in Pennsylvania, eventually serving as a justice in the state supreme court. During the Revolution, Brackenridge consciously wrote literary work for political effect, subordinating aesthetic quality to public duty and producing what one historian calls "patriotic litanies" (Ellis, *After the Revolution* 87). Later, when he returned to satiric writing, Brackenridge used the form he learned under Witherspoon's tutelage to pick apart the contradictions in American society. Brackenridge's novel is a mock romance, showcasing periodic digs at the ignorance of local political assemblies and the foolishness of both the Democratic-Republican and Federalist parties. While at Princeton, he internalized a republican commitment to improving citizen virtue through rhetorical effort. Thanks to Witherspoon's instruction, he "foresaw that public opinion was destined to exercise an unprecedented influence on arts and letters in America" (Ellis, *After the Revolution* 110).

Lectures 14 and 15 distinguished between the eloquence of the pulpit, the bar, and promiscuous assemblies, offering advice for discourse in each. These two lectures closely resemble Blair's own adaptation of the classical division among epideictic, judicial, and deliberative oratory. Lecture 16 offered the only treatment of taste and criticism. Witherspoon told students that taste was grounded in one's nature but improved through exposure to and rational appreciation of great art. He concluded this lecture by reminding students that a sense of moral virtue had no connection to a sense of taste. His repeated separation of aesthetics and civic virtue reveals a typically bourgeois republican inclination to enjoy the cultural fruits of commercial progress without falling into its corrupting excesses. Cultural historian Joseph Ellis notes that in this era "[h]ostility towards the arts was part of a larger hostility towards the liberal values of the marketplace" (*After the Revolution* 35). In his continual assertion that civic virtue has nothing to do with aesthetic refinement, in his efforts to stop stylistic bombast, in all his pains to step away from belletrism's genteel excesses, Witherspoon laid bare his republican concerns. While these reservations appealed to the era's dominant political discourse, they also appealed to the New Jersey freeholder's reservations about proprietary gentility.

Though Witherspoon adapted republican discourse to the interests of New Jersey's freeholding citizens, he was no modern-day Cicero. As it turned out, he openly opposed certain classically republican principles, such as the subordination of private commercial acquisition to the public good. In many regards, Witherspoon was a laissez-faire liberal, advocating free trade and commercial development while he served in Congress.[7] His liberalism not only appeared in speeches made about federal trade policy but also in his lectures on moral philosophy. Witherspoon championed a Lockean consensualist notion of citizenship, in which one's membership in a political order derives from free choice to enter a social compact. He began his lecture on politics by supposing "the state of natural liberty antecedent to society" (*WJW* 3: 417). From this premise, he advanced to other liberal mainstays, such as the right to property based on one's investment of labor into natural resources. Property, said Witherspoon, forms the basis for "universal industry," which is good for all (*WJW* 3: 422). He separated civil society from the state, defining the former as a free realm where reasonable citizens form contractual relationships without state interference. He even offered extensive reflection on the right to contract and the nature of contracts in a civil order. Witherspoon admired commerce and the prosperity it brought to New Jersey citizens. At the same time, he desperately worried about the corrupting influence of genteel culture. In all, Witherspoon articulated republicanism, laissez-faire economic policy, liberal notions of citizenship and property, and a pragmatic, respectable program of rhetorical education into a hegemonic cluster that appealed to the dominant political discourse of the day and to the economic, social, cultural, and political interests of New Jersey's emergent capitalist class. When examining these various articulations, it is hard to assert that Witherspoon's republican rhetorical *paideia* is a useful counter to modern-day liberal rhetorical pedagogy. His republicanism appears compromised, his pedagogy deeply invested in eighteenth-century New Jersey struggles for hegemony.

Witherspoon's Ascriptive, Liberal, Republican *Paideia*

If liberalism and republicanism, a developing commercialism and a fear of its cultural corruptions, were the sole elements at play at Princeton, then this analysis, and this book, would be concluded. But there's more. As noted in the introduction to this chapter, Protestantism had a central role in the college's mission and in the freeholding bourgeois resistance to genteel proprietors. Witherspoon himself was an unfaltering Calvinist, and his faith played an integral part in his politics and in the moral character that he promoted. In the words of one historian, the Princeton curriculum attempted to "harmonize, under the canopy of republican patriotism, a traditional Presbyterian faith and the moderate Scottish Enlightenment" (Noll 6). Though he referenced Montesquieu and Rousseau in his lectures on moral philosophy, his proposed civic virtue looks nothing like the commercial cosmopolitanism or the Spartan asceticism found in these writers' works. His religion informed his civic republicanism by providing a millennial view of time and by connecting public religious performance to the formation, distribution, and invocation of virtue. His efforts at the college can be summarized as an attempt to mix political liberalism, laissez-faire economic policy, republican discourse, and Calvinist evangelism.

Like many early American Calvinists, Witherspoon imagined the colonies as a chosen land where God's elect would build a perfect society to welcome Christ's second coming. He imagined the political animal as a religiously trained, divinely inspired, and civically minded rhetor/preacher. He embodied this ideal, as his political speeches attest. In his "Memorial and Manifesto of the U.S.," for instance, he argued that independence from Britain was "the purpose of God Almighty" (*WJW* 4: 370). In his "Speech in Congress on the Confederation," he said that "human science and religion have kept company together, and greatly assisted each other's progress in the world. I do not say that intellectual and moral qualities are in the same proportion in particular persons; but they have a great and friendly influence upon one another, in societies and larger bodies" (*WJW* 4: 350–51).

His sermons, likewise, conflated religious and political training, the millennium and the republic. In "The Dominion of Providence over the

Passions of Men" (1776), Witherspoon openly connected his liberal republican ideal to his Calvinist millennial vision, calling on God to "grant that in America true religion and civil liberty may be inseparable, and that the unjust attempts to destroy the one, may in the issue tend to the support and establishment of both" (*WJW* 3: 46).[8] Along with their tradition of millennial prophecy, British Atlantic Calvinists also had a long history of communitarian political organization. One historian of early American theology and politics, Alan Heimart, has argued that "the Calvinist pursuit of happiness was, almost by definition, a quest for the great community," a quest that easily mapped onto the civic republican imagination of, and hope for, a vibrant public sphere (103). The community of saints, in Calvinist theology, was bound together by a common sense that was inflected by notions of regeneration and invoked in sermon rhetoric: "An eloquent depiction of social beauty was their means of inducing harmonious union [. . .] Yet before European theorists had [. . .] reduced the rhetoric of sensation to its simplest elements, the Calvinist ministry, in its delineations of the united Church, were assuming this to be the orator's role" (Heimart 115–16). Witherspoon's notion of common sense, inflected by Scottish philosophy and a Calvinist belief in divine beauty as perceived by righteous saints, thus had a rhetorical element: demonstration of faith through oratorical performance that other saints would presumably recognize as moral. The agora of public presentation was not wholly inclusive since not all people are saved, and appropriate rhetorical performance must follow the dictates of regenerate taste. In short, Witherspoon's belief that good citizens are also good Protestants incorporated an ascriptive component to his republican ideal, one that directly contradicted his liberal claim that citizenship derives from consent.

The vita activa as presented in Witherspoon's lectures involved much arguing about political matters and also much praying for religious salvation. He opened his lectures on moral philosophy by isomorphically connecting political theory to Calvinist theology: "I am of opinion, that the whole Scripture is perfectly agreeable to sound philosophy" (*WJW* 3: 369). He also told his students that the moral sense had divine origins and was awakened by regeneration.[9] In his theological writings, he further connected the moral sense to salvation, saying that "a person possessed only of understanding and taste, may admire the sallies of holy fervor" (*WJW* 3:

371). In his sermons, particularly, Witherspoon promoted civic gatherings for public worship to create communal bonds along a divinely inspired and shared moral sense. In "Frequency and Importunity in Prayer," he said, "Serious persons, by associating together, direct each other by their counsels, embolden each other by their examples, and assist each other by their prayers" (*WJW* 3: 464). Likewise in the "Nature and Extent of Visible Religion," he argued for the civic duty of public prayer and worship, saying, "We are bound so to order our outward conversation, as that it may on the one hand, contribute nothing to the corruption of others, but rather that they may be invited to the practice, and persuaded of the excellence and amiableness of true religion" (*WJW* 3: 543). In this imagined civico-religious public sphere, rhetorical performance is the sharing conduit, promoting, reassuring, and spreading the common moral sense needed to achieve a millennial republic. While Witherspoon invited everyone to join this conversation, he also demanded that participants display a certain moral character and adhere to the rules of tasteful discourse in their performances. His lectures on moral philosophy taught students this Calvinist civic virtue.

Witherspoon's first five lectures on moral philosophy discussed the moral sense and its divine origin and offered hints about the republican millennium to come. Upon this foundation, the remaining ten lectures summarized and commented on eighteenth-century political theory, discussing and resonating both liberal and republican thinkers such as Locke, Rousseau, Pufendorf, and Montesquieu. These lectures laid eighteenth-century political theory on top of Protestant theology by putting the moral sense at the root of all human interaction and by praising certain aspects of bourgeois liberal democracy as the highest possible human achievement, the millennial perfection prophesied in jeremiads. Witherspoon particularly valued the division between civic and domestic life; a three-part government with checks and balances among the judiciary, executive, and legislative bodies; faith in the presumably extant social compact; an advanced legal system; and developed laws for property ownership and contract negotiation. But, despite his appreciation of and advocacy for many of its institutions, Witherspoon never promoted the secular commercial society that Franklin advocated. Instead, he offered an ascriptive, liberal republic where Protestantism and regenerate education would disseminate civic virtue.

Though his lectures on moral philosophy may have ended with bourgeois liberal notions about the rights to contract and property, they began with Protestant notions of religious duty. His lectures on divinity placed religious knowledge in the most privileged position, the foundation for all other intellectual and political pursuits. Echoing yet substantially revising Cicero, he said, "Piety without literature, is but little profitable; and learning, without piety, is pernicious to others, and ruinous to the possessor" (*WJW* 4: 11).[10] His sermon "On the Religious Education of Children" claimed that public (dis)approval, as guided by divine statutes into a salutary "visible religion," could and should mold the moral character of young children. Nevertheless, he said that public shame and praise should lead to the ultimate approval: "final acceptance with God through Christ" (*WJW* 2: 261). His "Letters on Education" focused on similar themes of authority and example. He said that a parent's first duty is to establish authority over the child by habitually playing seemingly cruel games like denying pleasant things solely to show that the parent can do so (*WJW* 4: 130–36). Parents should then shape the child's moral character in a religious mold: "It is a noble support of authority, when it is really and visibly directed to the most important end [. . .] the glory of God in the eternal happiness and salvation of children" (*WJW* 4: 140). Once authority is established, parents should teach by pious example. This model of education through religiously inflected authority and example is not only suited to a happy family but is necessary to a sound republic because it creates a morally sound populace. In a marvelous conflation of the republican belief in widespread citizen education and the Protestant belief in education for obedience to divine edict, Witherspoon said that "religion is the great polisher of the common people" (*WJW* 4: 146).

And, of course, rhetorical practice occupied a central position in this Protestant imaginary. While he taught civic republicanism at the College of New Jersey, he also taught its practice through instruction in English rhetoric, composition, and oratory, but always with one eye on a Calvinist God ruling over the millennial republic. Indeed, Witherspoon's constant reference to the vulgar public and his advice that students avoid corrupt, overly bombastic, ornate, or unchaste discourse morally resonated a message that good orators only speak in certain ways about certain things. In later writings, like the "Druid" articles, which he wrote as a series to be published in local newspapers, Witherspoon further advised against vulgar usage and hoped for the formation of national political character through dissemination of proper language. His concerns about "low phrases and vulgar terms" reflected both a bourgeois respectable reaction against the genteel culture of New Jersey proprietors and a Protestant concern that such cosmopolitanism would corrupt the civic virtue necessary for a millennial republic *(WJW* 4: 468). Witherspoon, like his fellow middle colony freeholders, articulated a version of commercialism to a Protestant reservation about cultural refinery, and he wrapped all this in a republican rhetorical theory obsessed with preserving virtuous style.

The rhetoric he taught in his lectures bears out this connection between religion and politics. Witherspoon's objection to overly flowery, ornamented, "unchaste," or bombastic discourse was typical of evangelical Calvinist ministers in early America and in Scotland. By adulating the plain style, and by claiming that sublimity related more to subject matter than to use of figures, Witherspoon taught a civically Calvinist rhetoric. In his lectures on divinity, he even said that Biblical authors offer the best examples of "propriety and taste" as well as "many examples of sublimity and majesty [. . .] superior to any uninspired writings whatsoever" (*WJW* 4: 30). He connected the two: religion and politics, pulpit and public sphere, preacher and politician. And he taught his students to participate in an ascribed arena of particularly educated and trained men debating in a strictly determined, moral language. All of this appealed to the New Jersey freeholding population, many of them Presbyterian, many suspicious of proprietary gentility, many speaking the same republican vocabulary of corruption and virtue.

Witherspoon's Republican Rhetorical Legacy

Though Witherspoon's immediate influence on early American civic education ended in 1794, he affected other curricula through his students. In effect, he directed Princeton well into the nineteenth century. During his tenure at the college, several of his students became successful instructors themselves. For instance, Samuel M'Corcle opened a prosperous gram-

mar school in Goshen (*Documents* 28: 382), and in 1771 Frederick Freling-
housen was appointed to teach English language and grammar at Queen's
College (Rutgers) (*Documents* 27: 607–09). Princeton's next two presidents had been Witherspoon's students, as well as professors during his
tenure as president. Samuel Stanhope Smith (president 1795–1812) was
the professor of moral philosophy, and he taught the course on eloquence
when Witherspoon was off performing his duties at Congress. Smith's lectures on moral philosophy mirror Witherspoon's common-sense bent.
Like his mentor, Smith grounded his entire system in a religious framework. He told students that all political philosophy takes root in divinely
implanted moral sense and human reason. Smith delivered twenty-one
lectures in all, but he spent the first sixteen discussing the biological and
theological roots of human morality. In lecture 14, for example, Smith
taught his students that all people have a sense on which is imprinted "the
moral law of the universe" (*Lectures Corrected* 1: 302). Like Witherspoon,
Smith also anchored everything that he taught in his Protestantism. While
his lectures on moral philosophy explored what he called "natural" religion (divine laws as found in nature), his lectures on divinity explored
revealed religion (divine truths received through revelation) (*Lectures on
the Evidences* 3). He opened by declaring that "[t]heology is the science of
divine truth" (*Lectures on the Evidences* 1). Smith even followed his teacher
by connecting Christian virtue to rhetorical style. He said that rhetorical
simplicity indicates true divine wisdom while bombast and an excess of
"sentiment" betray the corrupting invocations of false prophets (*Lectures on
the Evidences* 176–97).

Ashbel Green was professor of mathematics and natural philosophy,
and he returned to become president from 1812–22. Like Witherspoon,
Green was an evangelical Calvinist, and he promoted revival and revelation throughout his tenure as president. Both Smith and Green continued
Witherspoon's mission to train divinely inspired saints for appropriately
chaste debate informed by revelation and divinely granted reason and
aimed at achieving the millennial republic. This ascriptive republicanism eventually caused students, trustees, and faculty much grief. During
Witherspoon's presidency, it was easy to believe that the college was a
stop on the road to the millennial republic, but, while this framework
categorized success as sanctity's reward, it also categorized calamities as

divine punishments. When Nassau Hall burned to the ground in 1802, Smith attributed it to "the progress of vice and irreligion" (qtd. in Noll 157). In 1807, when student rebellions shook the college, a new wave of trustees redefined their goals, taking attention away from political science and focusing on religious revival. They decided that Protestant ascriptivism, not liberal republicanism, would save the college, and they diverted funds away from the pursuit of natural philosophy and political science and toward Bible and tract societies. At this time, Ashbel Green spearheaded a campaign to found a seminary at Princeton. When Green became president, he eliminated Smith's course in moral and political philosophy, replacing it with Bible study and William Paley's *Natural Theology*. Witherspoon's ascriptive, liberal republican civic education at the College of New Jersey collapsed when social circumstances put weight on this *paideia*'s internal contradictions.

As I began this chapter, so I began this book—with reservations about the politics of republicanism and with a desire to pick apart the real work actuated by republican invocations in early American society. In John Witherspoon, we find that early American republican civic education was a complex, conflicted affair directly participating in particular economic, social, political, and cultural struggles over hegemony. In the Revolution, in the Constitution, and in Ashbel Green's presidency, history delivered its own judgment of Witherspoon's pedagogical accomplishments. Like his republicanism, this judgment is mixed. My depiction is not meant to demonize a heretofore admired figure. There is something wonderfully admirable and hopeful in this story, even in the episodes about Witherspoon's Presbyterianism. After all, freeholders made good use of Protestant disdain for refinery in their efforts to resist and depose a parasitic feudal poseur class. And concerns about rhetorical display of vulgarity in virtuous political discourse are not peculiar to eighteenth-century Protestants nor are they unreasonable. Recent studies of discursive civility in the U.S. Congress indicate that when legislators avoid name-calling, aspersions, pejoratives, and vulgarities, they tend to be more cooperative and more productive (Annenberg). Whether rhetorical decorum is promoted by appeals to Christian morality or to legislative efficacy should not matter to those genuinely interested in productive democratic deliberation. In the end, we should find in John Witherspoon an interesting, an accomplished, and above all, a conflicted figure. Once we acknowledge his complicated articulations among rhetorical theory, pedagogy, republicanism, free-holding economic interests, political liberalism, laissez-faire capitalism, and Presbyterian Calvinism, we cannot continue to position Witherspoon in the halcyon days of civic education before liberal tenets plunged rhetorical pedagogy into what Gregory Clark and S. Michael Halloran have called an ideology of "individual conscience" (13). Such is the upshot of this entire study. Now, as in the eighteenth century, republicanism is not good nor is it necessarily bad. It is interesting and potentially useful if we're careful about how its applications get articulated to other political and economic factors that shape a particular historical moment.

Conclusion
We Are All Republicans

What "ought to be" is therefore concrete; indeed it is the only realistic and historicist interpretation of reality, it alone is history in the making and philosophy in the making, it alone is politics.

—Antonio Gramsci

On March 4, 1801, after winning a narrow victory in an acrimonious presidential election, Thomas Jefferson delivered his first inaugural address, which, in the spirit of reconciliation, included the following, now famous statement: "We have called by different names brethren of the same principle. We are all republicans—we are all federalists." Of course, in his use of the term "republican," Jefferson referred to his own Democratic-Republican Party, but there was something else, something subtler, something distinctly republican (not in the partisan sense), happening that morning in front of the incomplete Capitol building, before Chief Justice John Marshall and the anxious American citizenry. Jefferson asserted that the politics of republicanism united the nation, exceeded the bounds of partisan conflict, infected every patriot, and endured in every American breast. In his private writings, Jefferson made this claim more pointedly: "[T]he mass of our countrymen, even those who call themselves Federalists, are republicans" (qtd. in Elkins and McKitrick 753). In his first inaugural, he appealed to republican political discourse as a uniting force, a common ground on which everyone could (dis)agree.

While Jefferson appealed to republicanism as a unifying force, a set of rhetorically constructed and circulated ideals that transcend partisan identification, this discourse fell out of favor among Americans not long after his presidency ended, and liberal political discourse achieved dominance in articulatory practice. Jeffersonian emphasis on limited government and free-market tenets like the free pursuit of profit among competing interests had already begun the transition to a new hegemonic political discourse (Schlesinger 520–21). After Jefferson, the road to Jacksonian liberalism was short and easy. Liberalism's dominance in American political discourse begins with the age of Jackson and extends into the twenty-first century. Though liberalism today may be the dominant discourse, it has been articulated to conflicting efforts at rhetorical education, as well as to contemporary economic developments. Liberalism may provide a common vocabulary, but this vocabulary is contested, as are a host of liberal rhetorical norms and liberal approaches to rhetorical education. We may have a different set of players and a new rhetorical deck, but the hegemonic game remains the same, a point that can be illustrated by sketching the principal lines of liberal discourse and by analyzing its articulation to conflicting rhetorical pedagogies and to contemporary economic institutions.

Liberalism and the Present Hegemony

Liberalism initially appeared during the seventeenth century as a reaction against monarchism and as a viable political discourse in alliance with a developing mode of capitalist production. Seventeenth- and eighteenth-century western European liberalism promoted common assumptions about good government. Specifically the liberal state was (and still is) imagined as an effort to bring together a collection of autonomous individuals with separately shaped personalities and desires into a social collective that does not violate the freedoms and interests of those involved. Liberalism typically presents history as the progressive expansion of individual freedoms through increasingly enlightened governments that more efficiently negotiate among various interests. Liberalism, therefore, imports the following: a belief in autonomous individuals capable of rational, critical thought; a belief in the separation of the private (including the family and the market) and the public (including the state); a belief that history progressively advances (or should advance) toward greater human liberty; a negative definition of rights (rights are defined as freedoms from various encroachments); and an effort to protect individual liberty from encroachment by other individuals or the state (Held 75–87). In the seventeenth and eighteenth centuries, liberal political discourse was articulated to a rhetorical practice often located in an imaginary space of public engagement. This is the liberal public sphere, best described by Jürgen Habermas in his now famous study *The Structural Transformation of the Public Sphere* (1962). Though it is dangerous to assume that public interaction must follow a political discourse's ideals (Hauser, *Vernacular* 46–55), many would justify certain rhetorical practices by referencing theoretical arguments, so we should consider how a political discourse like liberalism can be articulated to norms of rhetorical exchange.

According to Habermas, participants in seventeenth- and eighteenth-century liberal public spheres behaved as if they were private individuals in an unregulated arena of open discussion that would allow citizens rationally to hash out political possibilities that they could then apply to the state in electoral proceedings. Though a part of civil society, these public spheres mediated between autonomous individuals and the state. Through the public sphere, private individuals exerted control over the organization established to protect and to enforce their interests. Discussion should therefore follow certain rules, principal among them the bracketing of "private" interests and social markers. This discourse, ideally, would be inclusive, rational, disinterested (Habermas, *Structural* 30, 54). Habermas offers us an idealized picture of liberal public exchange, yes, but this ideal was articulated to real rhetorical practices. His studies of coffeehouses, salons, and literary debates indicate that discourse did indeed reflect these ideals, and other sociological studies of eighteenth-century French and British society indicate that in many instances people behaved accordingly (Habermas, *Structural* 31–43; Sennett 80–83). Liberal political discourse was thus articulated to norms of rhetorical practice, as well as to a nascent commercial order. Habermas argues that discourse among autonomously active and privately interested individuals contributed to a representative democracy suitable to a commercial society ("Three" 23).

However, liberal political discourse has not always been articulated to the same norms of rhetorical exchange. In fact, several recent scholars articulate liberal political discourse to a radically egalitarian practice of public exchange, one that certainly did not exist in eighteenth-century Western societies (Benhabib, Mary P. Ryan, Eley). These scholars articulate liberal political theory to radical social change by recognizing the disparity between public spaces and liberal promises. Articulations of liberal political discourse to various efforts at public rhetorical exchange demonstrate that there is a struggle over power in contemporary society and that both rhetorical norms and liberal political discourse are crucial elements in this struggle. Specific actors variously articulate liberalism to specific norms of rhetorical exchange. Likewise, assorted pedagogies have been woven into this hegemonic fabric, as they are articulated to liberal political discourse and to norms of liberal public exchange. In the late twentieth century, Patricia Roberts-Miller finds two strands of liberalism—traditional-universalist and deontological—articulated to different rhetorical pedagogies in the hegemonic struggle over contemporary humanities curricula, a struggle now commonly referenced as the "culture wars" (*Deliberate Conflict* ch. 1).

Traditional-universalist liberalism assumes that everyone, by virtue of being human, shares a body of concerns. Publicity must be built upon these commonalities. In a classic traditional-universalist moment during the 1980s, Allan Bloom insisted that teachers focus on "human nature" and that they help students to ask the question "what is man?" (20–21). Bloom claimed that the liberal rhetor must bracket everything not universal among (hu)mankind. Humanities instructors should teach the great works of Western literature and philosophy and devote less attention to issues of race, class, and gender, since these lack universality.

The culture wars of the 1980s were largely fought between traditional-universalist liberals like Allan Bloom and deontological liberals like Henry Giroux. For the deontological liberal, there is no solidly determinable human nature, so democratic public inclusivity must embrace multiple identities, multiple concerns in public debate. Giroux, writing with Stanley Aronowitz, defended several common liberal theoretic assumptions about the public sphere and its proper relationship to the state. Giroux and Aronowitz defined the public as "a space where people create the conditions not only where they can explore and talk about their needs, but also where democratic traditions function to mediate the role of government action." Giroux and Aronowitz hoped for a pedagogy of "critical literacy" and "civic courage" (Aronowitz and Giroux 219–20). Based on deontological liberal assumptions, Giroux has more recently called for a "border pedagogy" that encourages students of multiple races, classes, and ethnicities to enter and be active in the ostensibly open public sphere (*Border Crossings* 122, 133). Giroux articulated his own liberalism to a multicultural pedagogy of civic engagement with various peoples.

So far, I have discussed various articulations between liberal rhetorical norms, political discourse, and rhetorical pedagogies, but there is another element that deserves attention if we are to understand our own hegemonic order and liberalism's place therein: economics. Public-sphere theorists have long been aware that a given rhetorical effort at publicity depends on particular economic conditions.[1] Likewise, one can surmise that economic conditions will affect any effort to train citizens for participation in specific public spaces. Economism, therefore, brings to the table an understanding that political discourse and rhetorical pedagogy never function alone in the construction of social institutions. Henry Giroux's deontological liberal pedagogy appears quite appealing by itself but, when set in the context of postindustrial capitalism, begins to look more problematic. Giroux has tied his pedagogy to postmodernism, shorthand for the emergent cultural and intellectual developments of contemporary American society. Among these developments, within the vast array of cultural formations labeled *postmodern,* is the radical celebration of difference and diversity, a party at which Giroux dances his border pedagogy.

Giroux's celebration of postmodern multiculturalism exhibits a blindness typical to those measuring pedagogy, political discourse, and public rhetorical norms without weighing economics into the balance. He never considers that postmodernism, the music for his pedagogical jig, might also set the rhythm for a questionable economic symphony. However, several theorists have recently argued that postmodernism is a cultural formation amenable to the persistence of postindustrial capitalism (Harvey 327–59; Jameson, *Postmodernism*). In the ideology and organizational patterns of contemporary transnational corporations, one finds a mirror image of Giroux's border pedagogy. Business primers celebrate diversity, frown on sexism and racism, and practice a politics of difference (Hardt and Negri 150–54). After all, if a corporation will truly be transnational, it must teach its workers to interrogate and constructively manage the complications of identity and difference. Or, in Giroux's words:

> At issue here is not a patronizing notion of understanding the Other, but a sense of how the self is implicated in the construction of Otherness, how exercising critical attention to such a relationship might allow educators to move out of the center of the dominant culture toward its margins in order to analyze critically the political, social, and cultural lineaments of their own values and voices as viewed from different ideological and cultural spaces. (*Border Crossings* 141)

I encourage you to re-read the above passage replacing the word "educators" with the word "marketers." This exercise illustrates that perhaps humanities instructors in Giroux's model teach economically advantaged students who will eventually manage profit-driven industry to perniciously appropriate constructed identities for the further exploitation of labor. When unable to get unions outlawed (as Motorola accomplished in Malaysia), foreign-owned factories in Asia often hire young women— whose identities have been constructed in a patriarchal culture—because they are obedient and unlikely to organize (Greider 98). Crossing borders does not always lead to social justice.[2]

Of course, we must avoid privileging economics as the sole cause of cultural institutions. Pedagogy, political discourse, and public rhetorical norms are not and should not appear to be epiphenomena of economic systems. Rather, as historical materialists have long since illustrated, economic systems shape human interests, divide societies into classes, bring large groups together into common pursuits, and contribute to the overall trajectory of human history *without absolutely determining the course*. A liberal public sphere, for instance, is not an epiphenomenon of capitalism but rather a space semi-separate from, influenced by, and influencing economic systems.[3] Though systems of economic production might lie at the base, they are not the last word in social formations, a point argued by materialist rhetoricians calling for further consideration of economics in rhetorical and pedagogical theory (Cloud, "Rhetoric"; Aune, *Rhetoric* 118– 20). States, political theories, public spheres, and educational institutions all mediate their respective economic conditions. If rhetoricians care to understand the politics of public discourse and pedagogy, they must also understand the economic history in which various public spheres and pedagogical institutions develop.

The Republican Challenge to Liberal Hegemony

While liberal political discourse may have pushed republicanism off the main stage in the early nineteenth century, in recent times, scholars in a variety of fields have made a concentrated effort to resuscitate republican political discourse. At the forefront of the republican revival are rhetoricians promoting a new republican pedagogy. Republicanism is making a comeback because liberalism seems so hopelessly sutured to institutions like free-market capitalism, to the liberal public sphere and its individualist mores as described above.

In their efforts to challenge contemporary liberal hegemony, many have articulated republican political theory to a communitarian politics. Several revisionist historians have revived republican political discourse by noticing its prevalence in eighteenth-century public discussions (Bailyn, *Ideological;* Wood; McCoy; Pocock; Appleby, *Liberalism*). A brief review of republican tenets demonstrates their utility in the effort to unseat liberal hegemony. Republicanism defines rights in positive terms—citizens have the right to political participation—and imagines the state not as a protector of individual liberty but as a power to actuate communal resolve. Thus, for the republican, there is no sharp or necessary divide between civil society and the state. Gerard Hauser argues that it was common in ancient Athenian society to articulate republican political discourse to a specific rhetorical practice, one in which relatively homogenous citizens came together in "*agonistic relations* tending towards the recognition of virtuosity or *arête*" ("Civil" 35). According to Hauser, the classical republican public sphere was not a collection of differing individual interests but was rather an open place where citizens could engage in agonistic debate aimed at mutual understanding and collective will formation. The sole and enduring criterion of evaluation in the republican public sphere, the only consistent end toward which republicanism reaches, is the public good. For this reason, the liberal, extended, and protected "private" realm (the family, the market) is of less concern for republicans.

Hannah Arendt retheorized republicanism in the twentieth century to counter liberalism and its articulation to a civil society tradition of public debate. As Hauser has argued, in present-day America, the classical republican public sphere has been replaced by a tradition in which people's relationships are formed around their own individuality rather than their commitments to the collective good ("Civil" 28). Arendt tried to counter this liberal norm of public rhetorical exchange by resuscitating republican political discourse and then articulating it to a classical republican rhetorical practice of agonistic debate and community investment. While liberal political theory valorizes privacy above a citizen's public obligations, Arendt argued that citizen privacy is only necessary to allow some protection from glaring public lights. She held that the twentieth-century hypertrophy of private wealth accumulation diminished the space of public deliberation and influence. Arendt worried that the liberal public sphere was a weak servant to the private, a reverse order of ancient Greek society in which the private search for wealth served the public by caring for the realm of necessity and by making possible a productive focus on active citizenship (*Human* 66–78). Once people's needs are met, they can get to the more fulfilling work of public action (*Human,* chs. 3 and 5).

Sociologists composing the now canonical *Habits of the Heart* (1985) have likewise argued that nineteenth-century liberalism undid a valuable political tradition that should be resuscitated. They argued that republicanism "can be reappropriated in ways that respond to our present need" (283). More recently, Robert Putnam has maintained that liberalism among the baby boomer generation leads to waning civic involvement and a weaker nation overall (258). Putnam's cure for the collapse of American community is a revitalized sense of citizenship—an active principle forged in civic activities, a turn away from liberal individualism and toward sacrifice for the greater good. (See *Bowling Alone,* particularly ch. 23.) In order to counter liberal rhetorical norms and bureaucratic managerialism in the twentieth century, Alasdair MacIntyre has advanced the classical republican traditions of virtue and agonistic deliberation. (See *After Virtue.*) Just as liberalism is woven into social and political trends that sociologists find baleful, it has also been articulated to many rhetorical pedagogies (Roberts-Miller, *Deliberate*). Just as contemporary sociologists revitalize republican political discourse to counter the present hegemonic order, so have a number of scholars revitalized republicanism to counter the articulation between liberal discourse and pedagogical trends that they find objectionable.

Seen in the context of a present-day struggle against liberal hegemony, the Edenic narrative described in the introduction looks less like an effort at reviving a time-honored tradition and more like an effort to alter the present order by narrating republican political discourse back into the American tradition and then by articulating this discourse to norms of republican rhetorical exchange and to a civically charged program of rhetorical education. Thomas Miller, for instance, claims that, though the civic republican tradition has its problems, it can be revived to resist the articulations between liberal political discourse and curricula that do not encourage students to engage public debate (*Formation* 278–79). S. Michael Halloran similarly argues that rhetorical education lost interest in public discourse because, among other things, liberal principles infected rhetorical pedagogies. Halloran and Gregory Clark call for a revitalization of the civic republican tradition to counter liberalism's effects on American rhetoric. (See Halloran's article "From Rhetoric to Composition" and the introduction to *Oratorical Culture,* cowritten with Clark.)

Gregory Clark even finds in early American republican pedagogy an exemplar for twenty-first-century civic education, saying "Education in America was once democratic [. . .] and rhetoric was once at its center, but is no longer." He champions a "rhetoric of public discourse," teaching students to engage in agonistic debate, to argue multiple sides of an issue, and to search for common ground on which to build collective ethical positions and political actions. Clark aims to teach students the tools of democratic exchange (*Dialogue* 63–65), emphasizing rhetorical norms that Arendt and Hauser located in classical Athenian rhetorical practice: debate exercises to explore common ground; critical exercises to locate the points of stasis or disagreement; communal construction of political will, ethical norms, and knowledge; continual recognition that any resolution will always be open to redefinition through further debate (*Dialogue* xvi, 21–30, 51–61). Clark has mobilized an Edenic narrative about American education to revive republican political discourse as articulated to specific norms of public exchange and to a specific program for educating good citizens. He has constructed this constellation in the interest of resisting the present hegemonic articulations among liberal political discourse, liberal rhetorical norms, and liberal rhetorical pedagogy.[4]

Other educators on the political left also argue for the revival of republicanism in a charge against liberal hegemony. James Aune, an avowed

Marxist, has called for the revival of republican citizenship to counter the liberal belief that human beings are individuals first. Aune hopes to counter free-market capitalism and certain fads among inheritors of the 1960s new left by rhetorically reviving the republican sense of citizens as "political animals who can best fulfill their natures by participating in government, and who require a sense of communal virtue to sustain republican institutions" (*Rhetoric* 148–49). Even Henry Giroux, once a culture warrior fighting beneath the deontological liberal flag, has discovered republicanism. Giroux's recent *Take Back Higher Education* (2004), co-authored with Susan Searls Giroux, proposes a republican renaissance in American higher education, presenting this effort as a direct response to neoliberalism in American politics, particularly to the hyper-capitalist effort to have "market values supplant civic values" (221). The Girouxs repeat the Edenic republican narrative outlined in the introduction, saying, "The early transition from classical rhetoric to literary study, which shifted emphasis from civic to aesthetic concerns, is really about trading one form of citizenship for another—one participatory and public, the other nationalistic and privatized" (156). They end with a call for a revitalized republicanism purged of ascriptive components (167). After reviewing Clark's, Aune's, and the Girouxs's proposals to revive republican political theory, one may think that the articulation between republicanism and a new hegemonic order is sutured tightly to the political left, but a brief glance at other recent appropriations of republican discourse teaches that republicanism is not hemmed inexorably to any partisan fabric.

Among those on the political right, one finds republican political discourse articulated to political and cultural programs that Clark, Aune, and Giroux would find quite objectionable. Ascriptive republicanism, always a danger in American civic discourse, has been reborn in recent efforts to define civic virtue in Anglo-Protestant terms. Samuel Huntington, writing in *Foreign Policy* (March/April 2004), claimed that a stable American republic must stand on its "Anglo-Protestant culture," a civic ideal threatened by waves of Latin immigrants who refuse assimilation. Says Huntington, "There is no Americano dream. There is only the American dream created by Anglo-Protestant society" (45). Similarly, Victor Davis, a classics professor at California State University–Fresno, has worried extensively about the threat that Latin immigrants pose to the Anglo-Protestant republic. Davis has even criticized educators who encourage racial and ethnic identification among students, calling them "ethnic shepherds" (5). In contrast, he wants students to define themselves "as individuals, and as Americans, rather than as part of a collective and dependent Mexican underclass" (4). Davis presents a *paideia* to encourage his Anglo-Protestant notion of virtue. Both Davis's and Huntington's efforts to articulate republicanism to protectionist and assimilationist policy are particular to this moment in American history, as the Southwest states take in and become dependent on foreign workers. Their republicanism, though continuing a long and regrettably ascriptive tradition, is peculiar to a socioeconomic drama resolving the conflicts created by the globalizing North American Free Trade Agreement (1994), itself born of liberal hegemony.

An especially developed articulation of republicanism to economic protectionism and to cultural ascriptivism occurs in Patrick Buchanan's work, particularly his books *The Great Betrayal* (1998), which details the perils of liberal globalization, and *A Republic, Not an Empire* (1999), which warns against expanding American military alliances beyond what is necessary to protect national security. Buchanan's definition of American patriotism recalls Lacedemonian conflation of civic virtue and love for Sparta: "True patriotism is love of country for inexpressible reasons, simply for who and what she is" (xxi). Buchanan's republicanism is articulated to a free-market posture dissociated from free trade and thereby separated from the pernicious effects of global capital, such as downsizing, deindustrialization, falling wages, and reduced benefits (Aune, *Selling* 144). Buchanan's vision of the American republic differs dramatically from Giroux's civically minded, multicultural republic and from Aune's socialism in one republic. This brief comparison of republican political discourse, as it has been articulated to political programs on both the left and the right, elaborates on a claim explained earlier: splitting the history of rhetorical education between halcyon civic republican days and the dead season of apolitical pedagogy will not help us to categorize or understand a blossoming variety of political discourses, rhetorical norms, pedagogies, and the varying ways that these institutions impinge one another in a given social ecology. An Edenic narrative, though laudably recalling us to civic pastures, does not help us to investigate or navigate the civic terrain. Like the republicanism to which it is often articulated, civic education is less a bucolic field and more a battleground where we encounter the complex struggle over hegemony. Though there may be merit in revitalizing the republican political tradition, such a reanimation by no means wins the war. Instead, republican salvos might change our positions, alter the lines of battle, forge new articulations, dig new cultural trenches, and establish new pedagogical bivouacs, re-situating rhetorical education in the battle over hegemony.

Given the various possibilities available in republicanism, the various articulations made across history to cultural positions, economic programs, social classes, and individual interests, it should be evident that the civic turn is one bend in a long and complicated path that begs more decisions, more divergences, more roads less traveled. Simply championing republicanism in American higher education will not suffice. Though I agree with Rogers M. Smith that the typical liberal multicultural response to ascriptive republicanism is often insufficient, I also have to worry that switching to any other political discourse, be it strict liberalism, classical republicanism, or even agonistic pluralism, won't do the trick either (477).

Without close analysis of the articulations among political discourses, public rhetorical practices, pedagogies, and economics, we should be wary of cries for any political discourse in our efforts to become civic educators. This book ends not with an argument for more or less republicanism. My analyses of eighteenth-century American politics, pedagogy, and public discourse illustrate that republicanism is one open component in the continual hegemonic struggle over democratic institutions. Rhetorical educators, like it or not, engage in that struggle daily. We need a way to map the field of engagement. If anything, we need more consideration of economic factors and more close analysis of how cultural institutions like education mediate economic interests in real moments of conjuncture. This is the hard critical work of becoming responsible civic educators. I hope we are up to the task.

Notes

Introduction

1. In communication studies, research contributes both to scholarly conversations and to local community concerns. Richard Cherwitz's Intellectual Entrepreneurship Program at the University of Texas at Austin (est. 1996), for instance, encourages local faculty to become "citizen-scholars." The Annenberg Public Policy Center (est. 1994) at the University of Pennsylvania brings communication studies scholarship to bear on pragmatic civic concerns such as the use of media in modern politics. While communication studies scholars research civically relevant topics, faculty in English departments theorize democratic education. Drawing from a number of intellectual, pedagogical, and political traditions, many encourage students to become civically active, politically charged, motivated public citizens. For a survey of these efforts, see Christian Weisser's *Moving Beyond Academic Discourse* (2002). For a careful description of one laudable effort at civic pedagogy engaging a contemporary public sphere in a service-learning composition course, see David Coogan's "Counterpublics in Public Housing" (2005).

2. For examples of this Edenic narrative about the history of rhetoric, see Gregory Clark's *Dialogue, Dialectic, and Conversation* (1990), particularly ch. 5; S. Michael Halloran's "From Rhetoric to Composition" (1990); the introduction to *Oratorical Cultures in Nineteenth-Century America* (1993) by both Clark and Halloran; Thomas Miller's *The Formation of College English* (1997), particularly the conclusion; and Janet Carey Eldred's and Peter Mortensen's *Imagining Rhetoric* (2002), particularly the introduction and ch. 1. Historians tracking the formation of English departments have grown fond of claiming that aesthetics did not preoccupy rhetoric teachers in late eighteenth- and early nineteenth-century American or British higher education. The aesthetic fixation in English studies begins to look like an aberration from rhetoric's more time-honored civic course. For an example, see Linda Ferreira-Buckley's article "'Scotch Knowledge' and the Formation of Rhetorical Studies in Nineteenth-Century England" (1998). Even historians of classical rhetoric get into this game. Their Edenic narrative depicts rhetoric's intellectual and

pedagogical tradition as a four-thousand-year consistent hymn to audience, immediately relevant politics, and democratic citizenship, a song interrupted by atavistic, staccato bursts of literary, apolitical, noise. For an example of a classical historian telling an Edenic history of rhetoric's past, see George Kennedy's *Classical Rhetoric and Its Christian and Secular Tradition from Ancient to Modern Times* (1980), particularly chs. 6 and 11. Takis Polulakis even goes so far as to argue that English faculty interested in the civic potential of cultural studies and critical pedagogy should turn to classical rhetoric, particularly to Isocrates, where they will find a program of rhetorical education suitable to the civic turn in twenty-first-century writing instruction. See his book *Speaking for the Polis* (1997), particularly the introduction.

3. It was common practice for students in the late nineteenth century to write descriptive essays about pictures included in textbooks, about natural scenes that they witnessed, or about their own personal feelings. These essays located authority in the students' empirical observations or in their own sincerity, not in communally held knowledge or shared principles (Schultz 108–09).

4. To my knowledge, Michael Ryan was the first to use the term *articulation* in the manner that I do here. Ryan tried to articulate Marxian political practice to deconstructive philosophy in the interest of promoting radical democratic politics in the early 1980s. Ryan conceded that Marxian politics and Derridean deconstructive philosophy were wholly separate institutions, but he believed that forging a connection between them would allow historical agents in postmodern America to actuate a radically inclusive political agenda sufficient to their own peculiar circumstances. (See Ryan's *Marxism and Deconstruction,* especially the introduction.)

5. A review of several articles illustrates that articulation theory among rhetoricians continues the emphasis on discourse as begun by Laclau, Mouffe, Hall, and Grossberg. Kevin DeLuca, for instance, defines articulation strictly as a rhetorical practice, though he does concede that there are "real" objects and institutions at stake. DeLuca says that the factory may be a real structure, but the realm of political action must be confined to the "competing discourses" of "Marxism and capitalism" which define this structure and its uses in very different ways (336). Raymie McKerrow likewise turns away from economic factors when discussing power and hegemony, strictly focusing, like DeLuca, on discourse. For McKerrow as for DeLuca, articulatory practice and social agency are rhetorically constructed: "Discourse is the tactical dimension of the operation of power in its manifold relations at all levels of society, within and between its institutions, groups and individuals" (98). For McKerrow, as for DeLuca, the "material" no longer refers to the economic basis of a given social formation but rather to the discursive practice among rhetorically constructed and active agents (McKerrow 102–03; DeLuca 341–42). Most recently, Nathan Stormer has added to the body of articulation theory among rhetoricians, arguing for an understanding that avoids "collapsing the distinction between ma-

teriality and meaning to advance a specific critical project." Rather, Stormer says that rhetorical critics should focus on "historicizing different configurations of materiality and meaning (collapsed, segregated, overlapping) as conditions for the coming into being of a given form of rhetoric" (261). While Stormer's (re)vision of articulation theory holds out promise for the consideration of economic factors in an analysis of hegemony, his discussion remains, like DeLuca's and McKerrow's, preoccupied principally with discursive connections. Despite Stormer's concern for the material, his analytic lens only captures discursive articulations.

6. Louis Althusser similarly argues that while economics might be the foundational and principal force shaping history, it never exists alone. Economic formations are always layered into complicated sociohistorical formations all contributing to moments of "overdetermined" rupture in revolution (100–01). Althusser says particularly of social institutions like ideology: "[I]n History, these instances, the superstructures, etc.—are never seen to step respectfully aside when their work is done or, when the Time comes, as his pure phenomena, to scatter before His Majesty the Economy as he strides along the royal road of the Dialectic. From the first moment to the last, the lonely hour of the 'last instance' never comes" (113).

7. Recently Ernesto Laclau has used terms common to rhetorical theory, like *identification* and *definition,* to discuss the discursive element of hegemony ("Identity" 57–58).

8. James Aune argues in *Rhetoric and Marxism* (1994) that social analysis cannot lose track of the economic foundations on which societies are built but must also recognize that rhetorical efforts synthesize "contradictory social reality" (22). Aune seeks a Marxism that does not fall into myths of transparent language or revolution without the rhetorical effort at common identification (43). His analytic framework considers both rhetoric and economics, both "the world of outer nature, system, and forces and relations of production" and "the understanding of the historical-hermeneutic space" (132).

Chapter 1

1. There is a host of recent scholarship treating the part language played in the formation of early American politics. Literary analysts Christopher Looby and Thomas Gustafson argue that early American language was an important if not principal factor in the construction of national identity. Looby finds in a variety of texts a common trope that America was "spoken into existence," indicating that even in the eighteenth century citizens recognized the importance of a common language in their national unity (22). In Charles Brockden Brown's *Wieland* and Hugh Henry Brackenridge's *Modern Chivalry* (see chs. 3–4) Looby also finds a dissonance that allowed contending visions of the early republic. Thomas Gustafson finds that eighteenth-century debates about proper language reflected and influenced government. Gustafson studies, among other things, "how theories of language and fears about the power and duplicity of words influenced political

thought and the form of American government" (12). Rhetoric scholars also find that eighteenth-century American public discourse, particularly oratory, contributed to the formation of a national public sphere. Sandra Gustafson analyzes the public performances of political leaders, particularly attorneys, demonstrating that they positioned themselves as public servants and translated narrow legal proceedings into a language a wide audience could understand, thereby making possible a national public sphere based on common interest in and discourse about legislative procedure and effect. (See ch. 4 of *Eloquence Is Power.*) Stephen Browne closely analyzes Thomas Jefferson's first inaugural address to locate several rhetorical efforts to bring a nation into existence by public oratory. (See *Jefferson's Call for Nationhood.*) Recent historians have argued along similar lines. Christopher Grasso, for instance, claims that an elite few in Connecticut attempted to create a public sphere through discursive "civic conversion of the people" (4). Jay Fliegelman contends that the eighteenth-century elocutionary movement made public oratory commonplace along the British Atlantic and led to a public sphere that permitted people to declare their common purpose in national unity (28–35). These various studies, spread across a number of disciplines, in some form or other, claim that early American national unity was affected by a common political discourse and that various publicities depended on the discourse shared by those called into the public sphere.

2. In the early-to-mid-twentieth century, theorists focusing on liberalism dominated the field (see Hartz's *The Liberal Tradition in America* [1952]). But, beginning in the 1960s, several revisionist historians began to investigate the place of republicanism in revolutionary and early national discourse. (See Joyce Appleby's essay "Liberalism and Republicanism in the Historical Imagination," pp. 1–33 in *Liberalism and Republicanism in the Historical Imagination* [1992], for an excellent description of these trends in historical scholarship.) Bernard Bailyn's *The Ideological Origins of the American Revolution* (1967) closely examines political pamphlets written between the Seven Years' War and the Constitutional Convention (1787) to determine that radical British Whiggish republicanism lay at the root of American politics and motivated people to resist British tyranny and to worry over their own oppressive institutions, particularly slavery. Bailyn reads the Federalist movement as an ideological reaction against such radical efforts. (See chs. 2–3 and the postscript "Fulfillment: A Commentary on the Constitution.") Gordon Wood similarly finds republican discourse at the root of the early national period in American politics. In his study *The Creation of the American Republic 1776–1787* (1969), Wood claims that American republicanism, grounded in British Whiggism, led to the U.S. Constitution (chs. 1–3). J. G. A. Pocock traces the origins of American politics back to classical republicanism as filtered through fifteenth- and sixteenth-century Florentine thinkers like Bruni, Savonarola, and Machiavelli (chs. 14 and 15). In response to these republican revisionists, Joyce Appleby has argued that, though republicanism was an important rhetorical factor in eighteenth-century America, liberalism held its ground and eventually

dominated American public discourse. (See her book *Liberalism and Republicanism in the Historical Imagination,* particularly ch. 5.) Also, Paul Rahe, in his mammoth study of ancient Greek, seventeenth-century British, and eighteenth-century American politics, *Republics, Ancient and Modern* (1992), argues that the American political experiment was distinct from classical and Florentine republics. Rahe, writing directly against the republican revisionists, argues that Americans built on Lockean liberal principles of government when shaping their political tradition, thereby breaking sharply from classical republicanism (552–72).

3. For Burke's description of the parlor conversation, see *The Philosophy of Literary Form,* pp. 110–13. While focusing on discourse, Burke also paid consistent deference to extra-discursive factors in the formation of human events, which is why his rhetorical theory is particularly well suited to my efforts at reading early American society as a conflicted formation of economic interests shaped by and articulated to political and rhetorical patterns. Burke described rhetorical actions as "*strategies* for dealing with *situations.* In so far as situations are typical and recurrent in a given social structure, people develop names for them and strategies for handling them" (*Philosophy* 297). Frederic Jameson has similarly worked toward a rhetorical criticism that is conscious of economics, proposing a "dialectical *Rhetoric,* in which the various mental operations are understood not absolutely, but as moments and figures, tropes, syntactical paradigms, of our relationship to the real itself, as, altering irrevocably in time, it nonetheless obeys a logic that like the logic of language can never be fully distinguished from its object" (*Marxism* 374). Political theorist Murray Edelman has used Burkean rhetorical theory to understand how people negotiate complicated economic differences in a conversation using commonly known symbols. (See *Constructing the Political Spectacle* and *The Symbolic Uses of Politics* for Edelman's application of Burkean rhetorical theory to contemporary politics and political science.) Like Burke, Edelman argues that politics involves *both* symbolic effect and rational reflection of economic interest (*Symbolic* 43).

4. Aristotle mentions the topics in his *Rhetoric* bk. 1, ch. 2, sec. 2, using the Greek word *topoi* to designate two kinds of topics: common topics (*koinoi topoi*), which apply to all situations and all arguments, and specific topics (*idioi topoi*), which are peculiar to particular debates or particular rhetorics. (Aristotle covers twenty-eight common topics in *On Rhetoric* bk. 2, ch. 23.) Quintilian discusses argumentative topics in his *Institutio Oratoria* (bk. 5, ch. 8, sec. 1, 8–9). Quintilian uses the Latin phrase *loci argumentorum* (places of arguments) throughout his discussion and focuses on the topics as a pedagogical tool for teaching students how to invent arguments. Cicero likewise discusses various *loci argumentorum* in his *De Inventione,* treating topics for invoking emotions (bk. 1, chs. 53–56, 149–63) and topics for prosecutors and defenders in criminal trials (bk. 2, ch. 22, 231–33). Neo-Aristotelian rhetoricians Chaim Perelman and Lucie Olbrechts-Tyteca cover common topics in *The New Rhetoric* (1958) (83–99). Though they focus on the common

topics, Perelman and Olbrechts-Tyteca recognize the value of mapping specific topics as well: "Although the more general *loci* primarily claim our attention, it is undoubtedly worthwhile to examine the more specific *loci* which are accepted in various societies and are thus characteristic of them" (85). My analysis of the discourse of American republicanism is an attempt to study the specific topics in this period. This analysis is indebted to two recent theorists, Rosa Eberly and Michael Leff. Eberly's description of argumentative topics as "bioregions of discourse" is a valuable reminder that rhetorical forms make production possible "from the common ground up" but also delimit what is sayable by only allowing certain arguments to take root (6). Leff delineates between the Aristotelian notion of topics (based on the process of inference or the argumentative form devoid of subject matter) and the Ciceronian notion of topics (based on the subject matter and devoid of interest in the argumentative form) (25–27). Burke's approach to the topics in the *Grammar* is Aristotelian, and my approach in this analysis is Ciceronian.

5. Burke theorized that any argument consists of five components in relation with one another. They are the pentad: scene, act, agent, agency, purpose. In part 1 of *A Grammar of Motives* (1945), he defined a rhetorical topic as the set of relations among the five components, and in part 2 he analyzed several philosophical schools to see which topics they deploy and how. In part 3, he discussed the "constitutive" act, or the deployment of topics, to articulate new agencies in a given historical moment. The pentad and the constitutive act always exist together in rhetorical action, since, for Burke, human agency inhabits and reconstitutes the rhetorical forms available in a given moment to innovatively connect with extra-discursive circumstances. My read of Burke's *Grammar* relies heavily on Robert Wess's *Kenneth Burke: Rhetoric, Subjectivity, Postmodernism* (1996) (135–85).

6. To be fair, I should note that Machiavelli did say that mixed government can avoid the cycle of monarchy and democracy. See the *Discourses on Livy* (bk. 1, sec. 2, 10–14).

7. Edward Schiappa has coined the term *definitional rupture* to describe what happens when people reject the standards of definition to argue over how to make sense of their worlds (9–10). Such disagreements over how to define objects have both metaphysical and practical implications. In the metaphysical sense, these disagreements reconstitute the order of people's realities, and in the pragmatic sense, they (re)arrange people's sense of "ought" by asking us to position certain objects within ethically heavy categories (40–46). To define all monarchy as an infringement on liberty, for instance, is to expand the definition of power and to take a resistant posture toward British rule, however beneficent. Richard Weaver made a similar point when he noticed that the argument from definition hinges on ideals and their application (87–88). Power and liberty were equally ideals, and their applications affected the way people perceived and managed the real events of their era. The definitional arguments that I map here are, in Perelman's and Olbrechts-Tyteca's vocabulary, "descriptive definitions." They "indicate what meaning is

given to a word in a certain environment at a particular time" (211). Schiappa calls definitional arguments based on any foundational notion " 'real' definitions" (35–39).

8. Samuel Adams learned a great deal about political resistance through direct action from sailors who skillfully fought British press gangs. Adams's Sons of Liberty, however, positioned themselves as a reasonable alternative to the uncontrollable plebian masses whose muscled shoulders and heavy fists threatened the privileged classes. See ch. 7, pp. 211–47, of Peter Linebaugh's and Marcus Rediker's *The Many-Headed Hydra: Sailors, Slaves, Commoners, and the Hidden History of the Revolutionary Atlantic* (2000). James Madison voiced a typical fear that direct democracy would lead to rule by the passionate mob. (See Federalist 10 in *Federalist Papers,* pp. 122–28.) Thomas Jefferson denigrated Patrick Henry's fiery oratory, which Jefferson associated with the uncultured working class and the frontierspeople (Fliegelman 94–102).

9. Phyllis Wheatley, an African-American slave, wrote numerous poems that invoke a language of evangelical Christianity, pleading for recognition and political agency. Benjamin Banekker, a brilliant African-American mathematician, wrote to Thomas Jefferson in 1791, arguing for the equality of all American citizens and the necessity of freeing African Americans held in slavery. Sadly, neither Wheatley nor Banekker would ever get much recognition in the republican public sphere. Thomas Jefferson dismissed them both out of hand (*Notes* 189).

10. Jeffrey Walker, for instance, offers an insightful analysis of enthymemes and emotional appeal in Paine's *Common Sense,* noting the difficulty of accounting for the fourth section of Paine's book. See his article "Enthymemes of Anger in Cicero and Paine," especially pp. 372–73.

11. Bernard Mandeville's *Fable of the Bees* (1723) presents the self-serving individual as the basic component of social existence. In Mandeville's portrait, people in their "State of Nature and Ignorance of the true Piety" are greedy, materialistic, and solely concerned with private gain (36). The economy celebrated by the likes of Mandeville, Thomas Hobbes, and Adam Smith promotes a citizen principally motivated by self-interest. In Smith's words, "It is not out from the benevolence of the butcher, the brewer, or the baker, that we expect our dinner, but from their regard to their own interest" (*Wealth* 15). Smith's *Wealth of Nations* (1776) popularized possessive individualism, but his *Theory of Moral Sentiments* (1759, 1761, and 1790) argues that people are (and should be) driven by their sympathy for others. Smith also taught an ethic of sympathy. He positioned people's capacity for sympathy as innate—forming the basis for public institutions and the common good (*Theory* 13–26). Smith was not alone among British philosophers theorizing sympathy. Anthony Ashley Cooper, third Earl of Shaftesbury, argued that people have an innate sense of and therefore enjoy pursuing the public good: "in the Passions and Affections of particular Creatures, there is a constant relation to the Interest of *a Species,* or *common Nature*" (48). Francis Hutcheson's famous notion of the moral sense

laid the foundation for Scottish eighteenth-century moral philosophy: "by a *Superior Sense,* which I call a *Moral one,* we perceive Pleasure in the Contemplation of such Actions in others, and are determined to love the Agent [. . .] without any View of further *natural Advantage* from them" (106). Even David Hume, though devoted to laissez-faire capitalism and willing to argue that "*self interest is the original motive to the* establishment *of justice,*" was so influenced by Hutcheson that he could not base society strictly in self interest, though he could no more easily base it in publicly directed virtue. Hume argued, like Hutcheson and Shaftesbury, that sympathy plays a vital role in the construction of social institutions, saying, "[S]ympathy is a very powerful principle in human nature [. . . I]t also gives rise to many of the other virtues; and [. . . these] qualities acquire our approbation, because of their tendency to the good of mankind" (*Treatise* 577–78).

12. Jean-Jacques Rousseau and Adam Ferguson both alluded to classical Greek republicanism, arguing against the capitalist state constructed solely to protect individual property rights. According to Rousseau, "with money one has everything, except morals and citizens" (52). Like Rousseau, Ferguson worried that a collection of profit-seeking individuals would cease to exist as a nation and would therefore crumble into anarchy, destroying the institutions that made commercial advancement possible: "Neither the parties formed in republics, nor the courtly assemblies which meet in monarchical governments, could take place, where the sense of mutual dependence should cease to summon their members together" (182).

13. Paul Rahe presents early American republicanism as a justification for laissez-faire capitalism in the third book of his study *Republics, Ancient and Modern.* Christopher Looby likewise argues that "[r]epublican rhetoric enabled the creation of a liberal market society to masquerade nostalgically as a reversion to an older order of things" (242).

14. To be fair, Appleby does caution against the depiction of Federalists as "mindless conservatives," and she stresses their own commitment to capitalism. However, she also emphasizes their unwillingness to entertain the more radical version of free-market economic policy that she finds among the Democratic-Republicans (*Capitalism* 59).

15. Carl Bridenbaugh locates various manufacturing industries throughout the northeast. In mid-eighteenth-century Philadelphia, he finds cooperage, rum distilling, iron manufacture, flour milling, tanning, woolen-stocking manufacture, paper mills, iron furnaces, linseed-oil mills, and smithies. In Newport, he finds a thriving manufacture in specialty items for export: cabinets, furniture, gravestones, and even clocks. By the mid-eighteenth century, Boston developed prosperous efforts at manufacturing large and complicated items such as furniture and carriages (*Cities in Revolt* 72–76).

16. Most recent economic analyses of early American society divide the economy into various interests depending on the principal mode of production and the area's geography. See John McCusker's and Russel Menard's *The Economy of British America, 1607–1789* (1985) and essays included in the *Cambridge Economic History of the United States, Volume One:*

The Colonial Era (1996). Both of these texts treat the eighteenth-century British Atlantic economy as a fragmented and conflicted terrain. Charles Beard has argued that these various economic interests affected how people voted during the Constitutional ratification process. See his *Economic Interpretation of the Constitution of the United States* (1913). Beard demonstrates that southern plantation owners and northeastern merchants voted in different ways based on very different economic interests. Beard's analysis of the Jeffersonian era, *Economic Origins of Jeffersonian Democracy* (1936), presents extensive research into voting records and the political beliefs of particular representatives (see chs. 2–3 especially). This analysis offers a convincing portrait of economic division in the early national period. Beard believed that in this era class division lay at the bottom of political division. He said as much in his 1916 lectures at Amherst College, whose principal thesis he summarized with these words: "[C]ivilized societies are divided into economic groups or interests, according to different degrees and kinds of property-possessions and occupations, whether private or bureaucratic; and forms of government rest upon this social configuration, and politics is concerned with conflicts among interests" (*The Economic Basis* 25). Carl Bridenbaugh finds that the manufacturing interest in northeastern urban centers also had a significant impact on people's decisions to support the American Revolution. See *Cities in Revolt* (1955), chs. 9–11, and an earlier study coauthored with Jessica Bridenbaugh, *Rebels and Gentlemen* (1942). Jackson Turner Main's *The Anti-Federalists* (1961), chs. 1–3, argues that the division between the Federalists and the Anti-Federalists was underpinned by the differing economic interests among northeastern urban merchants, southern agrarian plantation owners, and frontierspeople.

17. Jackson Turner Main's study *Society and Economy in Colonial Connecticut* (1985) says seventeenth-century Connecticut was egalitarian, but in the eighteenth century greater economic distinctions appeared; most notably the poor became a constant feature (116–30). Even still, Main notices that in the eighteenth century three-fourths of the laboring classes could hope to achieve a decent living on par with the broad middle class (196).

18. A number of literary critics have read Dwight's poetry as an effort to revive the Augustan cyclical notion of history and to position America as a society at the apex of its cycle and on the precipice of decay. Clearly, Dwight appropriated a great deal of classical republicanism for his own purposes, but it is questionable to argue that he adopted this political discourse wholesale. William Dowling in *Poetry and Ideology in Revolutionary Connecticut* (1990) has offered a nuanced picture of Dwight. In Dowling's depiction, Dwight appropriated classical republican thought, injecting into it his own Christian agenda, particularly his millennialism (67–87). More recently, however, Colin Wells, in *The Devil and Doctor Dwight* (2000), has argued that Dwight rejected Christian millennialism for a more traditionally classical notion of cyclical time. (See particularly ch. 1 in Wells's study.)

19. Joseph Schumpeter discussed the commonly held seventeenth- and eighteenth-century "populationist attitude," which he summarized as the belief that "*under prevailing*

conditions, increase in heads would increase real income per head" (251–52). Schumpeter notes that the Malthussian fear of population growth and full employment was peculiar to England in this era (252–58).

20. Two scholars focusing on early American republican discourse charge all econo-mistic interpretation with a reductionary perspective. Paul Rahe has claimed that efforts to consider economic interest when analyzing early American republicanism forget that "the articulation of humanity into nations and political communities is of greater funda-mental importance and deserves more careful study than its articulation into economic and social classes" (24). Thomas Pangle has accused all economistic analyses of an unwill-ingness or an inability to consider political theory on its own terms. According to Pangle, those privileging economic factors in their analysis lack "the essential moral or intellec-tual motivation to devote themselves to the requisite, the difficult, textual analysis" (12). It is not uncommon to find among rhetorical theorists an acknowledgment that economic interests affect rhetorical articulations, but there is rarely a deep consideration of this interplay between discursive and extra-discursive social forces. Kenneth Burke, a giant among twentieth-century rhetorical theorists, concedes that "human motives are not confined to the realm of verbal action" (*Grammar* 33) and then dedicates more than five hundred pages of his *Grammar of Motives* to the analysis of human motives as constituted in verbal action. Stephen Browne's rhetorical analysis of Jefferson's first inaugural address also acknowledges that Jefferson's rhetoric cannot be "abstracted from the material con-ditions that summoned them in the first place" (50). Despite this concession, Browne proceeds to analyze the address as if it happened without the impact of said materiality. His "rhetorical perspective" emphasizes "the centrality of symbols in setting horizons and limits of life, especially as it is lived among others in the conduct of public affairs" (6–7).

21. Antonio Gramsci also recognized that hegemony depends on education: "Every relationship of 'hegemony' is necessarily an educational relationship" (*Selections from the Prison Notebooks* 350). Gramsci even focused on rhetorical education, saying that "language=history" and that "[g]rammar is 'history' or a 'historical document' . . . the 'photograph' of a given phase of a national (collective) language that has been formed historically" (*Selections from Cultural Writings* 177, 179).

Chapter 2

1. Some historians of rhetoric have argued that rhetorical theory along the eighteenth-century British Atlantic was unimportant or entirely derivative of English sources. Warren Guthrie says as much in two articles: "The Development of Rhetorical Theory in America" (1946) and "The Development of Rhetorical Theory in America, 1635–1850" (1947). Though Guthrie is right to point out that American treatments of rhetorical theory prior to the mid-nineteenth century were heavily influenced by English and Scottish sources, his claim that Americans therefore had little influence is narrowly based on a notion of

intellectual history in which "influential" figures are cited and repeated by subsequent thinkers. Surely, none of the accepted, canonical rhetoric texts of the nineteenth century directly cited John Witherspoon's lectures, but that does not mean Witherspoon "had no immediate influence save at Princeton" (Guthrie "1635–1850" 50). Witherspoon's students taught rhetoric at Dickinson College, Queen's College (Rutgers), Princeton, and in numerous academies. Some, like James Madison, also became influential rhetors in their own rights.

2. David Potter transcribed the Latin versions of these disputation exercises along with his own English translations in appendices A and B of *Debating in the Colonial Charter Colleges* (1944), pp. 125–30. I rely on his transcriptions and translations for this discussion.

3. Reuben Guild reprinted the entire text of this debate in his article "The First Commencement of Rhode Island College and American Independence" (1885), pp. 281–98.

4. For more extensive reviews of the King's College controversy, see Robson, pp. 4–10 and Humphrey, chs. 2–4.

5. John McCusker and Russel Menard argue that the mix of agricultural and commercial interests provided the middle colonies with the most balanced economies in eighteenth-century America: "The middle colonies, it would seem, lived up to their name combining the best of two colonial worlds. Like the plantation colonies, they possessed a staple export much in demand overseas; like New England they supplied customers in a variety of markets, participated heavily in commerce with other mainland colonies, and earned substantial credits through the carrying trade" (198).

6. Russell Menard estimates that in 1776 tobacco, rice, and indigo accounted for 75 percent of southern exports (256).

7. B. W. Higman finds the following characteristics in British Caribbean colonial economies, all of which were repeated in South Carolina: "monocultural focus and dependence on external trade, the dominance of large-scale plantations and involuntary labor systems, the drain of wealth associated with a high ratio of absentee proprietorship, and the role of the servile population in the internal market" (297). Caribbean colonies did not revolt in 1776 because of their dependence on British markets, which is also why South Carolina plantation owners resisted independence (326).

8. For descriptions of the classical curriculum at William and Mary, see Lyon G. Tyler's "Early Courses and Professors at William and Mary College" (1905) and Courtlandt Canby's "A Note on the Influence of Oxford University upon William and Mary College in the Eighteenth Century" (1941).

9. For an example of such a Latin poem written at William and Mary in the late seventeenth century, see Julian Ward Jones's "A 'New' Latin Quitrent Poem of the College of William and Mary" (1988).

10. Description of the colonial gentry in Philadelphia can be found in Stephen Bro-

beck's "Revolutionary Change in Colonial Philadelphia: The Brief Life of the Proprietary Gentry" (1976). Carl and Jessica Bridenbaugh's *Rebels and Gentlemen: Philadelphia in the Age of Franklin* (1942) also provides descriptions of both the proprietary gentry and the emergent bourgeoisie, their conflict in the revolutionary period, and the gentry's eventual political defeat.

11. Richard D. Brown notes that "[a]mong merchants, wealth and social rank were so closely joined that learning was merely ornamental" (121). Brown also argues that professional, middle-class men, such as lawyers, relied heavily on a practical literacy to ply their trades. As a result, they did not value nor benefit from the classical education that Franklin abjured.

12. In a November 1750 letter, Johnson commended Franklin on his endeavor but lamented, "you say nothing of Rhetoric and Oratory considered as an Art, perhaps you might have done well to prescribe in that year the learning of some system of Rhetoric so as to have a good notion of Tropes and Figures." In a response, written November 22, 1750, Franklin says, "I approve exceedingly of the Additions you propose."

13. For more on Kinnersley's work in electricity and his relationship with Benjamin Franklin, see Leo Lemay's *Ebenezer Kinnersley: Franklin's Friend* (1964).

14. For a more extended discussion of Ciceronian decorum and its potential in modern rhetorical theory, see Robert Hariman's *Political Style* (1995), particularly ch. 4 and the conclusion. Hariman succinctly defines the classical notion of decorum as "a set of conventions and as a theory of conventions. In either case, such conventions blended significant aspects of rhetorical practice, social awareness, and political structure into an aesthetic sensibility that could be applied uniformly to literary texts, rhetorical performances, and official conduct" (180).

15. In his *Notes on the State of Virginia,* Jefferson praised the oratorical capacity of Amerindian leaders (99–100).

16. Among the more influential histories of rhetorical theory and pedagogy, one finds a consistent emphasis on intellectual trends or major figures. Wilbur Samuel Howell's *Eighteenth-Century British Logic and Rhetoric* (1971), for instance, focuses exclusively on intellectual developments among Enlightenment empiricists and major thinkers like John Locke and George Campbell. Thomas Miller's *The Formation of College English* (1997) provides much more information about the economic and political contexts in which these theories and figures operated, but Miller also focuses several chapters on major figures like Hugh Blair, Adam Smith, and George Campbell. In the scholarship about nineteenth-century rhetoric, one often finds a similar focus on intellectual trends and major figures. Sharon Crowley's *The Methodical Memory* (1990) carefully traces the epistemological origins of current-traditional rhetoric without acknowledging in any fashion the economic and political contexts of late nineteenth-century America. Nan Johnson's *Nineteenth-*

Century Rhetoric in North America (1991) divides the American rhetorical tradition into categories like belletrism and psychological rhetoric, focusing on theoretic trends without close attention to the circumstances of their appropriation. Finally James Berlin's *Rhetoric and Reality* (1987) divides the history of modern composition rhetoric into three trends, current-traditional, expressive, and social-epistemic rhetorics, giving only the occasional nod to the political and economic circumstances to which these theoretic developments were articulated.

Chapter 3

1. My use of the terms "dominant," "residual," and "emergent" derives from Raymond Williams's discussion of historical change in *Marxism and Literature* (1977) (125–27). Williams, like Marx, has recognized that no historical moment is dominated by one culture or able to escape nascent growth of new or the residue of old socioeconomic patterns. Williams says, "*No mode of production, and therefore no dominant social order and therefore no dominant culture ever in reality includes or exhausts all human practice, human energy, and human intention*" (125).

2. Elizabeth Flower and Murray Murphy illustrate that the American Puritan faith in the accuracy of ectypal knowledge in part stemmed from Ramistic confidence in the representational powers of language (1: 23, 41).

3. Ames even goes so far as to draw on British political theory, describing the church as a mixed government with Christ as monarch, the ministers as an aristocracy, and the congregation as a democracy (*Marrow* 169).

4. Samuel Johnson's technologia is reprinted in the four-volume collection, *Samuel Johnson, President of King's College: His Career and Writings* (1929), abbreviated hereafter as *SJCW,* followed by the volume and the page numbers.

5. Unless otherwise noted, the historical details about Yale and its curriculum printed in this chapter derive from Brooks Mather Kelley's *Yale: A History* (1974). I have also relied on Thomas Clap's *The Annals of the History of Yale College* (1766) and Franklin B. Dexter's *Biographical Sketches of the Graduates of Yale College with Annals of the College* (1885–1911).

6. One of the first mentions that I have found of English forensic disputation at Yale occurs in a letter, dated December 24, 1751, from Benjamin Franklin to Jared Eliot, Yale trustee, commending Yale faculty for bringing forensic disputation into the college's regular routine. This letter is reprinted in Dexter's *Biographical Sketches,* vol. 2, pp. 275–76. David Potter has found English forensic disputations recorded in Napthali Daggett's student notebook, dated 1747.

7. These broadsides were all printed in New Haven in limited quantity. Many are available in the Yale University archives and in the Early American Imprints micro-card collection, as referenced by the Charles Evans bibliography. The broadsides were printed

in Latin until the 1790s. English versions offered here are my own translations, occasionally accompanied by the original Latin. The scholar's obligation to publicly exhibit and defend his knowledge derives from a medieval European tradition. In the colonial colleges, this exercise became a formal show at commencement, more of a pageant display than an actual public examination.

8. According to Perry Miller, Puritans believed that "method was not merely simple and clear, but objectively true, that the content of every science falls of itself into dichotomies, that all disciplines can be diagrammed in a chart of successive foliations" (*New England* 127). Walter Ong has most fully explored the implications of Ramistic method for rhetorical invention and for the place of rhetoric in the liberal arts curriculum. See *Ramus, Method, and the Decay of Dialogue* (1958).

9. For Locke, simple ideas come directly from sensation or reflection. They constitute the most rudimentary empirical observations and the most reliable knowledge. The mind forms complex ideas by combining, comparing, and abstracting simple ideas. Locke says, "These simple ideas, the materials of all our knowledge, are suggested and furnished to the mind only by those two ways above mentioned, viz. sensation and reflection. When the understanding is once stored with these simple ideas, it has the power to repeat, compare, and unite them, even to an almost infinite variety, and so can make at pleasure new complex ideas. But it is not in the power of the most exalted wit, or enlarged understanding, by any quickness or variety of thought, to *invent* or *frame* one new simple idea in the mind" (*Essay* 1: 145). Later in the *Essay* (vol. 1, pp. 213–15), Locke argued that the mind is passive in receiving simple ideas but active in forming complex ones. In 1759, students defended logical theses fully in agreement with Locke: (1) "All simple ideas are adequate," and (2) "The mind is always active in forming complex ideas."

10. Recent historians have argued convincingly that belletrism was among the principal contributing intellectual forces to the formation of a long textbook tradition in the United States, reaching from the nineteenth and into the twentieth centuries. See Robert Connors's *Composition-Rhetoric* (1997) and Nan Johnson's *Nineteenth-Century Rhetoric in North America* (1991).

11. Hume's essay "Of Eloquence" exhibits this tension, and Adam Potkay has illustrated the political ramifications of Hume's rhetorical theory in ch. 2 of *The Fate of Eloquence in the Age of Hume* (1994).

12. Compare Dwight's passage with the lines that he imitated in Pope's *Essay.*
Dwight's *Dissertation on the History, Eloquence, and Poetry of the Bible* (1772):

> Unincumbered by critical manacles, they [the Bible's authors] gave their imaginations an unlimited range, called absent objects before the sight, gave life to the whole inanimate creation, and in every period, snatched the grace

which is beyond the reach of art, and which, being genuine offspring of elevated Genius, finds the shortest passage to the human soul. (p. 4)

Pope's *Essay Concerning Criticism,* part one, lines 152–57:

> Great Wits sometimes may *gloriously offend,*
> And *rise* to *Faults* true Criticks *dare not mend;*
> From *vulgar Bounds* with *brave Disorder* part,
> And *snatch* a *Grace* beyond the Reach of Art,
> Which, without passing thro' the *Judgment,* gains
> The *Heart,* and all its End *at once* attains. (p. 149)

13. There were ten essays in "The Meddler" series, published in the *Boston Chronicler* between September 4, 1769, and January 22, 1770. There were thirty-eight essays in "The Correspondent" series, published in the *Connecticut Journal* between February 23, 1770, and September 3, 1773.

14. Two student notebooks inform this discussion: David Lewis Daggett's 1807 notebook, published by Vincent Freimarck as "Rhetoric at Yale in 1807," and John Pierpont's 1803 notebook, published by Abe C. Ravitz as "Timothy Dwight: Professor of Rhetoric." These are parenthetically cited in the body text as "Freimarck" and "Ravitz" respectively.

Chapter 4

1. Richard Bushman's *The Refinement of America* (1992) provides a history of the transition from genteel to respectable cultures and the political implications of each formation. Bushman comments that though bourgeois citizens adopted many genteel artifacts and mannerisms, they were never comfortable in the fully developed genteel parlor: "This vision of a purely polite society grew from a cultural memory of an aristocratic past. The whole family shared enough of the vision and memory to create a room filled with the current tokens of genteel culture—mahogany table, brass andirons, gilt mirror, and stuffed and claw-footed chairs—but the incongruities with their ordinary friends and everyday existence made them shun the parlor in favor of the kitchen" (267).

2. The newspaper accounts of King's College commencement exercises were edited by Milton Halsey Thomas and reprinted as "King's College Commencement in the Newspapers" *Columbia University Quarterly* 22 (June 1930): 226–50. My discussion references this reprinting.

3. For more on the socially conservative Quakers in early eighteenth-century Philadelphia and their distrust of genteel culture, particularly belletristic rhetoric, see Dennis Barone's "Hostility and Rapprochement" (1989).

4. Franklin's eventual abjuration was politically affected, as was Smith's appointment

as provost. In a letter (28 July 1759) to Ebenezer Kinnersley, Franklin reflected, "The scheme of public parties made it requisite to lessen my influence wherever it could be lessened" (qtd. in Cheyney 109).

5. This connection between natural philosophy and Christianity constitutes no innovation on Smith's part, since seventeenth-century English thinkers like Robert Boyle and Isaac Newton wrestled with the intersection of science, religion, and rhetoric and arrived at conclusions similar to what Smith taught in Philadelphia. Robert Markley illustrates in his book *Fallen Languages* (1993) that English thinkers trying to reconcile religion with physical science (physico-theologians) searched in vain to find a language that could represent the perfection of God's kingdom as encountered in scientific and mathematical inquiry. Markley argues that these thinkers never arrived at such a language and so always had to mediate the contingency of human experience and the unchanging perfection of God's world through imperfect discourse.

6. This quote comes from Smith's *A General Idea of the College of Miriana,* reprinted in the *Works of William Smith,* hereafter parenthetically cited as *WWS* followed by the volume and the page numbers. Since vol. 1 of this work is split into two sections with separate pagination, whenever vol. 1 is referenced, it will be followed by a numerical indication of the section referenced. This parenthetical (*WWS* 1.2: 203), for instance, refers to vol. 1, sec. 2, p. 203.

7. Smith's description of natural philosophy as another realm teaching the same lessons found in revealed religion parallels Robert Boyle's seventeenth-century physico-theology by repeating the lesson that the book of nature and the book of God isomorphically exist, allowing one to read either in search of the same divine message. See Markley's *Fallen Languages,* pp. 40–50 and 95–110.

8. Ned O'Gorman's essay "Longinus's Sublime Rhetoric" (2004) argues convincingly that this tendency to mystify the sublime is present even in the original Greek text. O'Gorman says, "Longinus moves rhetoric beyond the traditions of character and persuasion, traditions which directly or indirectly bind rhetoric to external criteria for judgment, and brings rhetoric to autonomy" (75).

9. The anonymously published Cato letters, printed in the *Pennsylvania Gazette* March 13–April 24, 1776, provide one of the clearest and fullest articulations of Smith's loyalism. Gegenheimer (178) attributes these letters to Smith based on a prospectus for Smith's collected works. There is still some debate about whether or not Smith authored the loyalist pamphlet *Plain Truth,* most often attributed to James Chalmers.

Chapter 5

1. Unless otherwise noted, all references to Witherspoon's writings come from *The Works of John Witherspoon* (1802). The specific passages will be referenced parenthetically hereafter as *Works of John Witherspoon* (*WJW*) followed by the volume and page numbers.

2. Witherspoon bragged about these purchases in his *Address to the Inhabitants of Ja-maica on Behalf of the College of New Jersey* (1772), reprinted in vol. 4 of *The Works of John Witherspoon.*

3. Thomas Miller demonstrates that Witherspoon was principally influenced by Francis Hutcheson, whose lectures he attended while studying in Scotland ("Introduc-tion" 6–7). As mentioned in ch. 4, the division between common-sense realism and Christian idealism was one of the principal fissures in early American philosophy, and it led to real tensions among college faculty (Flower and Murphy 1: 215–49; Hoeveler 122–23). Witherspoon arrived at the college to find several idealists, including Jonathan Edwards Jr., working as tutors. After chafing against their curricula for a brief time, he fired them all.

4. For more on the literary societies, see Jacob N. Beam's *The American Whig Society of Princeton University* (1933) and J. Jefferson Looney's *Nurseries of Letters and Republicanism* (1996).

5. British and colonial soldiers occupied Nassau Hall during the Revolution and de-stroyed much of the college's archives dating prior to 1786. Nassau Hall also burned down in 1802, destroying much of what survived the Revolution.

6. Blair delivered and published forty-seven lectures in all. Lectures 20–24 examine the aesthetic beauty in texts written by Joseph Addison and Jonathan Swift. Lecture 30 closely examines Bishop Atterbury's sermons with a similar attention to aesthetic appre-ciation. Lectures 38–47 discuss poetry and drama as distinct genres worthy of apprecia-tion and examination. All of these lectures taught students to appreciate, not produce, the kinds of writing discussed.

7. For a particularly interesting glimpse into Witherspoon's liberalism, see his "Essay on Money" (*WJW* 4: 203–44). In this document, written as an insertion into a raucous debate about government issuance of specie, Witherspoon repeats much of John Locke's liberal advice about government intervention into commerce and manufacturing.

8. For more on Witherspoon's connection between the civic republican and the mil-lennial ideals, see Richard Sher's "Witherspoon's *Dominion of Providence* and the Scottish Jeremiad Tradition" (1990).

9. See lectures 3 and 4 for more on the divine origins of the moral sense. In lecture 3, Witherspoon placed God's will at the foundation of moral and political action: "[W]e ought to take the role of duty from [divinely inspired] conscience, enlightened by reason, experience, and every way which we can be supposed to learn the will of our Maker, and his intention of creating us as such as we are" (*WJW* 3: 388).

10. Compare Witherspoon's statement to Cicero's: "I have been led by reason itself to hold this opinion first and foremost, that wisdom without eloquence does little for the good of the states, but that eloquence without wisdom is generally highly disadvanta-geous and is never helpful" (*De Inventione* bk. 1, ch. 1, sec. 1, 3).

Conclusion

1. Habermas has noticed that developing commercial economies made liberal public exchange possible. Particularly the institutions of commodity ownership and exchange encouraged the liberal notion of an autonomous actor driven by self-interest. The liberal public sphere served as a useful bourgeois mechanism to curtail the interventions of mercantilism, an economic system established prior to and at odds with laissez-faire capitalism. Establishing an arena of discourse to question and influence the state helped a bourgeois citizenry to inhibit mercantilist interventions like trade restriction, price fixing, tariffs, and restrictions on incorporation, all of which slowed capital growth and restricted individual profit (*Structural* 73–79; see also Hauser, "Civil" 25–31). Reflecting on more recent possibilities for constructing a democratic public sphere, Nancy Fraser likewise recognizes the importance of economic institutions and their relation to civil society. Fraser acknowledges that her proposed proliferation of multiple and interacting publics requires an economic parity not achievable among citizens in "laissez faire capitalism" (132). Though she never lays out an economic program, Fraser seems to lean toward welfare capitalism as a prerequisite for her ideal of public debate. Richard Harvey Brown questions the possibility of forming any cohesive public space in the fragmented world of transnational capitalism. Brown argues that a functional deliberation requires some revitalization of the republican political tradition, including appropriation of the *res publica* (355). All of these public-sphere theorists recognize that particularly fashioned norms of rhetorical exchange depend not just on their articulation to a political discourse or even to a rhetorical pedagogy but also upon their connection to an economic environment.

2. To illustrate the possible articulation between deontological liberalism and post-industrial capitalism, one need only consider a curious alliance over college entrance requirements in the summer of 2003. As the U.S. Supreme Court heard challenges to the University of Michigan Law School's efforts to give special consideration to nonwhite candidates, both deontological liberals like Giroux and private corporations like Kellog Co., Bank One, and Saks Fifth Avenue came together to champion institutions that maintain racial and cultural diversity in higher education (France and Symonds).

3. Oskar Negt and Alexander Kluge argue that the bourgeois public sphere is necessary to the hegemony of a certain class in twentieth-century capitalism, but they never claim that capitalism determines the formation of public space. Rather, Negt and Kluge characterize the public sphere as a space where citizens, both exploited and exploiting, can leverage economic effect through cultural work (1–3).

4. Liberalism and republicanism, though certainly available trends in American political discourse, by no means exhaust Western efforts to theorize democratic government, to publicly debate issues, or to impart rhetorical skills. Also, the above discussion

of articulations made among political discourses, publicities, and rhetorical pedagogies does not exhaustively cover the possibilities available to those orchestrating twenty-first-century rhetoric classrooms. Habermas himself has in his most recent work moved away from both liberalism and republicanism, arguing instead for another model of democracy, what he calls a "discourse theory." For Habermas's discussion of the troubles with liberalism and republicanism, see *Between Facts and Norms* (1992), 3.1.4, pp. 99–104. See also his article "Three Normative Models of Democracy" (1996) for a very concise explanation of how liberalism and republicanism are wanting and how his "discourse theory" of democracy derives from and builds on both. Concerned about contemporary "communitarian" republican leanings (which bring Clark a fair amount of criticism—see Greg Myers, Reynolds), Habermas hopes to preserve the valuable tendencies of both liberalism and republicanism in a theory of democracy built on "communicative action," the collectively accepted and constructed principles of law, which then become a quasi-foundational structure through which individual interests can contend. From republicanism Habermas learns the importance of deliberation to construct community ethos, and from liberalism he learns the value of competing interests. In the law, he finds a space "between facts and norms" where a nonliberal, nonrepublican, nonfoundational democratic practice can appear, allowing apparently autonomous actors to vie for personal gain without threatening the public good, private rights, or communally constructed morals (*Between* 9–16). Habermas's discourse theory of democracy and its devotion to a public sphere comprised of and debating over the quasi-foundational institution of modern law finds its pedagogical extension in Susan Wells's efforts to teach students how to function in public spheres that are temporarily constructed on the norms negotiated and accepted by their participants. Wells finds in Habermas's theory of communicative action a valuable understanding of how to teach students to enter and construct public spaces "based on shared problems and possible solutions" (336). Wells's discourse-democratic pedagogy teaches students "the forms of agreement, the criteria of interdependence, that support particular communicative situations" (337). Discourse-democracy, liberalism, and republicanism still do not exhaust the possibilities for democratic political theory or civic democratic pedagogy. There are others, including: radical democracy as proposed by Karl Marx and the Frankfurt School, deliberative-dialogic democracy as proposed by James Bohman (*Public Deliberation,* chs. 1–2), and agonistic pluralism as outlined by Chantal Mouffe (*The Democratic Paradox,* chs. 2–3).

Works Cited

Adams, John Quincy. *Lectures on Rhetoric Oratory, Delivered to the Classes of Senior and Junior Sophisters in Harvard University.* 2 vols. Cambridge: Hilliard and Metcalf, 1810.

Althusser, Louis. *For Marx.* Trans. Ben Brewster. New York: Verso, 1996.

Ames, William. *The Marrow of Sacred Divinity, Drawne Out of the Holy Scriptures, and the Interpreters Thereof, and Brought into Method.* London: Printed by Edward Griffin for Henry Overton, 1642.

———. *Technometry.* Trans Lee W. Gibbs. Philadelphia: University of Pennsylvania Press, 1979.

Anderson, Benedict. *Imagined Communities: Reflections on the Origin and Spread of Nationalism.* New York: Verso, 1991.

Andrews, John. *Elements of Logick. The Second Edition, with Corrections and Additions.* Philadelphia: B. B. Hopkins and Co., 1807.

———. *Elements of Rhetorick and Belles Lettres Compiled for the Use of Schools.* Philadelphia: Moses Thomas, 1813.

Annenberg Public Policy Center of the University of Pennsylvania. "Civility in the House of Representatives: The 106 Congress." 9 March 2001. <http://www.annenbergpublicpolicycenter.org/03_political_communication/civility/2001_civility106th.pdf> (accessed 9 July 2004).

Appleby, Joyce. *Capitalism and the New Social Order: The Republican Vision of the 1790s.* New York: New York UP, 1984.

———. *Liberalism and Republicanism in the Historical Imagination.* Cambridge: Harvard UP, 1992.

Arendt, Hannah. *The Human Condition.* Intro. Margaret Canovan. 3rd ed. Chicago: U of Chicago P, 1998.

——. "What is Authority?" *Between Past and Future: Eight Exercises in Political Thought.* New York: Viking Press, 1968. 91–141.

Aristotle. *On Rhetoric: A Theory of Civic Discourse.* Trans. George Kennedy. Oxford: Oxford UP, 1991.

——. *The Poetics. Criticism: Major Statements.* Ed. Charles Kaplan and William Anderson. 3rd ed. New York: St. Martin's Press, 1991. 21–54.

——. *The Politics and the Constitution of Athens.* Ed. Benjamin Everson. Trans. Benjamin Jowett. Cambridge: Cambridge UP, 1996.

Aronowitz, Stanley, and Henry Giroux. *Education Under Siege.* 2nd ed. Westport: Bergin and Garvey, 1993.

Asen, Robert. "A Discourse Theory of Citizenship." *Quarterly Journal of Speech* 90.2 (2004): 189–211.

Aune, James Arnt. *Rhetoric and Marxism.* Boulder: Westview Press, 1994.

——. *Selling the Free Market: The Rhetoric of Economic Correctness.* New York: Guilford Press, 2004.

Bailyn, Bernard. *The Ideological Origins of the American Revolution.* Enlarged ed. Cambridge: Harvard UP, 1992.

——. *The New England Merchants in the Seventeenth Century.* Cambridge: Harvard UP, 1955.

Balibar, Etienne. "The Basic Concepts of Historical Materialism." *Reading Capital.* By Louis Althusser and Etienne Balibar. Trans. Ben Brewster. New York: Verso, 1997. 199–308.

Banekker, Benjamin. "Copy of a Letter from Benjamin Banekker to the Secretary of State, with His Answer." *Unchained Voices: An Anthology of Black Authors in the English-Speaking World of the 18th Century.* Ed. Vincent Carretta. Lexington: UP of Kentucky, 1996. 319–24.

Baron, Dennis E. *Grammar and Good Taste: Reforming the American Language.* New Haven: Yale UP, 1982.

Barone, Dennis. "Before the Revolution: Formal Rhetoric in Philadelphia During the Federal Era." *Pennsylvania History* 54 (1987): 244–62.

——. "Hostility and Rapprochement: Formal Rhetoric in Philadelphia before 1775." *Pennsylvania History* 56 (1989): 15–32.

Beam, Jacob N. *The American Whig Society of Princeton University.* Princeton: Published by the Society, 1933.

Beard, Charles. *The Economic Basis of Politics.* Intro. Clyde W. Barrow. New Brunswick: Transaction Publishers, 2002.

————. *An Economic Interpretation of the Constitution of the United States.* Intro. Forrest McDonald. New York: Free Press, 1986.

————. *Economic Origins of Jeffersonian Democracy.* New York: Macmillan Company, 1936.

Bellah, Robert, Richard Madsen, William Sullivan, Ann Swidler, and Stephen Tipton. *Habits of the Heart: Individualism and Commitment in American Life.* Berkeley: U of California P, 1996.

Benhabib, Seyla. "Models of Public Space: Hannah Arendt, the Liberal Tradition, and Jürgen Habermas." Calhoun 73–98.

Bercovitch, Sacvan. *The Puritan Origins of the American Self.* New Haven: Yale UP, 1975.

Berkeley, George. *Principles of Human Knowledge and Three Dialogues Between Hylas and Philonous.* Ed. Roger Woolhouse. New York: Penguin, 1988.

Berlin, James. *Rhetoric and Reality: Writing Instruction in American Colleges, 1900– 1985.* Carbondale: Southern Illinois UP, 1987.

Blackwell, Anthony. *The Sacred Classics Defended and Illustrated: Or an Essay Humbly Offer'd Towards Proving the Purity, Propriety, and True Eloquence of the Writers of the New Testament.* London: C. Rivington, 1727.

Blair, Hugh. *Lectures on Rhetoric and Belles Lettres.* 2 vols. London: W. Strahan and T. Cadell, 1783.

Blair, Samuel. *An Account of the College of New Jersey.* New Jersey: James Parker, 1764.

Bloom, Allan. *The Closing of the American Mind.* New York: Simon and Schuster, 1987.

Bohman, James. *Public Deliberation: Pluralism, Complexity, and Democracy.* Cambridge: MIT Press, 1996.

Bridenbaugh, Carl. *Cities in Revolt: Urban Life in America, 1743–1776.* New York: Alfred A. Knopf, 1955.

————. *Cities in the Wilderness: The First Century of Urban Life in America, 1625–1742.* New York: Ronald Press Company, 1938.

Bridenbaugh, Carl, and Jessica Bridenbaugh. *Rebels and Gentlemen: Philadelphia in the Age of Franklin.* New York: Reynal and Hitchcock, 1942.

Broaddus, Dorothy C. *Genteel Rhetoric: Writing High Culture in Nineteenth-Century Boston.* Columbia: U of South Carolina P, 1999.

Brobeck, Stephen. "Revolutionary Change in Colonial Philadelphia: The Brief Life of the Proprietary Gentry." *William and Mary Quarterly* 3rd ser. 33 (1976): 410–35.

Brody, Miriam. *Manly Writing: Gender, Rhetoric, and the Rise of Composition*. Carbondale: Southern Illinois UP, 1993.

Bronson, Walter. *The History of Brown University, 1764–1914*. Providence: Published by the University, 1914.

"Brothers in Unity, Secretary's Records, 1783–1803." Mss. 40.56.8. Yale University, Sterling Memorial Library. Yale Manuscripts and Archives.

Brown, Richard D. *Knowledge Is Power: The Diffusion of Information in Early America, 1700–1865*. Oxford: Oxford UP, 1989.

Brown, Richard Harvey. "Global Capitalism, National Sovereignty, and the Decline of Democratic Space." *Rhetoric and Public Affairs* 5.2 (2002): 347–57.

Brown, William Hill. *The Power of Sympathy. The Power of Sympathy and The Coquette*. Ed. Carla Mulford. New York: Penguin, 1996. 1–104.

Browne, Stephen Howard. *Jefferson's Call for Nationhood: The First Inaugural Address*. College Station: Texas A&M UP, 2003.

Brubacher, John S. *Higher Education in Transition: An American History, 1636–1956*. New York: Harper and Row, 1958.

Buchanan, Patrick. *A Republic, Not an Empire: Reclaiming America's Destiny*. Washington D.C.: Regnery Publishing, 2002.

Burke, Kenneth. *A Grammar of Motives*. Berkeley: U of California P, 1969.

———. *The Philosophy of Literary Form: Studies in Symbolic Action*. 3rd ed. Berkeley: U of California P, 1973.

———. *A Rhetoric of Motives*. Berkeley: U of California P, 1969.

Bushman, Richard. *From Puritan to Yankee: Character and the Social Order in Connecticut, 1690–1765*. Cambridge: Harvard UP, 1967.

———. *The Refinement of America: Persons, Houses, Cities*. New York: Alfred A. Knopf, 1992.

Butterfield, L. H. *John Witherspoon Comes to America: A Documentary Based Largely on New Materials*. New Jersey: Princeton UP, 1953.

Buxbaum, Melvin H. "Benjamin Franklin and William Smith: Their School and Their Dispute." *Historical Magazine of the Protestant Episcopal Church* 39 (1970): 361–82.

Calhoun, Craig, ed. *Habermas and the Public Sphere*. Cambridge: MIT Press, 1992.

Canby, Courtlandt. "A Note on the Influence of Oxford University upon William and Mary College in the Eighteenth Century." *William and Mary Quarterly* 2nd ser. 21 (1941): 243–47.

Castiglione, Baldesar. *The Book of the Courtier.* Trans. George Bull. New York: Penguin, 1976.

Channing, Edward T. *Lectures Read to the Seniors in Harvard College.* Boston: Ticknor and Fields, 1856.

Cheyney, Edward Potts. *History of the University of Pennsylvania, 1740–1940.* Philadelphia: U of Pennsylvania P, 1940.

Cicero. *De Inventione, De Optima Genere Oratorum, Topica.* Trans. H. M. Hubbell. Cambridge: Harvard UP, 1949.

———. *De Oratore.* Trans. and ed. J. S. Watson. Intro. Ralph Micken. Carbondale: Southern Illinois UP, 1970.

Clap, Thomas. *The Annals of the History of Yale College.* New Haven: Printed by John Hotchkiss and B. Mecon, 1766.

———. *An Essay on the Nature and Foundation of Moral Virtue and Obligation.* New Haven: B. Mecon, 1765.

Clark, Gregory. *Dialogue, Dialectic, and Conversation: A Social Perspective on the Function of Writing.* Foreword by Robert J. Connors. Carbondale: Southern Illinois UP, 1990.

———. "The Oratorical Poetic of Timothy Dwight." Clark and Halloran, 57–77.

———. *Rhetorical Landscapes in America: Variations on a Theme from Kenneth Burke.* Columbia: U of South Carolina P, 2004.

Clark, Gregory, and S. Michael Halloran. Introduction. "Transformations of Public Discourse in Nineteenth-Century America." *Oratorical Culture in Nineteenth-Century America.* Ed. Clark and Halloran. Carbondale: Southern Illinois UP, 1993.

"Cliosophic Society Archives, Clerk's Documents, Final Minutes, 1792–1801." Mss. Princeton University, Seeley J. Mudd Manuscript Library.

Cloud, Dana. "The Materiality of Discourse as Oxymoron: A Challenge to Critical Rhetoric." *Western Journal of Communciation* 58 (1994): 141–63.

———. "Rhetoric and Economics: Or, How Rhetoricians Can Get Some Class." *Quarterly Journal of Speech* 88.3 (2002): 342–62.

Collins, Varnum Lansing. *The Continental Congress at Princeton.* Princeton: Princeton UP, 1908.

———. *President Witherspoon: A Biography.* 2 vols. Princeton: Princeton UP, 1925.

Connors, Robert. *Composition-Rhetoric: Backgrounds, Theory, and Pedagogy.* Pittsburgh: U of Pittsburgh P, 1997.

Coogan, David. "Counterpublics in Public Housing: Reframing the Politics of Service-Learning." *College English* 67.5 (2005): 461–82.

Court, Franklin. *The Scottish Connection: The Rise of English Literary Study in Early America.* Syracuse: Syracuse UP, 2001.

Cremin, Lawrence. *American Education: The Colonial Experience, 1607–1783.* New York: Harper Torchbooks, 1970.

———. *American Education: The National Experience: 1783–1876.* New York: Harper and Row, 1980.

Crowley, Sharon. *The Methodical Memory: Invention in Current-Traditional Rhetoric.* Carbondale: Southern Illinois UP, 1990.

Davidson, Cathy. *Revolution and the Word: The Rise of the Novel in America.* New York: Oxford UP, 1986.

Davis, Victor. *Mexifornia: A State of Becoming.* San Francisco: Encounter Books, 2003.

Day, Jeremiah. "Notebook, 1755." Mss. 175.2.18.271. Day Family Papers. Yale University, Sterling Memorial Library.

DeLuca, Kevin. "Articulation Theory: A Discursive Grounding for Rhetorical Practice." *Philosophy and Rhetoric* 32 (1999): 334–48.

de Tocqueville, Alexis. *Democracy in America.* Trans. George Lawrence. Ed. J. P. Mayer. New York: Harper Collins, 1969.

Dexter, Franklin B. *Biographical Sketches of the Graduates of Yale College with Annals of the College.* 6 vols. New York: Henry Holt and Company, 1885–1911.

Diamond, Peter J. "Witherspoon, William Smith, and the Scottish Philosophy in Revolutionary America." *Scotland and America in the Age of the Enlightenment.* Ed. Richard Sher and Jeffrey R. Smitten. Princeton: Princeton UP, 1990. 114–32.

Dickinson, Jonathan. *Letters from a Farmer in Pennsylvania, to the Inhabitants of the British Colonies.* Intro. Robert Halsey. New York: Outlook Company, 1903.

Documents Relating to the Colonial History of the State of New Jersey. 31 vols. Ed. William Nelson and A. Van Doren Honeyman. Paterson: Call Printing and Publishing Co., 1897–1923.

Dowling, William C. *Poetry and Ideology in Revolutionary Connecticut.* Athens: U of Georgia P, 1990.

D'Souza, Dinesh. *What's So Great about America.* New York: Penguin, 2002.

Duché, Jacob. *Observations on a Variety of Subjects, Literary, Moral, and Religious.* Philadelphia: J. Dunlop, 1774.

———. *A Poem by a Student of the College of Philadelphia.* Philadelphia: B. Franklin and D. Hall, 1756.

Duncan, William. *The Elements of Logick. In Four Books.* London: Pall-Mall, 1748.

Dwight, Timothy. *America; Or a Poem on the Settlement of the British Colonies Addressed to Friends of Freedom, and their Country.* New Haven: Printed by Thomas and Samuel, 1771.

———. *A Dissertation on the History, Eloquence, and Poetry of the Bible, Delivered at the Public Commencement at New Haven.* New Haven: Printed by Thomas and Green, 1772.

———. *An Essay on Education; Delivered at the Public Commencement at Yale College, in New Haven, September 9th, 1772.* New Haven: Thomas and Samuel Green, 1772.

———. "The Friend XI." *The New-Haven Gazette and the Connecticut Magazine* 22 June 1786.

———. *Greenfield Hill: A Poem in Seven Parts.* New York: Childs and Swain, 1794.

———. *President Dwight's Decisions of Questions Discussed by the Senior Class in Yale College, in 1813 and 1814. From Stenographic Notes by Theodore Dwight.* New York: Jonathan Leavitt, 1833.

———. *Sermon on the Means of Public Happiness. The True Means of Establishing Public Happiness, a Sermon, Delivered on the 7th of July, 1795, before the Connecticut Society of Cincinnati.* New Haven: Greens and Beers, 1795.

———. *Sermons by Timothy Dwight.* 2 vols. New Haven: Hezekiah and Durrie and Peck, 1828.

———. *Theology; Explained and Defended in a Series of Sermons.* 5 vols. Middletown, NY: Clark and Lyman, 1818.

———. *Travels in New England and New York.* 4 vols. New Haven: S. Converse, 1821.

———. *A Valedictory Address to the Young Gentlemen, Who Commenced Bachelors of Arts at Yale College, July 25th, 1776.* New Haven: Thomas and Samuel Green, 1776.

"The Early Days of Phi Beta Kappa, 1776–1781." Vol. 2 of *A Documentary History of Education in the South Before 1860.* 5 vols. Ed. Edgar W. Knight. Chapel Hill: U of North Carolina P, 1950. 243–59.

Eberly, Rosa A. *Citizen Critics: Literary Public Spheres.* Urbana: U of Illinois P, 2000.

Edelman, Murray. *Constructing the Political Spectacle.* Chicago: U of Chicago P, 1988.

———. *The Symbolic Uses of Politics.* Urbana: U of Illinois P, 1967.

Edwards, Jonathan. *"The Mind" of Jonathan Edwards, a Reconstructed Text*. Ed. Leon Howard. Berkeley: U of California P, 1963.

———. *Religious Affections*. Ed. John E. Smith. New Haven: Yale UP, 1959.

Eldred, Janet Carey, and Peter Mortensen. *Imagining Rhetoric: Composing Women of the Early United States*. Pittsburgh: U of Pittsburgh P, 2002.

Eley, Geoff. "Nations, Publics, and Political Centuries: Placing Habermas in the Nineteenth Century." Calhoun 289–339.

Elkins, Stanley, and Eric McKitrick. *The Age of Federalism: The Early American Republic, 1788–1800*. Oxford: Oxford UP, 1993.

Ellis, Joseph. *After the Revolution: Profiles of Early American Culture*. New York: W. W. Norton and Company, 1979.

———. *The New England Mind in Transition: Samuel Johnson of Connecticut, 1696–1772*. New Haven: Yale UP, 1973.

Engerman, Stanley L., and Robert E. Gallman, eds. *The Cambridge Economic History of the United States, Volume One: The Colonial Era*. Cambridge: Cambridge UP, 1996.

Ennals, Thomas. *An Account of the Commencement in the College of Philadelphia: May 17th, 1775*. Philadelphia: 1775.

Evans, Nathaniel. *Poems on Several Occasions, with Some Other Compositions*. Philadelphia: J. Dunlap, 1772.

An Exercise Containing a Dialogue and Ode . . . Performed at the Commencement in the College of Philadelphia, May 23rd, 1761. Philadelphia: W. Dunlap, 1761.

Farnaby, Thomas. *Indexus Rhetoricus*. London: Felice Kyngstonio, 1625.

Farrell, Thomas. *Norms of Rhetorical Culture*. New Haven: Yale UP, 1993.

Ferguson, Adam. *An Essay on the History of Civil Society*. Ed. Fania Oz-Salzberger. Cambridge: Cambridge UP, 1995.

Ferreira-Buckley, Linda. "'Scotch Knowledge' and the Formation of Rhetorical Studies in 19th-Century England." *Scottish Rhetoric and Its Influences*. Ed. Lynee Lewis Gaillet. New York: Hermagoras Press, 1998. 163–75.

Fiering, Norman. "President Samuel Johnson and the Circle of Knowledge." *William and Mary Quarterly* 28.2 (1971): 199–236.

Fish, Stanley. "Why We Built the Ivory Tower." *New York Times* 21 May 2004: A23.

Fliegelman, Jay. *Declaring Independence: Jefferson, Natural Language, and the Culture of Performance*. Stanford: Stanford UP, 1993.

Flower, Elizabeth, and Murray G. Murphy. *A History of Philosophy in America*. 2 vols. New York: Capricorn Books, 1977.

Foster, Hannah Webster. *The Coquette: The Power of Sympathy and the Coquette.* Ed. Carla Mulford. New York: Penguin, 1996. 1–104.

Four Dissertations on the Reciprocal Advantages of a Perpetual Union between Great Britain and Her American Colonies Written for Mr. Sargeant's Prize-Medal. Philadelphia: Thomas Bradford, 1766.

France, Mike, and William Symonds. "Diversity Is About to Get More Elusive, Not Less." *BusinessWeek* 7 July 2003: 30.

Franklin, Benjamin. *The Autobiography of Benjamin Franklin.* Ed. Leonard W. Labaree, Ralph Ketcham, Helen Boatfield, and Helene H. Fineman. New Haven: Yale UP, 1964.

———. "The Idea of an English School." *The Papers of Benjamin Franklin.* Ed. Leonard W. Labaree and Whitfield Bell Jr. Vol. 4. New Haven: Yale UP, 1961. 101–108.

———. Letter to Samuel Johnson, 22 November 1750. *The Papers of Benjamin Franklin.* Ed. Leonard W. Labaree and Whitfield Bell Jr. Vol. 4. New Haven: Yale UP, 1961. 75–76.

———. "Observations Relative to the Intentions of the Original Founders of the Academy in Philadelphia." *The Writings of Benjamin Franklin.* Ed. Albert Henry Smith. Vol. 10. New York: Haskell House Publishers Ltd., 1970. 9–29.

———. "On the Need for an Academy." *The Papers of Benjamin Franklin.* Ed. Leonard W. Labaree and Whitfield J. Bell Jr. Vol. 3. New Haven: Yale UP, 1961. 385–86.

———. "Proposals Relating to the Education of Youth in Pennsylvania." *The Papers of Benjamin Franklin.* Ed. Leonard W. Labaree and Whitfield J. Bell Jr. Vol. 3. New Haven: Yale UP, 1961. 397–421.

Fraser, Nancy. "Rethinking the Public Sphere: A Contribution to the Critique of Actually Existing Democracy." Calhoun 109–142.

Freimarck, Vincent. "Rhetoric at Yale in 1807." *The Proceedings of the American Philosophical Society* 110 (1966): 235–55.

Gale, Benjamin. *A Letter to a Member of the Lower House Assembly of the Colony of Connecticut.* New Haven, CT: n.p., 1759.

———. *The Present State of the Colony of Connecticut Considered.* New London, CT: n.p., 1755.

Galenson, David W. "The Settlement and Growth of the Colonies: Population, Labor, and Economic Development." *The Cambridge Economic History of the United States, Volume One: The Colonial Era.* 135–208.

Garnham, Nicholas. "Political Economy or Cultural Studies: Reconciliation or Divorce?" *Critical Studies in Mass Communication* 12.1 (1995): 62–71.

Gegenheimer, Albert Frank. *William Smith, Educator and Churchman: 1727–1803.* Philadelphia: U of Pennsylvania P, 1943.

Giroux, Henry. *Border Crossings: Culture Workers and the Politics of Education.* New York: Routledge, 1992.

Giroux, Henry, and Susan Searls Giroux. *Take Back Higher Education: Race, Youth, and the Crisis of Democracy in the Post–Civil Rights Era.* New York: Palgrave, 2004.

Goodson, Sarah, Ludwell Johnson, Richard B. Sherman, Thad W. Tate, and Helen C. Walker. *The College of William and Mary: A History, Volume I 1693–1888.* Williamsburg, VA: King and Queen Press, 1993.

Gramsci, Antonio. *Selections from Cultural Writings.* Ed. David Forgacs and Geoffrey Nowell Smith. Trans. William Boelhower. Cambridge: Harvard UP, 1991.

———. *Selections from the Prison Notebooks.* Ed. and trans. Quintin Hoare and Geoffrey Nowell Smith. New York: International Publishers, 1971.

Grasso, Christopher. *A Speaking Aristocracy: Transferring Public Discourse in Eighteenth-Century America.* Chapel Hill: U of North Carolina P, 1999.

Graydon, Alexander. *Memoirs of His Own Time with Reminiscences of the Men and Events of the Revolution.* Ed. John Stockton Litteli. Philadelphia: Lindsay and Blakiston, 1846.

Greene, Ronald Walter. "Rhetoric and Capitalism: Rhetorical Agency as Communicative Labor." *Philosophy and Rhetoric* 37.3 (2004): 188–206.

Greider, William. *One World, Ready or Not: The Manic Logic of Global Capitalism.* New York: Simon and Schuster, 1997.

Grossberg, Lawrence. "Strategies of Marxist Cultural Interpretation." *Critical Perspectives on Media and Society.* Ed. Robert K. Avery and David Eason. New York: Guilford Press, 1991.

———. *We Gotta Get Out of This Place: Popular Conservatism and Postmodern Culture.* New York: Routledge, 1992.

Guild, Rueben. "The First Commencement of Rhode Island College and American Independence." *Collections of the Rhode Island Historical Society.* Vol. 7. Providence: Kellogg Printing Company, 1885. 267–98.

Gustafson, Sandra. *Eloquence Is Power: Oratory and Performance in Early America.* Chapel Hill: U of North Carolina P, 2000.

Gustafson, Thomas. *Representative Words: Politics, Literature, and American Language, 1776–1865.* Cambridge: Cambridge UP, 1992.

Guthrie, Warren. "The Development of Rhetorical Theory in America." *Speech Monographs* 8 (1946): 14–22.

———. "The Development of Rhetorical Theory in America, 1635–1850." *Speech Monographs* 14 (1947): 38–54.

Habermas, Jürgen. *Between Facts and Norms: Contributions to a Discourse Theory of Law and Democracy.* Trans. William Rehg. Cambridge: MIT Press, 1996. First published in 1992.

———. *The Structural Transformation of the Public Sphere: An Inquiry into a Category of Bourgeois Society.* Trans. Thomas Burger. Cambridge: MIT Press, 1991.

———. "Three Normative Models of Democracy." *Democracy and Difference: Contesting the Boundaries of the Political.* Ed. Seyla Benhabib. Princeton: Princeton UP, 1996. 21–30.

Hall, Stuart. *The Hard Road to Renewal: Thatcherism and the Crisis of the Left.* New York: Verso, 1988.

———. "On Postmodernism and Articulation: An Interview with Stuart Hall." Ed. Lawrence Grossberg. *Journal of Communication Inquiry* 10.2 (1986): 45–60.

———. "The Problem of Ideology—Marxism without Guarantees." *Journal of Communication Inquiry* 10.2 (1986): 28–44.

———. "Signification, Representation, Ideology: Althusser and the Post-Structuralist Debates." *Critical Studies in Mass Communication* 2 (1985): 91–114.

Halloran, S. Michael. "From Rhetoric to Composition: The Teaching of Writing in America to 1900." *A Short History of Writing Instruction.* New York: Hermagoras Press, 1990. 151–82.

Hamilton, Alexander. "Report on Manufactures, Communicated to the House of Representatives, December 5, 1791." *The Works of Alexander Hamilton.* Ed. Henry Cabot Lodge. Vol. 4. New York: G. P. Putnam's Sons, 1904. 70–198.

Hardt, Michael, and Antonio Negri. *Empire.* Cambridge: Harvard UP, 2000.

Hariman, Robert. *Political Style: The Artistry of Power.* Chicago: U of Chicago P, 1995.

Hartz, Louis. *The Liberal Tradition in America.* Intro. Tom Wicker. New York: Harcourt, Brace and Company, 1991.

Harvey, David. *The Condition of Postmodernity: An Inquiry into the Origins of Cultural Change.* Cambridge: Blackwell, 1990.

Hastings, George Everett. *The Life and Works of Francis Hopkinson*. Chicago: University of Chicago Press, 1926.

Hatch, Nathan O. *The Democratization of American Christianity*. New Haven: Yale UP, 1989.

———. *The Sacred Cause of Liberty: Republican Thought and the Millennium in Revolutionary New England*. New Haven: Yale UP, 1977.

Hauser, Gerard. "Civil Society and the Principle of the Public Sphere." *Philosophy and Rhetoric* 31.1 (1998): 19–40.

———. *Vernacular Voices: The Rhetoric of Publics and Public Spheres*. Columbia: U of South Carolina P, 1999.

Heimart, Alan. *Religion and the American Mind: From the Great Awakening to the Revolution*. Cambridge: Harvard UP, 1966.

Held, David. *Models of Democracy*. 2nd ed. Stanford: Stanford UP, 1996.

Higman, B. W. "Economic and Social Development of the British West Indies, from Settlement to ca. 1850." *The Cambridge Economic History of the United States, Volume One: The Colonial Era*. 297–336.

Hobbes, Thomas. *Leviathon*. Ed. Edwin Curley. Indianapolis: Hackett Publishing Company, 1994.

Hoeveler, J. David. *Creating the American Mind: Intellect and Politics in the Colonial Colleges*. New York: Rowman and Littlefield, 2002.

Holcomb, Christopher. *Mirth Making: The Rhetorical Discourse of Jesting in Early Modern England*. Columbia: U of South Carolina P, 2001.

Holmes, John. *The Art of Rhetoric Made Easy*. London: A. Parker, 1783. First published in 1739.

Hopkinson, Francis. "On Education." *Pennsylvania Gazette* 21 (Nov. 1754).

Howard, Leon. *The Connecticut Wits*. Chicago: U of Chicago P, 1943.

Howe, John. *Language and Political Meaning in Revolutionary America*. Amherst: U of Massachusetts P, 2004.

Howell, Wilbur Samuel. *Eighteenth-Century British Logic and Rhetoric*. New Jersey: Princeton UP, 1971.

Hume, David. "Of Commerce." *Hume's Political Discourses*. Intro. William Robertson. London: Walter Scott Publishing Company, 1906. 1–14.

———. "Of Eloquence." *Essays Moral, Political, and Literary*. Cambridge: Oxford UP, 1963. 98–111.

———. "Of Refinement in the Arts." *Hume's Political Discourses*. Intro. William Robertson. London: Walter Scott Publishing Company, 1906. 15–26.

————. *A Treatise of Human Nature.* Ed. L. A. Selby-Bigge and P. H. Nidditch. Oxford: Clarendon Press, 1978.

Humphrey, David. *From King's College to Columbia: 1746–1800.* New York: Columbia UP, 1976.

Hunt, Isaac. *A Humble Attempt at Scurrility.* Philadelphia: n.p., 1765.

Huntington, Samuel. "The Hispanic Challenge." *Foreign Policy* March/April 2004: 30–45.

Hutcheson, Francis. *An Inquiry into the Original of Our Ideas of Beauty and Virtue.* Hildeshem, UK: George OLMS, 1971. Vol. 1 of *The Collected Works of Francis Hutcheson.* 8 vols.

Isocrates. *Areopagiticus.* Trans. George Norlin. Cambridge: Harvard UP, 1929. Vol. 2 of *Isocrates.* 99–158.

Jaeger, Warner. *Paideia: The Ideals of Greek Culture.* Trans. Gilbert Highet. 3 vols. New York: Oxford UP, 1939.

Jameson, Frederic. *Marxism and Form: Twentieth-Century Dialectical Theories of Literature.* Princeton: Princeton UP, 1971.

————. *Postmodernism; or, the Cultural Logic of Late Capitalism.* Durham, NC: Duke UP, 1991.

Jefferson, Thomas. "First Inaugural." *Basic Readings in U.S. Democracy.* <http://usinfo.state.gov/usa/infousa/facts/democrac/11.htm> (accessed 12 July 2004).

————. *Notes on the State of Virginia. The Portable Thomas Jefferson.* Ed. Merrill D. Peterson. New York: Penguin, 1975. 23–232.

Jennings, Francis. *The Creation of America: Through Revolution and Empire.* Cambridge: Cambridge UP, 2000.

Johnson, Nan. *Nineteenth-Century Rhetoric in North America.* Carbondale: Southern Illinois UP, 1991.

Johnson, Samuel. Letter to Benjamin Franklin, November 1750. *The Papers of Benjamin Franklin.* Ed. Leonard W. Labaree and Whitfield Bell Jr. Vol. 4. New Haven: Yale UP, 1961. 74–75.

————. *Samuel Johnson, President of King's College: His Career and His Writings.* Ed. Herbert and Carol Schneider. 4 vols. New York: Columbia UP, 1929.

Jones, Julian Ward, Jr. "A 'New' Latin Quitrent Poem of the College of William and Mary." *Virginia Magazine of History and Biography* 96.4 (1988): 491–504.

Kames, Henry Home Lord. *Elements of Criticism.* 6th ed. 2 vols. Edinburgh: Printed for John Bell and William Creech and for T. Cadell and G. Robinson, 1785.

Kelley, Brooks Mather. *Yale: A History.* New Haven: Yale UP, 1974.

Kennedy, George. *Classical Rhetoric and Its Christian and Secular Tradition from Ancient to Modern Times.* Chapel Hill: U of North Carolina P, 1980.

"King's College Commencement in the Newspapers." Ed. Milton Halsey Thomas. *Columbia University Quarterly* 22 (June 1930): 226–50.

Klein, Milton M., ed. *The Independent Reflector, or Weekly Essays on Sundry Important Subjects More Particularly Adapted to the Province of New York by William Livingston and Others.* Cambridge: Belknap Press of Harvard UP, 1963.

Laclau, Ernesto. "Identity and Hegemony: The Role of Universality in the Constitution of Political Logics." *Contingency, Hegemony, Universality: Contemporary Dialogues on the Left.* New York: Verso, 2000. 44–89.

Laclau, Ernesto, and Chantal Mouffe. *Hegemony and Socialist Strategy: Towards a Radical Democratic Politics.* London: Verso, 1985.

Landis, Charles I. "Jasper Yeates and His Times." *Pennsylvania Magazine of History and Biography* 46 (1922): 199–231.

Leff, Michael. "The Topics of Argumentative Invention in Latin Rhetorical Theory from Cicero to Boethius." *Rhetorica* 1.1 (1983): 23–44.

Lemay, Leo. *Ebenezer Kinnersley: Franklin's Friend.* Philadelphia: U of Pennsylvania P, 1964.

Linebaugh, Peter, and Marcus Rediker. *The Many-Headed Hydra: Sailors, Slaves, Commoners, and the Hidden History of the Revolutionary Atlantic.* Boston: Beacon Press, 2000.

"Linonian Society Records, 1760–1789." Mss. 40.206.2.5. Yale University, Sterling Memorial Library, Yale Manuscripts and Archives.

Locke, John. *Essay Concerning Human Understanding.* Intro. Alexander Campbell Frasier. 2 vols. New York: Dover Publications, 1959.

———. *Some Thoughts Concerning Education: The Educational Writings of John Locke.* Intro. James L. Axtell. Cambridge: Harvard UP, 1968. 111–326.

———. *Two Treatises of Government.* Ed. Peter Laslett. Cambridge: Cambridge UP, 1960.

Looby, Christopher. *Voicing America: Language, Literary Form, and the Origins of the United States.* Chicago: U of Chicago P, 1996.

Looney, J. Jefferson. *Nurseries of Letters and Republicanism: A Brief History of the American Whig-Cliosophic Society and Its Predecessors, 1765–1941.* Princeton: Trustees of the American Whig-Cliosophic Society, 1996.

Lyon, Janet. *Manifestoes: Provocations of the Modern.* Ithaca, NY: Cornell UP, 1999.

Machiavelli, Niccolo. *Discourses on Livy.* Ed. Harvey C. Mansfield and Nathan Tarcov. Chicago: U of Chicago P, 1996.

MacIntyre, Alasdair. *After Virtue.* Notre Dame: U of Notre Dame P, 1984.

Madison, James, Alexander Hamilton, and John Jay. *The Federalist Papers.* Ed. Isaac Kramnick. New York: Penguin Press, 1987.

Magaw, Samuel. "On the Several Branches of Education." *Pennsylvania Gazette* 21 Nov. 1754.

Main, Jackson Turner. *The Anti-Federalists: Critics of the Constitution, 1781–1788.* New York: W. W. Norton and Company, 1974.

———. *Society and Economy in Colonial Connecticut.* Princeton: Princeton UP, 1985.

———. *The Social Structure of Revolutionary America.* Princeton: Princeton UP, 1965.

Mandeville, Bernard. *The Fable of the Bees: Or, Public Vices, Private Benefits.* 2nd ed. London: Edmund Parker, 1723.

Markley, Robert. *Fallen Languages: Crises of Representation in Newtonian England, 1660–1740.* Ithaca: Cornell UP, 1993.

Martin, Josiah. "On the Several Branches of Science." *Pennsylvania Gazette* 28 Nov. 1754.

Marx, Karl. *A Contribution to the Critique of Political Economy.* Ed. Maurice Dobb. Trans. S. W. Ryazanskaya. New York: International Publishers, 1970.

Mather, Cotton. *Bonifacius: An Essay upon the Good.* Boston: Printed by B. Green for Samuel Gerrish, 1710.

———. *The Christian Philosopher: A Collection of the Best Discoveries of Nature with Religious Improvement.* London: Printed for Eman Matthews at the Bible in Pater-Noster Row, 1721.

———. *Manuductio ad Ministerium: Directions for a Candidate of the Ministry.* Boston: Printed for Thomas Hancock, 1725.

May, Eleazor. "Notebook, 1750–2." Mss. 360.1.3. Yale University, Beinecke Library.

McCaughey, Elizabeth. *From Loyalist to Founding Father: The Political Odyssey of William Samuel Johnson.* New York: Columbia UP, 1980.

McClean, James. *History of the College of New Jersey, from its Origin in 1746 to the Commencement of 1854.* 2 vols. Philadelphia: J. B. Lippincott and Co., 1877.

McConville, Brendan. *These Daring Disturbers of Public Peace: The Struggle for Property and Power in Early New Jersey.* Ithaca: Cornell UP, 1999.

McCoy, Drew. *The Elusive Republic: Political Economy in Jeffersonian America.* Chapel Hill: U of North Carolina P, 1980.

McCusker, John J. "British Mercantilist Policies and the American Colonies." *Cambridge Economic History of the United States, Volume One: The Colonial Era.* 337–62.

McCusker, John J., and Russel R. Menard. *The Economy of British America, 1607–1789.* Chapel Hill: U of North Carolina P, 1985.

McKerrow, Raymie. "Critical Rhetoric: Theory and Practice." *Communication Monographs* 56 (1989) 91–111.

Menard, Russel R. "Economic and Social Development of the South." *Cambridge Economic History of the United States, Volume One: The Colonial Era.* 249–96.

Meranze, Michael, ed. *Essays: Literary, Moral, Philosophical.* Schenectady, NY: Union College Press, 1988.

Miller, Perry. *Jonathan Edwards.* Toronto: William Sloan and Associates, 1949.

———. *The New England Mind: The Seventeenth Century.* Cambridge: Belknap Press of Harvard UP, 1939.

Miller, Thomas P. *The Formation of College English: Rhetoric and Belles Lettres in the British Cultural Provinces.* Pittsburgh: U of Pittsburgh P, 1997.

———. "Introduction." *Selected Writings of John Witherspoon.* Ed. Miller. Carbondale: Southern Illinois UP, 1990. 1–38.

———. "Where Did College English Come From?" *Rhetoric Review* 9.1 (1990): 50–68.

———. "Witherspoon, Blair, and the Rhetoric of Civic Humanism." *Scotland and America in the Age of the Enlightenment.* Ed. Richard B. Sher and Jeffrey Smitten. Princeton: Princeton UP, 1990.

Mitchill, Samuel Latham. *The Present State of Learning at the College of New York.* New York: T and J Swords, 1794.

Montesquieu, Charles Le Secondat. *The Spirit of the Laws.* Ed. and trans. Anne Cohler, Basia Miller, and Harold Stone. Cambridge: Cambridge UP, 1989.

Montgomery, Thomas Harrison. *A History of the University of Pennsylvania from its Foundation to A.D. 1700.* Philadelphia: George W. Jacobs and Co., 1900.

Morgan, Edmund. *The Gentle Puritan: A Life of Ezra Stiles, 1727–1795.* New Haven: Yale UP, 1962.

Morison, Samuel. *Three Centuries of Harvard: 1636–1936.* Cambridge: Belknap Press of Harvard UP, 1963.

Mouffe, Chantal. *The Democratic Paradox.* New York: Verso, 2000.

———. "Hegemony and Ideology in Gramsci." *Gramsci and Marxist Theory.* Ed. Chantal Mouffe. London: Routledge, 1979. 168–204.

Myers, Greg. "Reality, Consensus, and Reform in the Rhetoric of Composition Teaching." *College English* 48.2 (1986): 154–73.

Myers, Minor, Jr. "A Source for Eighteenth-Century Harvard Master's Questions." *William and Mary Quarterly* 3rd ser. 38 (1981): 261–67.

Negt, Oskar, and Alexander Kluge. *Public Sphere and Experience: Toward an Analysis of the Bourgeois and Proletarian Public Spheres.* Trans. Peter Labany, Jamie Owen Daniel, and Assenka Oskiloff. Minneapolis: U of Minnesota P, 1993.

Newton, Roger. "Notebook, December 1783–December 1784." Mss. 261. Yale University, Beinecke Library.

Noll, Mark A. *Princeton and the Republic, 1768–1822: The Search for A Christian Enlightenment in the Era of Samuel Stanhope Smith.* Princeton: Princeton UP, 1989.

O'Gorman, Ned. "Longinus's Sublime Rhetoric, or How Rhetoric Came into its Own." *Rhetoric Society Quarterly* 34.2 (2004): 71–89.

Ong, Walter. *Ramus, Method, and the Decay of Dialogue: From the Art of Discourse to the Art of Reason.* Cambridge: Harvard UP, 1958.

Paine, Thomas. *The Age of Reason.* Intro. Philip S. Foner. Secaucus, NJ: Carol Publishing Group, 1998.

———. *Common Sense.* New York: Barnes and Noble Books, 1995.

Pangle, Thomas. *The Spirit of Modern Republicanism: The Moral Vision of the American Founders and the Philosophy of John Locke.* Chicago: U of Chicago P, 1988.

Perelman, Chaim, and Lucie Olbrechts-Tyteca. *The New Rhetoric: A Treatise on Argumentation.* Trans. John Wilkinson and Purcell Weaver. Notre Dame: U of Notre Dame P, 1969.

Plain Truth: Addressed to the Inhabitants of America, Containing the Remarks on a Late Pamphlet, Intitled Common Sense. Philadelphia: n.p., 1776.

Pocock, J. G. A. *The Machiavellian Moment: Florentine Political Thought and the Atlantic Republican Tradition.* Princeton: Princeton UP, 1975.

Pomfret, John E. *Colonial New Jersey: A History.* New York: Charles Scribner's Sons, 1973.

Pope, Alexander. *Essay on Criticism. The Poems of Alexander Pope.* Ed. John Butt. New Haven: Yale UP, 1963. 143–68.

Potkay, Adam. *The Fate of Eloquence in the Age of Hume.* Ithaca, NY: Cornell UP, 1994.

Potter, David. *Debating in the Colonial Charter Colleges: An Historical Survey, 1642–1900.* New York: Bureau of Publications, Teachers College, 1944.

Poulakos, Takis. *Speaking for the Polis: Isocrates' Rhetorical Education.* Columbia: U of South Carolina P, 1997.

"Presidents' Declaration on the Civic Responsibility of Higher Education." *Campus Compact.* 15 July 1999. <http://www.compact.org/presidential/declaration.html> (accessed 3 June 2004).

Priestley, Joseph. *A Course of Lectures on the Theory of Language and Universal Grammar.* Warrington, UK: W. Eyres, 1762.

Purcell, Robert J. *Connecticut in Transition: 1775–1818.* Middletown: Wesleyan UP, 1963.

Purvis, Thomas. *Proprietors, Patronage, and Paper Money: Legislative Politics in New Jersey, 1703–1776.* New Brunswick: Rutgers UP, 1986.

Putnam, Robert. *Bowling Alone: The Collapse and Revival of American Community.* New York: Simon and Schuster, 2001.

Quintilian. *Institutio Oratoria.* Trans. H. E. Butler. 4 vols. Cambridge: Harvard UP, 1921.

Rahe, Paul. *Republics, Ancient and Modern: Classical Republicanism and the American Revolution.* Chapel Hill: U of North Carolina P, 1992.

Ramus, Peter. *Arguments Against Quintilian. Translation and Text of Peter Ramus's Rhetoricae Distinctiones in Quintilianum (1549).* Trans. Carole Newlands. DeKalb: Northern Illinois UP, 1986.

Rathbun, Lyon. "The Ciceronian Rhetoric of John Quincy Adams." *Rhetorica* 18.2 (2000): 175–215.

Ravitz, Abe C. "Timothy Dwight: Professor of Rhetoric." *New England Quarterly* 29 (1956): 63–71.

Reid, Thomas. *Essays on the Intellectual Powers of Man.* Intro. Baruch A. Brody. Cambridge: MIT Press, 1969.

Reinhold, Meyer. "Opponents of Classical Learning in America during the Revolutionary Period." *Proceedings of the American Philosophical Society* 112.4 (1968): 221–34.

Reynolds, Nedra. "Who's Going to Cross This Border? Travel Metaphors, Material Conditions, and Contested Places." *Journal of Advanced Composition* 20.3 (2000): 541–64.

Richard, Carl J. *The Founders and the Classics: Greece, Rome, and the American Enlightenment.* Cambridge: Harvard UP, 1994.

Richardson, Alexander. *The Logicians School-Master: Or a Comment on Ramus Logicke.* London: Printed for John Bellamie, 1629.

The Rise and Progress of the Young Ladies Academy of Philadelphia, Containing an Account of a Number of Examinations and Commencements; the Charter and Bye-Laws; Likewise a Number of Orations Delivered by the Young Ladies and Several Trustees of Said Institutions. Philadelphia: Stewart and Cochran, 1794.

Roach, Helen. *History of Speech Education at Columbia College, 1754–1940.* New York: Teachers College, Columbia UP, 1950.

Roberts-Miller, Patricia. *Deliberate Conflict: Models of Democracy and the Teaching of Argument.* Carbondale: Southern Illinois UP, 2004.

———. "John Quincy Adams's Amistad Argument: The Problem of Outrage; Or, the Constraints of Decorum." *Rhetoric Society Quarterly* 23.2 (2002): 5–25.

———. *Voices Crying in the Wilderness: Public Discourse and the Paradox of Puritan Rhetoric.* Tuscaloosa: U of Alabama P, 1999.

Robson, David. *Educating Republicans: The College in the Era of the American Revolution, 1750–1800.* Westport: Greenwood Press, 1985.

Roche, Jacob. *The Colonial Colleges in the War for American Independence.* New York: National University Publications, 1986.

Rollin, Charles. *The Method of Teaching and Studying the Belles Lettres . . . Translated from the French.* 5 vols. London: Printed for C. Hitch, L. Hawes, and Paternoster Row, 1758.

Rousseau, Jean-Jacques. *The First and Second Discourses.* Ed. Roger D. Masters. Trans. Roger D. and Judith R. Masters. Boston: Bedford/St. Martin's Press, 1964.

Rudolph, Frederick. *The American College and University: A History.* New York: Alfred A. Knopf, 1962.

Rush, Benjamin. "Observations on the Study of Latin and Greek Languages, as Branch of Liberal Education, with Hints of a Plan of Liberal Education without them, Accommodated to the Present State of Society, Manners and Government in the United States." Meranze 13–34.

———. "Of the Mode of Education Proper in a Republic." Meranze 5–13.

———. "A Plan for Establishing Public Schools in Pennsylvania and For Conducting Education Agreeably to a Republican Form of Government. Addressed to the Legislature and Citizens of Pennsylvania, in the Year 1786." Meranze 1–5.

———. *Thoughts on Female Education . . . Addressed to the Visitors of the Young Ladies Academy in Philadelphia 28 July 1787*. Boston: John W. Folsom, 1791.

Russell, David. *Writing in the Academic Disciplines: A Curricular History*. 2nd ed. Carbondale: Southern Illinois UP, 2002.

Ryan, Mary P. "Gender and Public Access: Women's Politics in Nineteenth-Century America." Calhoun 259–88.

Ryan, Michael. *Marxism and Deconstruction: A Critical Articulation*. Baltimore: Johns Hopkins UP, 1982.

Sanderson, Robert. *Logicae Artis Compendium*. Ed. E. J. Ashworth. Bologna, It.: Editrice, 1985.

"Satires against the Tories. Written in the Last War Between the Whigs and Cliosophic." 1770. Mss. Historical Society of Philadelphia.

Schiappa, Edward. *Defining Reality: Definitions and the Politics of Meaning*. Carbondale: Southern Illinois UP, 2003.

Schlesinger, Arthur, Jr. *The Age of Jackson*. Boston: Little, Brown and Company, 1945.

Scholes, Robert. *The Rise and Fall of English: Reconstructing English as a Discipline*. New Haven: Yale UP, 1998.

Schudson, Michael. *Discovering the News: A Social History of American Newspapers*. New York: Basic Books, 1978.

Schultz, Lucille M. *The Young Composers: Composition's Beginning in Nineteenth-Century Schools*. Carbondale: Southern Illinois UP, 1999.

Schumpeter, Joseph A. *A History of Economic Analysis*. Ed. Elizabeth B. Schumpeter. New York: Oxford UP, 1954.

Scott, Blake. "John Witherspoon's Normalizing Pedagogy of Ethos." *Rhetoric Review* 16 (1997): 58–75.

Sennett, Richard. *The Fall of Public Man*. New York: W. W. Norton and Company, 1974.

Shaftesbury, Anthony Ashley Cooper. *An Inquiry Concerning Virtue, or Merit*. Manchester, UK: Manchester UP, 1977.

Sher, Richard B. *Church and University in the Scottish Enlightenment: The Moderate Literati of Edinburgh*. Princeton: Princeton UP, 1985.

———. "Witherspoon's *Dominion of Providence* and the Scottish Jeremiad Tradition." *Scotland and America in the Age of the Enlightenment.* Ed. Richard Sher and Jeffrey Smitten. Princeton: Princeton UP, 1990. 46—64.

Shields, David. *Civil Tongues and Polite Letters in British America.* Chapel Hill: U of North Carolina P, 1997.

Sloan, Douglas. *The Scottish Enlightenment and the American College Ideal.* New York: Teachers College Press, 1971.

Sloane, Thomas. *On the Contrary: The Protocol of Traditional Rhetoric.* Washington, DC: Catholic University of America Press, 1997.

Smith, Adam. *Lectures on Rhetoric and Belles Lettres.* Ed. J. C. Bryce. Indianapolis: Liberty Fund, 1985.

———. *The Theory of Moral Sentiments.* Ed. D. D. Raphael and A. L. Macfie. Indianapolis: Liberty Fund, 1984.

———. *The Wealth of Nations.* Ed. Edwin Cannan. New York: Modern Library, 1994.

Smith, J. W. Ashley. *The Birth of Modern Education: The Contribution of the Dissenting Academies, 1660–1800.* London: Independent Press, 1954.

Smith, Rogers M. *Civic Ideals: Conflicting Visions of Citizenship in U.S. Society.* New Haven: Yale UP, 1997.

Smith, Samuel Stanhope. *The Lectures Corrected and Improved, Which Have Been Delivered for a Series of Years in the College of New Jersey; on the Subject of Moral and Political Philosophy.* 2 vols. Trenton: James J. Wilson, 1812.

———. *Lectures on the Evidences of Christian Religion, Delivered to the Senior Class, on Sundays, in the Afternoon, in the College of New Jersey.* Philadelphia: Fry and Kummerer, 1809.

Smith, William. "Extract of a Letter from a Gentleman in Queen's Country, to His Friend in New York." *New York Mercury* 30 April 1753.

———. *Indian Songs of Peace with a Proposal, in a Prefatory Epistle, for Erecting Indian Schools, and a Postscript by the Editor, Introducing Yarizo, and Indian Maid's Letter, to the Principal Ladies of the Province and City of New York.* New York: J. Parker and W. Wayman, 1752.

———. "To the Public." *New York Mercury* 9 July 1753.

———. "To the Public." *New York Mercury* 17 Sept. 1753.

———. *A Sermon Preached on Sunday, Sept. 1st, 1754, in Christ-Church Philadelphia; Occasioned by the Death of a Beloved Pupil, Who Departed His Life, August 28th, 1754, in the 16th Year of His Age.* Philadelphia: B. Franklin and D. Hall, 1754.

———. *A Short History of the Rise and Progress of the Charitable Scheme, Carrying on by a Society of Noblemen and Gentlemen in London for Relief and Instruction of Poor Germans, and Their Descendents, Settled in Pennsylvania, and the Adjacent British Colonies in N. America.* Philadelphia: B. Franklin and D. Hall, 1755.

———. *Some Thoughts on Education with Reasons for Erecting a College in the Province, and Fixing the Same in the City of New York [. . .]* New York: J. Parker, 1752.

———. *The Works of William Smith, D.D. Late Provost of the College and Academy of Philadelphia.* 2 vols. Philadelphia: Hugh Maxwell and William Fry, 1803.

Sterling, John. *A System of Rhetoric.* London: Thomas Astley, 1733.

Stiles, Ezra. *The Literary Diary of Ezra Stiles.* Ed. Franklin Bowditch. 6 vols. New York: Charles Scribner's Sons, 1901.

Stormer, Nathan. "Articulation: A Working Paper on Rhetoric and *Taxis.*" *Quarterly Journal of Speech* 90 (2004): 257–84.

Stout, Harry. *The New England Soul: Preaching and Religious Culture in Colonial New England.* Oxford: Oxford UP, 1986.

Taylor, Robert. *Colonial Connecticut: A History.* New York: Kto Press, 1979.

Thomson, Robert Polk. "Colleges in the Revolutionary South: The Shaping of a Tradition." *History of Higher Education Quarterly* 10.4 (1970): 399–412.

Tiedemann, Joseph. *Reluctant Revolutionaries: New York City and the Road to Independence, 1763–1776.* Ithaca: Cornell UP, 1997.

Tompkins, Daniel D. *A Columbia College Student in the Eighteenth Century: Essays by Daniel D. Tompkins.* Ed. Ray W. Irwin and Edna L. Jacobsen. New York: Columbia UP, 1940.

Tracy, Patricia J. *Jonathan Edwards, Pastor: Religion and Society in Eighteenth-Century Northampton.* New York: Hill and Wang, 1979.

Trenchard, John, and Thomas Gordon. *Cato's Letters, or Essays on Liberty, Civil and Religious and Other Important Subjects.* 2 vols. Ed. Ronald Hamowy. Indianapolis: Liberty Fund, 1995.

Trumbull, John. "The Correspondent 11." *Connecticut Journal* 26 Feb. 1773.

———. "The Correspondent 23." *Connecticut Journal* 23 May 1773.

———. *An Essay on the Uses and Advantages of the Fine Arts, Delivered to the Public Commencement in New Haven, Sept. 18th, 1770.* New Haven: Printed by T. and S. Green, 1770.

———. *A Letter to an Honourable Gentleman of the Council-Board, for the Colony of Connecticut.* New Haven: B. Mecom, 1766.

———. "The Meddler 9." *Boston Chronicle* 11–15 June 1770.

———. *The Poetical Works of John Trumbull LL.D.* 2 vols. Hartford: Samuel G. Goodrich, 1820.

Tucker, Louis. *Puritan Protagonist: President Thomas Clap of Yale College.* Chapel Hill: U of North Carolina P, 1962.

Tyler, Lyon G. "Early Courses and Professors at William and Mary College." *William and Mary Quarterly* 14.2 (1905): 71–83.

Ulman, H. Lewis. *Things, Thoughts, Words, and Actions: The Problem of Language in Late Eighteenth-Century British Rhetorical Theory.* Carbondale: Southern Illinois University Press, 1994.

Vance, Clarence Hayden. "Myles Cooper." *Columbia University Quarterly* 22.3 (1930): 261–86.

Vasquéz, Mark G. *Authority and Reform: Religious and Educational Discourses in Nineteenth-Century New England Literature.* Knoxville: U of Tennessee P, 2003.

Vickers, Daniel. "The Northern Colonies: Economy and Society, 1600–1775." *Cambridge Economic History of the United States, Volume One: The Colonial Era.* 209–48.

Walker, Jeffrey. "Enthymemes of Anger in Cicero and Thomas Paine." *Constructing Rhetorical Education.* Eds. Marie Secor and Davida Charney. Carbondale: Southern Illinois UP, 1992. 357–81.

Walker, Obediah. *Of Education: Especially of Young Gentlemen.* Oxon: At the Theater, 1673.

Walmsley, Peter. *The Rhetoric of Berkeley's Philosophy.* Cambridge: Cambridge UP, 1990.

Warner, Michael. *The Letters of the Republic: Publication and the Public Sphere in Eighteenth-Century America.* Cambridge: Harvard UP, 1990.

———. *Publics and Counterpublics.* New York: Zone Books, 2002.

Warnick, Barbara. *The Sixth Canon: Belletristic Rhetorical Theory and Its French Antecedents.* Columbia: U of South Carolina P, 1993.

Watts, Isaac. *Logick, or the Right Use of Reason in the Inquiry after Truth [. . .].* 5th Amer. ed. Boston: Wells and Richardson, 1812.

Weaver, Richard. *The Ethics of Rhetoric.* Chicago: Henry Regnery Company, 1953.

Weber, Max. *The Protestant Ethic and the Spirit of Capitalism.* Trans. Talcott Parsons. Intro. Anthony Giddens. London: Routledge, 1992.

Webster, Noah. *Dissertations of the English Language: With Notes, Historical and Critical.* Boston: Isaiah Thomas and Co., 1789.

———. "On the Education of Youth in America." *A Collection of Essays and Fugitive Writings on Moral, Historical, Political, and Literary Subjects*. Boston: I. Thomas and E. T. Andrews, 1790. 1–37.

Weisser, Christian R. *Moving Beyond Academic Discourse: Composition Studies and the Public Sphere*. Carbondale: Southern Illinois UP, 2002.

Wells, Colin. *The Devil and Doctor Dwight: Satire and Theology in the Early American Republic*. Chapel Hill: U of North Carolina P, 2001.

Wells, Susan. "Rogue Cops and Health Care: What Do We Want from Public Writing?" *College Composition and Communication* 40.3 (1996): 325–41.

Wemyss Smith, Horace. *The Life and Correspondence of William Smith*. 2 vols. Philadelphia: Ferguson Bros. and Co., 1880.

Wess, Robert. *Kenneth Burke: Rhetoric, Subjectivity, Postmodernism*. Cambridge: Cambridge UP, 1996.

Wheatley, Phillis. *The Collected Works of Phillis Wheatley*. Ed. John Shields. Oxford: Oxford UP, 1988.

"Whig Society Archives, Clerk's Documents, Final Minutes, 1802–1806." Mss. 1.1. Princeton University, Seeley J. Mudd Manuscript Library.

Williams, Raymond. *Marxism and Literature*. Oxford: Oxford UP, 1977.

Witherspoon, John. *The Works of John Witherspoon*. Intro. Dr. John Rodgers. 4 vols. Philadelphia: William W. Woodward, 1802.

Wood, Gordon. *The Creation of the American Republic, 1776–1787*. Chapel Hill: U of North Carolina P, 1998.

Yeates, Jasper. "Brief Compen. of Metaphysics begun July 10th, 1759." Mss. 3.27.1652. University of Pennsylvania, Archives General Collection, 1740–1820.

———. "The Substance of a Course of Lectures on Rhetoric. Read in the College of Philadelphia by the Reverend Doctor William Smith, 1760." Mss. 3.27.1658. University of Pennsylvania Archives, General Collection 1740–1820.

Index